One Marriage under God

One Marriage under God

The Campaign to Promote
Marriage in America

Melanie Heath

NEW YORK UNIVERSITY PRESS
New York and London

NEW YORK UNIVERSITY PRESS
New York and London
www.nyupress.org

References to Internet websites (URLs) were accurate at the time of writing.
Neither the author nor New York University Press is responsible for URLs
that may have expired or changed since the manuscript was prepared.

Library of Congress Cataloging-in-Publication Data
Heath, Melanie.
One marriage under God : the campaign to promote marriage in America / Melanie Heath.
p. cm. — (Intersections)
Includes bibliographical references and index.
ISBN-13: 978-0-8147-3712-5 (cl : alk. paper)
ISBN-13: 978-0-8147-3713-2 (pb : alk. paper)
ISBN-13: 978-0-8147-4490-1 (ebook)
ISBN-13: 978-0-8147-4491-8 (ebook)
1. Marriage — United States. 2. Marriage — Religious
aspects — Christianity. 3. United States — Social conditions.
4. Heterosexuality — United States. I. Title.
HQ536.H427   2012
306.810973 — dc23   2011043846

New York University Press books are printed on acid-free paper,
and their binding materials are chosen for strength and durability.
We strive to use environmentally responsible suppliers and materials
to the greatest extent possible in publishing our books.

Manufactured in the United States of America
c 10 9 8 7 6 5 4 3 2 1
p 10 9 8 7 6 5 4 3 2 1

In memory of my parents,
A. Norman and Grace L. Heath

Contents

Acknowledgments

This book owes a great debt to the Oklahomans who were willing to share with me their experiences and understandings of marriage politics and ideology in the United States. First, I want to thank all of the staff at the Oklahoma Marriage Initiative for their willingness to allow me to study the initiative so closely and for welcoming my presence at events, activities, and workshops. A special thanks to George Young who opened his church to me and was incredibly supportive of my research. I also thank other church leaders I interviewed for their support and for welcoming me into their churches. I am indebted to the lesbians and gay Oklahomans who shared with me their experiences of discrimination and their dreams for a better Oklahoma, many of whom became friends and will always occupy a place in my heart. Finally, I want to thank the participants, the teachers, the students, and all of the others in Oklahoma who took time out from their busy schedules to share with me their experiences of marriage classes.

During my residence in Oklahoma, there were many individuals who offered assistance and support. The friends I made in Oklahoma were fond of reminding me that a person arriving in Los Angeles with no contacts and little information about the city or state would not fare nearly as well as I did on my arrival as a nonnative in Oklahoma. I thank Louise Goldberg and Mary Reynolds for helping me to settle in my first few months in Oklahoma. The faculty at the University of Oklahoma were always helpful, especially the sociology chair, Craig St. John, who hired me to teach for a semester and who was incredibly supportive of my research. I owe special thanks to Allan Brown for his friendship and support while I was in Oklahoma. Karen Weldon and Susanne Bain were incredibly gracious and kind. Joan and Carolyn were always helpful, and a special thanks to Toby Jenkins for his support of my research.

I am deeply grateful to my mentors who have made this book possible. I can't express enough my deepest gratitude to Judith Stacey for her steadfast support and mentorship. This book would not have been possible without her. I thank Michael Messner, whose encouragement throughout my graduate education and beyond has been indispensable. I send a special thanks to Sharon Hays, who gave amazing input on this manuscript in its earlier form. Thank you to Don Miller and Jon Miller for their support, and the support from the Center for Religion and Civic Culture at the University of Southern California for a generous grant that funded my research in Oklahoma. I also thank David Cruz for his contributions on the legal aspects of marriage. The research for this project was also supported through a Letters of Arts and Sciences Dissertation Fellowship from the University of Southern California. I also want to express my appreciation to the Association for the Sociology of Religion for awarding me the Fichter Research Grant, to the Center for Feminist Research for a travel grant, and to the Department of Sociology at USC for numerous research grants and other financial support.

A postdoctoral fellowship at Rice University enabled me to take extra time to revise this work. I thank Elizabeth Long and Holly Heard for reading the manuscript and for offering such helpful advice concerning revisions.

Ilene Kalish, my editor at New York University Press, showed great enthusiasm for the project and provided me invaluable feedback and encouragement. An earlier version of chapter 2 appeared originally in *Gender & Society* 23, no. 1 (2009). My thanks to the anonymous reviewers at NYU Press and at *Gender & Society*, all of whom offered critical feedback. I especially thank Dana Britton for offering constructive criticism and lively debate, and her managing editorial staff for all their assistance.

I am grateful to other numerous people who have offered input and support while I was conceptualizing and working on this project. I thank my colleagues at McMaster who have been supportive. Much appreciation goes to Neil McLaughlin, Tina Fetner, Charlene Miall, and Dorothy Pawluch. Many thanks to Verta Taylor, Leila Rupp, Kathleen Hull, Amy Binder, Celine-Marie Pascale, Shari Dworkin, James Thing, and Cheryl Cooky.

Finally, my abundant thanks to my family for their encouragement and support. I thank Rosi and Dwight Edwards for encouraging me to pursue my dreams and for being amazing role models. Finally, I want to thank my many friends for helping me remember to laugh, keeping me sane, and comforting me through personal difficulties.

Preface

During the process of writing and discussing the research for this book, people have often assumed that I chose to study marriage promotion in Oklahoma because it is the state where I was born and raised. Having spent most of my life in California, I found myself bristling at the suggestion. No, I would explain, I did research in Oklahoma because it has a pioneer state-wide program to promote marriage. Later, I would wonder why the defensive reaction? Besides the obvious differences between California and Oklahoma—blue versus red state, liberal versus conservative, the coast versus the heartland—I recognized a deeper ambivalence about the strong connection I felt during my time there.

Growing up in a middle- to upper-middle-class, predominantly white community on the central coast of California, I knew from a young age that my family was different from most of my friends, neighbors, and classmates. Although also white, we had a lot less money than those around us. More than this, though, was my family's religious conservatism. I was raised in a fundamentalist Christian environment and attended a Christian school for junior high and part of high school that mandated a pledge to the Christian flag *and* the American flag every morning. We attended the most conservative Baptist church in the area three times a week. My mother taught a weekly Bible class to the neighborhood children in our home, and, as part of a campaign to get out the good news, we went door to door handing out pamphlets and talking to neighbors about how to be "born again." I often was an outsider because most of my friends and schoolmates were not religious or conservative. Reflecting on this history, I realized that if I had been born in Oklahoma, religious conservatism would not have been an issue.

For me, much has changed since my childhood upbringing. Even from a young age, I had questioned the moral and theological worldview I was immersed in. After renewing my commitment to being born again in high school (I was born again as a very young child but wandered from the more righteous path in my early teens), I spent two years at Biola, a Christian university that requires a minor in biblical studies. I began to have serious doubts about the Christian theology I was taught, but it was during my undergraduate work at the University of California at Berkeley that these questions could no longer be ignored. Through an arduous, protracted process I began to cultivate a feminist consciousness in place of the antifeminist stance I had assumed from my upbringing. Years later, I realized that feminism and Christianity are not necessarily contradictory; however, Christianity no longer held an appeal for me. After completing my undergraduate degree, I eventually did research on gender, sexuality, and the religious right, first on the Promise Keepers, the movement of Christian men who gained notoriety in the 1990s for advocating the "spiritual" leadership of men. This research led to my interest in the "marriage movement" with its unique blend of secularism and religion.

All these aspects of my past have given me particular insight into the dynamics of marriage politics. Being bisexual, I sympathized and rallied with lesbian, gay, and bisexual activists to fight the passage of a state constitutional amendment to ban same-sex marriage. Simultaneously, I attended the conservative Christian church of a pastor who was a major player in the activism to pass the amendment. My background afforded me a distinctive insider-outsider perspective. I was an outsider to Oklahoma's culture, but Oklahomans are incredibly friendly, and I was heartened by the generosity and openness of all the groups and individuals I came in contact with. While never genuinely an insider, I was able to relate to the perspectives—from antipoverty to moral battle—that I found motivated marriage politics. As I reflected on the standpoints I encountered, I struggled to balance a critical stance to analyze the motivations of marriage promotion while also empathizing with the goal of improving relationships and teaching communication skills. Marie Griffith has named this stance "critical empathy," and the analysis that follows is an attempt to acknowledge the motivation, intentions, and perspectives of all those involved in marriage politics.[1]

My primary motivation for conducting this research has been to shed light on the cultural, political, and economic dynamics that create injustice and inequality in relation to marriage. In the United States, lesbians and gay men are systematically barred from the privileges, benefits, and responsibilities of married life. Broadly, marriage has been a central mechanism to privatize dependency by making the family responsible to meet a large portion of the needs of U.S. citizens.[2] In contrast to other industrial democracies that offer a safety net of social services to ameliorate inequality and poverty, in the United States these are exacerbated to create a widening gap between the rich and poor through declining social supports and the proliferation of low-wage, dead-end jobs. In the context of such inequality, what does it mean to promote marriage as a cure to poverty? Clearly, marriage plays a strong symbolic role as a "sacred institution" in debates over lesbian and gay rights and over the significance of its decline in society. My fundamentalist Baptist upbringing gives perspective on why a sexually conservative morality has been central to a particular vision of marriage.

Ultimately, my journey to Oklahoma uncovered a landscape populated by those doing their best to put their beliefs about marriage into practice to affect social change. Leaders of marriage promotion, whether drawing on a religious or secular orientation, sought to reestablish an ephemeral and elusive social stability through marriage-strengthening efforts that they believe essential to a cohesive (American) society. In writing this book, I have mulled over the symbolic importance of marriage and why its significance is so charged for Americans. I have come to the conclusion that the public meaning of marriage in the United States speaks to fundamental issues of boundaries, citizenship, and national and cultural identity. The debates over same-sex marriage have made these tensions more visible. My hope is that *One Marriage under God*, through its in-depth examination of the politics of marriage on the ground, will contribute to the ongoing intellectual debate to ponder the public purpose of marriage and the role it might play in a just society.

Introduction

*Marriage Promotion, Heterosexuality,
and "Being American"*

What can be done to nourish the cultural ideal that must be
restored if we are to revive the nuclear family: voluntary lifelong
monogamy? [We must] spread the word about the emotional,
economic, and health benefits of lifelong monogamy, and about
how it is superior to other family forms, and continue to privilege marriage through public policy.
—David Popenoe, "Can the Nuclear Family Be Revived?"[1]

We in the United States are currently in the midst of what might
be called a marriage moment—a time of unusual, perhaps
unprecedented, national preoccupation with the status and
future of marriage. One reason for this is the growing public
and scholarly concern over the weakness of the institution. . . .
A second reason, closely connected to the first, is the emergence
of the marriage movement. A third reason, currently dominant,
is the controversy over same-sex marriage, which erupted in
full force in the United States in mid 2003, making the marriage
debate much hotter and more political.
—David Blankenhorn, *The Future of Marriage*[2]

It was a sunny but chilly February day in Oklahoma City as I gathered at the
state capitol with approximately four hundred people to rally for an issue that
David Blankenhorn—the founder and president of the Institute for American Values, a pro-marriage organization—has characterized as a "national
preoccupation."[3] The Protect Marriage and the Traditional Family rally drew
a mostly white crowd, along with approximately forty-five elected local, state,
and federal officials, radio personalities, and religious leaders. Adults and
children held handmade signs with phrases like, "Kids need both a mom

and a dad"; "God made us male and female because he loves us"; and "The sacred union between a man and a woman, where would you be without it?" The surge of activism in Oklahoma against same-sex marriage in 2004 represented only a segment of efforts to deal with "the status and future of marriage." Starting in 1999, Oklahoma became one of the first states at the vanguard of national marriage promotion policies when it instituted an initiative financed with $10 million of its welfare grant.

In the United States, a self-identified marriage movement emerged in the late 1990s, uniting a coalition of clergy and religious leaders, family practitioners, welfare officials and employees, politicians, think-tank personnel, and other community activists to promote a "renaissance" for heterosexual marriage to stem its relentless decline.[4] Officially set in motion in 2000 with the release of "The Marriage Movement: A Statement of Principles," its 113 signatories include prominent family scholars and researchers, such as William Doherty, Jean Bethke Elshtain, Amitai Etzioni, William Galston, Norval Glenn, Steven L. Nock, David Popenoe, Linda J. Waite, Judith Wallerstein, Barbara Dafoe Whitehead, and James Q. Wilson. The movement has combined grassroots efforts with broader goals to expand the role of government in promoting marriage at the state and national level.[5] Diane Sollee, a family therapist, founded the Coalition for Marriage, Family, and Couples Education (CMFCE) in 1996, a clearinghouse for the movement that sponsors the annual Smart Marriages conference to bring together those interested in rebuilding a marriage culture.[6] While "marriage education" is a spinoff of the secular family-therapy movement of the 1970s, a strong component also involves faith-based programs like Marriage Savers, a ministry that works with local congregations to promote Community Marriage Policies and Covenants, which require engaged couples to complete four months of premarital counseling.

Nationally, the movement's growth has been closely tied to state and federal funding of statewide and community marriage initiatives. The Personal Responsibility and Work Opportunity Reconciliation Act (PRWORA), the law signed by former President Clinton in 1996 to end over sixty years of federal welfare benefits to poor families, specifically designated marriage promotion in addition to job preparation and work as a sanctioned use of Temporary Assistance to Needy Families (TANF). In 1999, Oklahoma became the first state to set aside a significant amount of its TANF block grant money to promote marriage, establishing a precedent for other states to follow. Overall, Oklahoma has a punitive welfare system that ranks it among the lowest states in the amount of cash assistance offered to the poor. The fervent antiwelfare stance of many policymakers and politicians, as well as the state's religious conservatism, helped to create a receptive environment for the philosophy of marriage promotion, and specifically for the idea of a "marriage cure" for poverty.

Following this initial activity, funding for marriage promotion began to increase substantially by 2002 when the Bush administration launched its Healthy Marriage Initiative within the U.S. Department of Health and Human Services, Administration for Children and Families (HHS/ACF), funding demonstration projects nationwide to disseminate a public message on the value of marriage. It diverted over $100 million from existing programs, including $6.1 million from the Child Support Enforcement Program, $9 million from the Refugee Resettlement Program, $14 million from the Child Welfare Program, and $40 million from the Social and Economic Development Strategies Program focusing on Native Americans.[7] By 2004 every state in the union had undertaken at least one activity or made at least one policy change designed to promote marriage.[8] Bush signed into law the Deficit Reduction Act in 2005, which reauthorized welfare reform and sanctioned an appropriation of up to $150 million more per year from 2006 to 2010 to promote healthy marriages and responsible fatherhood.[9] Recently, President Obama proposed spending $500 million in his 2011 budget on a new Fatherhood, Marriage, and Family Innovation Fund, and Congress ultimately approved $75 million for marriage promotion activities and $75 million for funding responsible fatherhood initiatives for the current fiscal year. At the state level, three states—Ohio, Utah, and Texas—have followed Oklahoma's lead to dedicate a portion of their TANF funds to create statewide initiatives (Texas allocated $16 million for fiscal year 2008–2009), and ten other states have also committed substantial amounts.[10] These policies and programs have thus gained a substantial foothold.

While the marriage movement has turned to federal and local government agencies to promote marriage, conservative politicians, religious leaders, and other activists likewise seek federal and state legislation to "protect" it. Dating back to the 1970s but gaining momentum in the 1990s, the fight for same-sex marriage became a central organizing principle for lesbians and gay men as a result of the vociferous backlash of the "religious right"—a movement of conservative religious (and predominantly Christian) organizations that advocate social and political conservatism—to the possible legalization of same-sex marriage in Hawaii.[11] The case of Hawaii spurred the passage of the federal Defense of Marriage Act (DOMA) in 1996, which provided the first federal definitions of "marriage" and "spouse" as one man and one woman, and it ensured that no state is compelled to recognize the same-sex marriage contract of another state. Most individual states have passed their own DOMAs and some passed "super-DOMAs," laws that block recognition not only of same-sex marriage but also of civil unions and domestic partnerships. In 2003, public controversy over same-sex marriage followed the decision by the Massachusetts Supreme Judicial Court in *Goodridge v. Department of Public Health* that established a right to marry for same-sex couples in the state's constitution. Currently, marriage licenses to same-sex couples are granted by six states: Connecticut, Iowa, Massachusetts, New Hampshire, New York, Vermont, and in Washington, D.C. At both the state and national level, opponents have sought to pass constitutional amendments to ban legal same-sex marriage. Former president George W. Bush endorsed a Federal Marriage Amendment that would have amended the U.S. Constitution to define marriage as the union of one man and one woman, and the amendment would have prohibited states from legalizing same-sex marriage. Although the federal amendment failed, states continued to pass their own amendments. The battle is now being played out in California where the passage of Proposition 8 in 2008 made it the twenty-sixth state to approve such a measure. After a federal court ruled the amendment to be unconstitutional discrimination in 2010, the appeal case is expected to make its way to the U.S. Supreme Court.

The politics of marriage in the United States draws attention to the uncertainty Americans feel over major shifts in sexual morality, values, and family life in postindustrial societies. Moving with unparalleled momentum in the past few decades, such transformations have cast doubt on the future of marriage. The historian Stephanie Coontz contends that anxiety over a crisis in marriage is nothing new. Over time, many have heralded a crisis of the family.[12] What is new, according to Coontz, is the speed in which the forms and values of marriage have changed since the late eighteenth century to idealize love as *the* fundamental reason to marry. From its inception, this "revolutionary new marriage system" contained the seeds of instability that have led to the current waning significance of the institution of marriage.[13] While family transformations occur on a global scale—especially in Euro-American societies—America appears unique in its pervasive national preoccupation with what marriage advocates refer to as the "m-word." Not only has the United States witnessed a burgeoning marriage movement, it has exported elements of it to other countries such as England, Australia, New Zealand, and Norway.[14] Likewise, the intensity of the acrimony over same-sex marriage in the United States distinguishes it from other countries, such as in the case of Spain and Canada where both countries legalized same-sex marriage in 2005 with relatively minor upheaval. Why has marriage in the United States become an issue of pervasive national preoccupation and anxiety?

This question has motivated my research on the politics of marriage. To think about the organization of these politics, I examine marriage as an ideology that draws together national cultural repertoires of the middle-class, married, heterosexual family as *the* model of American citizenship. Ideologies organize group attitudes and knowledge to facilitate specific courses of action as appropriate and deviations as nonnormative and misguided. It is through cultural repertoires as systems of ideas, values, and strategies that individuals make sense of the social conditions they confront.[15] Relying on an ideology of marriage, advocates claim that revitalizing the institution is key to solving a vast array of America's social problems, including crime, poverty, teen pregnancy, educational failure, and welfare "dependency." In what might be described as a feedback loop, these cultural repertoires complement social policies and institutional practices that sustain inequalities based on gender, supporting beliefs on the essential role of male breadwinners and fathers; on race, reinforcing an ideology of the American dream and bourgeois normality to assimilate racial others; on class, through institutional policies that perpetuate poverty, especially for poor women of color; and on sexuality, buttressing the importance of the heteronormative family model. Thus, marriage ideology and politics both rely on *and* contribute to inequality, often in unexpected ways.

In the pages that follow, I uncover the social consequences of efforts to reinstitutionalize a concept of "one marriage" in the United States through government, legal, and cultural intervention. The historian John Gillis has astutely remarked, "We all have two families, one that we live *with* and another we live *by*."[16] This book examines symbolic contests over marriage—over the "one marriage" we live by—to illuminate what is the case for the families we live with. To study these politics, I conducted ethnographic research in Oklahoma, viewing its policies as both "extending out" and being influenced by national marriage promotion politics.[17] I examine the ways that ideologies to reinforce a boundary of heterosexual marriage lead to uneven and contradictory consequences on the ground.

The Politics of Marriage

Contemporary political battles over marriage and family in the United States grew in the late 1970s, a time when the divorce rate peaked and a national White House Conference on The Family, planned under the Carter administration, splintered into three polarized regional conferences during the Reagan administration.[18] While liberalizing trends in cultural understandings and practices of sexuality began long before the 1960s, transformations in family and sexual mores accelerated during this decade due to social and economic developments. Over a twenty-year period, the divorce rate more than doubled from the mid-1960s, leveling off somewhat to the point where almost half of all marriages are estimated to dissolve.[19] In the early 1980s, one out of six births occurred outside marriage, a much higher ratio than two decades earlier.[20] By the twenty-first century, this figure had grown to one out of three.[21] Similar and higher figures are found in Canada, the United Kingdom, Ireland, and Nordic countries.[22] Today, roughly one in twenty U.S. couples are cohabitating and most marriages begin after cohabitation.[23] Nearly a quarter of families are headed by single parents.[24]

In the United States, a renewed focus on the family resulted from the growth of the women's movement, debates over a "culture of poverty" among African American families, and the rise of the religious right. The women's liberation movement characterized the nuclear family as an axis of patriarchal power, rallying for the end of gender discrimination in the workplace and at home.[25] Controversy over the family also grew alongside the rise of unwed motherhood in the 1960s. Aid to Dependent Children (ADC) was renamed Aid to Families of Dependent Children (AFDC) in 1962 and was specifically designed to enhance the family wage system to help poor single mothers raise their children at home, replacing the breadwinning father with the paternal state. A series of legal victories eradicated the restrictive policies that barred many poor women, and particularly poor women of color, from receiving benefits. These factors partly contributed to welfare's most dramatic growth since its inception: the number of families it served nearly tripled from 787,000 to 2,208,000 between 1960 and 1970.[26] During this period, public concern began to grow over the increase in female-headed households that many pointed to as proof of the dysfunctional nature of black families. Daniel Patrick Moynihan's 1965 report added fuel to the fire with his depiction of black single-mother families as a "tangle of pathology."[27] Finally, the 1970s witnessed the emergence of antifeminist, anti-abortion, and antigay evangelical movements, which merged together under the umbrella of the Moral Majority to advance "family values" and the state's role in promoting marriage and family life.[28] The Moral Majority laid the groundwork for the focus on the family during the Reagan-Bush years.

After the Republicans' defeat of 1992 with Bill Clinton's election, there was reason to believe that the predominance of family-values ideology would subside. Instead, in the 1990s, Judith Stacey describes the rise of a "neo-family-values campaign" that embraced "an explicitly centrist politics, rhetoric, and ideology," grounded its claims "in secular social science instead of religious authority," and rejected "anti-feminism for a post-feminist ethic."[29] By the turn of the century, this campaign had mobilized into the self-identified marriage movement, uniting a network of scholarly and policy institutes, including the Institute for American Values, with David Blankenhorn (the author of *Fatherless America*)[30] as president, and the National Marriage Project, a research and public education initiative once based at Rutgers and originally codirected by David Popenoe, who is a professor of sociology at Rutgers, and Barbara Dafoe Whitehead, who is a journalist. The project has been housed since 2009 at the University of Virginia.

Judith Stacey details the important role that social scientists played in shaping the field of marriage promotion and its knowledge claims.[31] Elsewhere, I have described these configurations of knowledge in terms of an "epistemic culture," a domain constructed by the practices of experts that make up how we know what we know.[32] I argue that examining the "machineries" of knowledge production sheds light on the practices involved in public policy formation within knowledge societies.[33] In solidifying expert knowledges for their cause, leaders within movements like marriage promotion explicitly politicize scientific knowledge as a way to garner support from governments and policymakers for social change. In the case of marriage promotion, elite players at academic institutions lead and participate in this politicization.

Policy institutes and think tanks that embrace marriage promotion deploy social scientific knowledge to argue in favor of the universal benefits of marriage. In a 2002 document, the Institute for American Values spells out "Why Marriage Matters: Twenty-Six Conclusions from the Social Sciences." A sampling includes, "Marriage is a virtually universal human institution; Marriage has important biosocial consequences for adults and children; Marriage reduces poverty and material hardship for disadvantaged women and their children."[34] Statements such as these present knowledge about marriage without contextualization of scholarly debates and complexities. For example, historians, anthropologists, and sociologists have called into question marriage's universality.[35] Likewise, there is debate about whether *marriage* itself can reduce poverty.[36] Arguments made by marriage advocates simplify the facts and suggest unanimity among social scientists. A fact sheet from the Institute for American Values explicitly espouses the "scholarly consensus on marriage": "Marriage is an important social good, associated with an impressively broad array of positive outcomes for children and adults alike. Marriage is an important public good, associated with a range of economic, health, educational, and safety benefits that help local, state, and federal governments serve the common good."[37] Dissemination of these facts is meant to influence public opinion concerning the importance of marriage: "That current rates of divorce, family conflict, and unwed childbearing are not good for children, for adults, or for society."[38] Marriage advocates seek to solidify the "case for marriage" because "married people are happier, healthier, and better off financially."[39]

Supporters of the religious right and other conservative organizations have worked together to also promote marriage's benefits. The sociologist Scott Coltrane traces the growth of marriage and fatherhood policies to think tanks funded with millions of dollars from conservative foundations, underscoring the connections between hybrid political-religious organizations, such as the National Fatherhood Initiative and the Promise Keepers.[40] Conservative think tanks such as the Heritage Foundation and the Family Research Council have been directly involved in marriage promotion policies. They also are vocal on their views of the negative moral impact that same-sex marriage would have on American society. For these players, a marriage renaissance in American culture is necessary to reestablish the cultural, social, and legal hegemony of heterosexual marriage. They advocate public declarations about the superiority of the two-parent, biological, married family. One example is rewarding those who marry. Senator Sam Brownback (R-KS)—a politician with ties to the religious right and who made a failed run for the Republican nomination for president in 2008—implemented a program in Washington, D.C., to give couples earning under $50,000 a year a marriage bonus of up to $9,000 to buy a house or to pay for job training/education. Such policies seek to influence culture in a pro-marriage direction.

Others have focused on the issue of poverty and government efforts to promote marriage among low-income populations. These marriage advocates point to the relationship between single motherhood and poverty as an important reason for public policies to promote marriage. Census data show that children living with married parents have on average a higher family income than children living outside a married family. In 2000, 6 percent of married two-parent families lived in poverty compared to 33 percent of single-mother families.[41] Mothers who never marry face conditions of poverty more than any other group, including those who divorce.[42] Marriage advocates argue that there is a "marriage gap" dividing America and begetting a rigid caste society: "A self-perpetuating single-mother proletariat on the one hand, and a self-perpetuating, comfortable middle class on the other."[43] Several policy analysts from the Center for Law and Social Policy (CLASP), a liberal think tank whose mission is promoting "progressive policies on welfare reform, child support, [and] child care," have written extensively about marriage promotion and poverty.[44] Some assert that if poor women and men married, poverty rates would diminish. Robert Rector and others from the Heritage Foundation conducted a study that simulated the effects of higher marriage rates by using data from the U.S. Census Bureau for the year 2000 by "marrying" single mothers with men of identical demographic characteristics. They found that 80 percent would be "lifted out of poverty."[45] Isabel Sawhill and Adam Thomas of the Brookings Institution simulated marriage rates by restoring marriage to 1970 levels. Using income to measure poverty, they concluded that the 1998 child poverty rate would have been 4.4 percentage points lower than its actual 18.3 percent level. Such simulations, however, do not take into account the social and historical factors affecting poor mothers in the past fifty years.[46] Using retrospective family life history data, the sociologists Lichter, Graefe, and Brown found that there may be a slight economic benefit of marriage for poor women, but, taking into account structural barriers, marriage is no "panacea."[47]

Scholars who are critical of marriage promotion have raised concerns about government policies that could lead to negative outcomes for women and children. The feminist scholars Stephanie Coontz and Nancy Folbre argue that the current pro-marriage agenda is misguided for at least four reasons. First, nonmarriage often results from poverty and not the other way around. Second, the quality of relationships is important to child outcomes, so encouraging couples to marry might leave these families worse off if there is abuse or divorce. Third, two-parent families in the United States are also susceptible to economic stresses that can have a negative effect on children. Fourth, single parenthood does not necessarily lead to poverty.[48] In countries with a more adequate social safety net, single-parent families are much less likely to be impoverished. One of the greatest concerns for critics of marriage promotion is the issue of domestic violence. Studies show that between 50 and 60 percent of women on welfare have experienced domestic violence, compared to 22 percent of the general population.[49] Women and children in poverty are particularly vulnerable to domestic abuse. Critics fear that promoting marriage could compel poor women to stay with an abusive partner. The word "healthy" was added to the national marriage initiative in order to underscore the goal of keeping women safe. However, the commitment of government officials to prioritize combating domestic violence is somewhat questionable. The welfare reform bill of 2006 failed to include proposed guarantees to require qualified domestic-violence experts, and it did not ensure that all marriage promotion programs would be voluntary.[50]

Another criticism of marriage promotion is its potential to discriminate against the unmarried—especially those who are not allowed legal entry. Jen Heitel Yakush, a senior public policy associate of the Sexuality Information and Education Council (SEICUS), criticizes the federal government for spending billions of dollars to promote heterosexual marriage as a way of "preaching ideology and a narrow definition of morality."[51] Early on, marriage advocates staved off a discussion of same-sex marriage by staying silent and downplaying the marriage debate. Not long after, however, a *USA Today* article spelled out the conundrum: "The key question that the movement's leaders—and critics—are grappling with is how one can be a proponent of marriage in general but oppose marriages between gays."[52] On this question, David Blankenhorn confesses in the article that marriage promoters are split. On the one hand, a large group unreservedly rallies to ensure marriage remains exclusively heterosexual and, on the other, a very smaller faction believes marriage would benefit lesbians and gay men.

While internal disagreements are endemic to movements and organizations that seek social change (in this case to reinstitutionalize marriage), the ultimate goal of marriage promotion has two faces. The first promotes a heterosexual marriage culture that positions same-sex couples as outsiders. The second attempts to strengthen marriage's boundary by assimilating a group who has challenged its limits: poor single mothers. In this book, I argue that marriage promotion relies on an understanding of marriage that espouses a hierarchical gender and sexual order, and an ideology that demonizes welfare "dependency" as an assault on freedom and responsible citizenship. While marriage advocates espouse a rainbow of political and religious persuasions, all in varying degrees draw on a tradition of Christian morality that has shaped the meaning of marriage in the United States and inspires a nostalgia for a time when marriage was the unquestioned norm for organizing family life. Moreover, marriage advocates predominantly embrace a free-market capitalist ideology that prioritizes the nuclear family unit as an essential component of American identity. The next section discusses the contributions of this research to theories of sexuality studies and inequality.

Boundary Work and Marital Outsiders

The historians John D'Emilio and Estelle Freedman document the historical emergence of dominant meanings of sexuality and family life in the United States. Their analysis underscores the ways that sexuality is constructed in relation to the social organization and history of a "system of sexual regulation."[53] Sexuality scholars who theorize the interrelationship of marriage and sexual regulation have brought about a renewed focus on the institution of heterosexuality.[54] The emergence of "critical heterosexuality studies," originating in radical lesbian feminist critiques of "compulsory heterosexuality" as a patriarchal institution, calls into question taken-for-granted understandings of heterosexuality as coherent and universal, and it investigates its multiplicity of meanings, institutional arrangements, and hierarchies.[55] It further points a critical lens on the ways that heterosexuality serves as the standard for all "sexual-socio behavior."[56] The emergence of queer theory in the 1990s also invigorated critical analyses of heterosexuality, such as the work of Jonathan Katz, who documents the recent invention of the concept of heterosexuality in the past hundred years.[57] Early queer theorists have elucidated the emergence of "the homosexual" as a category of person distinct from "the heterosexual" in the later part of the nineteenth century, and the subsequent amassing of medical, legal, psychological, and literary discourses based on the heterosexual/homosexual binary.[58]

In her seminal work on the epistemology of the closet, Eve Kosofsky Sedgwick proposes that "many of the major nodes of thought and knowledge in twentieth-century Western culture as a whole are structured—indeed fractured—by the now endemic crisis of homo/heterosexual definition, indicatively male, dating from the end of the nineteenth century." The closet, which according to Sedgwick characterizes gay oppression in this century, is a structure that is connected to broader configurations of secrecy and disclosure, of the private and the public, with the ability to dislocate the dominant heterosexist culture. It contains a "dangerous incoherence" that requires individuals to negotiate being "in" or "out" in a manner that links to injurious designations of homosexuality.[59] In this book, I argue that marriage ideology draws on these mappings of the closet to prohibit an implicit homosexuality that troubles marriage's unproblematic hegemony. This ideology organizes knowledge of heterosexuality, citizenship, and national belonging to uphold marriage as the "natural" and universal family formation. In the past two centuries, transformations in intimacy and family life have focused the act of marriage as a private, discreet choice that represents personal commitment and love. This private mapping obscures marriage's public nature and its regulation of sexuality, gender, and citizenship.[60] Thus, this ideology hides the work of concealing homosexuality's shadow and presents a simple choice based on consensual, romantic (heterosexual and monogamous) love.[61]

As the cultural theorist Neil Gross argues, there has been a decline in the "regulative tradition" of "lifelong, internally stratified marriage" (LISM) or the cultural context for regulating the heterosexual dyad through state control or a religiously sanctified commitment, based on an unequal division of labor and power between genders.[62] In addition to this regulative tradition are "meaning-constitutive traditions" that shape social action from generation to generation. Thus, while it has become easier for people to enter and exit relationships of their choosing, there still exists an ideal and hegemonic form of coupledom extolled by the regulative tradition of LISM. Meaning-constitutive traditions condition "the thinkability of particular acts and projects."[63] These traditions act as a commonsense way to mark how things have "always" been done. Celine-Marie Pascale examines the ways that commonsense knowledge of race, class, and gender is both "moral and ideological."[64] Its moral purpose works to construct boundaries between "us" and "them" through everyday, unconscious practice. On an ideological level, commonsense knowledge is naturalized as participating in a universe of facts.

Many marriage advocates draw on a universe of facts in order to view marriage in relation to nostalgia for a past when the "traditional" nuclear family and home life were thought to constitute the ideal, and when marriage was not troubled by high rates of divorce, out-of-wedlock childbearing, or what, for some, is the "threat" of same-sex marriage.[65] The historian Stephanie Coontz first wrote about "nostalgia as ideology" in *The Way We Never Were: American Families and the Nostalgia Trap*, arguing that nostalgic ideals of a morally superior family are based on ahistorical assumptions embraced by the right and even the left.[66] The political scientist Mary Caputi further maps out how the conservative movement in the United States is inspired by an image of "home" that offers a common ground in the face of the diversity, fractiousness, and dissonance that have always been central to American identity.[67] In recent decades, this image of home has brought comfort in the face of the massive identity dislocations of the 1960s and 1970s. Speaking of this period, the sociologist Fred Davis argues that Americans experienced perhaps "the most wide-ranging, sustained, and profound assault on native belief concerning the 'natural' and 'proper' that has ever been visited on a people over so short a span of time."[68] In response, the Reagan Revolution tied together America's free-market corporate culture, moral/religious traditions, and suburban family life in a zeitgeist to enable Americans "to *go back* to our former identity, search the past for forgotten meanings, and re-create a former, more innocent version of ourselves."[69]

Marriage ideology draws on the past when marriage was supposedly unburdened by the specters of homophobia, class divisions, and gender and racial politics. Identity-based politics that have emerged alongside the conditions of postindustrialism and globalization represent possibilities and excitement, as well as sweeping angst. As an "escape from freedom," the heterosexual family has often served as a pillar of steadfastness by promoting an ideology of conservative gender norms.[70] The historian Elaine Tyler May documents how a focus on the "traditional" family during the postwar period of the 1950s offered a response to the threat of international communism residing not only outside national borders but invading America from within, at home. The emphasis on conservative gender norms, patriotism, authority, and hygiene acted as buffers to the panic that American society might unravel from within.[71] McCarthyism sought to rout out internal threats such as "the homosexual." The 1990s were also anxious times marked by the paranoid beliefs of homespun extremist groups that culminated in events like the Oklahoma City bombing and that continued in post-9/11 America with its fear of terrorism and an increased culture of security. It is in these times that the politics of marriage have become more visible and strident, bringing to the fore the question of the relationships among marriage, heterosexuality, gender, and nostalgia, as Americans face the growing challenges posed by structural changes in global economies, transformation in family life, and movements for lesbian and gay rights.

Marriage advocates, and even many supporters of same-sex marriage, argue that the case to promote marriage is based on the "polarizing and politically charged assertion that children do best when their parents are married."[72] Such language is rooted in the normative claim that the benefits of marriage guard against the harms of illegitimacy and familial pathology, ideas that draw on a discourse once used to describe the "tangle of pathology" among African American single-mother families. The American and New Jersey Psychological Association's brief, submitted in the case challenging New Jersey's ban against same-sex marriage, characterized the discrimination that lesbian and gay families face as a stigma due to illegitimacy: "When same-sex partners cannot marry, their biological children are born 'out-of-wedlock,' conferring a status that has historically been stigmatized as 'illegitimacy' and 'bastardy.'"[73] The Indiana appeals court in *Morrison v. Sandler*, in favor of the state's same-sex marriage ban, found that the state "could legitimately create the institution of opposite-sex marriage, and all the benefits accruing to it, in order to encourage male-female couples to procreate within the legitimacy and stability of a state-sponsored relationship and to discourage unplanned, out-of-wedlock births resulting from 'casual' intercourse."[74] The abundance of the discourses of illegitimacy in court cases, the media, and popular culture demonstrates a subtle racialization that speaks to the "normality," respectability, and security of the white, middle-class, nuclear family.

Contemporary rhetoric against illegitimacy employed by commentators and scholars of all stripes reflects dominant cultural repertoires that link to ideas about an era when divorce, out-of-wedlock childbearing, and sex outside marriage were unambiguously stigmatized and resulted in public shunning. Not all marriage advocates agree on whether single-mother and divorced families should again be publicly stigmatized; however, they do argue for the necessity of upholding the public meaning of marriage where society, as the conservative commentator Maggie Gallagher notes, "formalizes its definition, and surrounds it with norms and reinforcements, so we can raise boys and girls who aspire to become the kind of men and women who can make successful marriages."[75] Marriage thus acts as an important apparatus of the state to produce the right kind of citizenry. In her history of marriage in America, Nancy Cott argues that the founders held a political theory of marriage that conceived marital and political governance on a continuum where consent and the Christian ideal of marital union mirrored state authority over citizens who were thought to freely consent to the rule of law.[76]

In the making of the nation, moral and political thinkers reinforced the ideal of "one marriage," based on the Anglo-American ideal of Christian, heterosexual monogamy, thus venerating it as morally superior to the ongoing practice of polygamy and other complex marriage practices that were predominant among cultures in the global South and among natives of North and South America. The laws of marriage also regulated racial relationships. In slaveholding states before the Civil War, marriage law prohibited slaves from marrying, making it easier to break up families when expedient.[77] White southerners defended slavery, including the rape and molestation of slave women, by pointing to a paternalistic social order in which the white master protected his family, "black and white."[78] From the founding of the nation until the U.S. Supreme Court's *Loving v. Virginia* (1967) decision, racially based state laws nullified and criminalized interracial marriage to keep the white race unmixed.[79] The federal government persistently scrutinized the marital lives of any group deemed nonwhite.

To regulate sexuality, the anthropologist Gayle Rubin points to the persistence of a hierarchy of sexual behavior that places marital (reproductive) heterosexuality alone at the top of an erotic pyramid.[80] As a sociologist of sexuality, Jeffrey Weeks points out that morality and sexual behavior have been intimately connected—"to the extent that 'immorality' in the English language almost invariably means sexual misbehaviour, and 'moral', to a lesser but still potent extent, implies adherence to certain agreed norms of behaviour."[81] Valorizing this hierarchy, U.S. federal and state laws attach a considerable number of benefits to marriage: retirement and death benefits, family leave policies, health-care decision making and access, taxation, immigration, and numerous others. In this way, knowledge about "proper" sexuality is ultimately tied to knowledge about the American family that relies on Christian principles of monogamy, nationalism, and heteronormativity—the view that heterosexuality comprises the standard for sexual and intimate relations. Thus, the power of state practice rests not only on specific law and policy, but also on the ability to conceal the work involved in maintaining the unitary "nature" of institutionalized heterosexuality. In recent years, it has become necessary to visibly reinforce the ideal of "one marriage" through laws like federal and state Defense of Marriage Acts and constitutional amendments to define marriage as exclusively heterosexual (as well as monogamous).

In this study of marriage promotion in the United States, I argue that marriage ideology is anchored in (1) a moral "meaning-constitutive tradition" that draws on current conceptions of family values to guard against homosexuality and espouse a hierarchical gender order and (2) an ideology of welfare "dependency" as an assault on freedom and responsible citizenship. Marriage advocates hold different perspectives on politics and religion. Nevertheless, they agree on the importance of marriage in American society to the fabric of the social order. Most also embrace a free-market capitalist ideology that prioritizes the nuclear family unit as an essential component of American identity. This understanding promotes a "bourgeois normality," in the words of the marriage advocate and author Kay Hymowitz, which organizes key elements of American identity according to the American dream, personal freedom, assimilation, and individual responsibility.[82]

Thus, marriage promotion combines the contradictory threads of "market fundamentalism," religion, and morality that shape the American view of marriage—Americans must take personal responsibility to beget children within the confines of heterosexual marriage. The sociologist Margaret Somers defines market fundamentalism as the "drive to subject all of social life and the public sphere to market mechanisms."[83] The philosophy of market fundamentalism is amenable to mainstream beliefs of a positive relationship between unfettered markets and individual freedom. Deeply embedded in American culture and social institutions, individualism represents the dominant frame of freedom and prosperity that is fundamental to the American way of life. Bellah and colleagues provide a portrait of the evolution of American individualism to argue that its pervasiveness and ambiguities beget isolation and inequality by proscribing an alternative.[84] Within the American imaginary, it is just commonsense to place responsibility squarely on the individual's shoulders for determining life's chances. It is this philosophy that generates the beliefs and cultural repertoires that sustain and perpetuate capitalism. The dominance of individualist language in American society facilitates an easy embrace of the morally rational actor and obscures the visibility of structural constraints (e.g., lack of education, skills, or work experience). Bringing together campaigns of traditional and "neo-family values," marriage advocates often seek to promote a "strong and free America."[85]

To examine the ideology and implementation of marriage promotion, I apply a cultural analysis of boundary work that traces how social scientific research is translated into policies and practices that reinforce and produce inequality between middle-class families and the poor. A growing field in cultural sociology has investigated how conceptual distinctions in everyday practice produce, maintain, and contest institutionalized and ongoing social difference.[86] Symbolic boundaries, the conceptual "tool kits" that are a site of struggle and consensus of shared meaning, are essential to the production of social boundaries, the unequal distribution of material and nonmaterial resources and opportunity.[87] Through comparative research, for example, Michèle Lamont elucidates the categories or "mental maps" that people use when drawing moral and symbolic boundaries between "us" and "them."[88] On an interactional level, individuals do cognitive work in their everyday lives that can build and is built on institutional division and difference. "Boundary work," according to the sociologist Christena Nippert-Eng, constitutes "the strategies, principles, and practices we use to create, maintain, and modify cultural categories."[89]

Blurred lines of intimacy and sexuality that mark a distinction between the "pure" and the "polluted" have spurred boundary work to reframe what counts as a right, such as the right to sexual privacy and to marry.[90] These debates illuminate weighty global questions about the place of sexual outsiders in U.S. society. The sociologist Arlene Stein, for example, studied how individuals in a small Oregon community negotiated boundaries when faced with civic disputes involving lesbian and gay rights. She found that economic shifts and changing social norms fueled anxiety and fear over "the stranger next door"—lesbians and gay men living in their midst who were not as easily identifiable as were other outsiders such as Latinos. For many, the growing presence of strangers, along with economic dislocations that wreaked havoc on the "family wage," threatened stable heterosexual, nuclear families and their tight-knit community.[91]

Examining the politics of marriage on the ground, *One Marriage under God* uncovers the striking social consequences of attempts to redraw a boundary of heterosexual marriage. For example, in the following pages I detail the ways that the marriage initiative in Oklahoma uses state welfare money to fund free workshops for the nonpoor, which represents a redistribution of welfare funds away from poor single mothers (see chapter 3). I investigate the boundary work that seeks to encourage one group—poor single mothers—to marry while endeavoring to exclude another group— gay men and lesbians—from the ability to marry. The conceptual frame of family values based on Christian morality and free-market capitalism, with its philosophy of personal responsibility and choice, motivates this boundary work that upholds marriage as essential to American identity. Theoretically, an examination of the politics of marriage extends social scientific and cultural investigations of how boundaries and identities produce inequality based on race, class, gender, and sexuality in everyday life and institutionally. Marriage advocates, for varied and sometimes disparate reasons, work to uphold the heterosexual, married family as the prototype of "the family," and a good amount of public policy and funding is being geared in that direction. As marriage promotion takes on more prominence as a potential solution to poverty, it becomes crucial to understand what this policy shift means for poor Americans, who are overrepresented by communities of color and women. It is also critical to consider the consequences of these politics on the lives of those who are legally barred from a seat at the marriage table.

Ethnographic Tales from Oklahoma

Initially, my plan to study the politics of marriage had not focused on Oklahoma. Even though the initiative in Oklahoma was a prototype of the national marriage movement, I had set my sights on Arizona, a state much closer to California that had allocated $1 million in federal welfare funds to pilot a marriage education program. I conducted preliminary research in Phoenix at a marriage conference sponsored by the National Association of Marriage Enhancement (NAME), which on the last day unveiled the "marriage mobile," a project that was to be funded with federal welfare dollars to turn semi-trailer trucks into mobile marriage education classrooms to take to low-income areas in Arizona. A month before I was ready to leave, I called NAME to ask about the next scheduled trip and learned that they had not received federal funding due to Congress's failure to reauthorize the welfare reform budget. The marriage mobile, which had only taken one trip, was not scheduled to take another any time soon.

Reconsidering, I changed course to do research in Oklahoma, a state whose marriage initiative had solid funding and had been operating for over four years by the beginning of 2004. During my preliminary research, I had met with two marriage initiative employees from Oklahoma at the Smart Marriages conference, and they had expressed enthusiasm for my project. My change of plan proved fortuitous as Oklahoma has become a national leader in its statewide initiative to promote marriage, and its unique confluence of political conservatism, lagging economics, and entrenched poverty set the stage. For the first few years after the passage of welfare reform in 1996, the focus on marriage promotion had little impact. Most states focused their attention on the work-related provisions of the law to reduce the welfare rolls. In 2000, Wade Horn, then the president of the National Fatherhood Initiative, wrote in his weekly column about "Fatherly Advice" that he had been traveling around the country for four years trying to convince state officials to spend some of their welfare dollars on activities to promote marriage. He lamented: "Everywhere I went, my exhortations resulted either in disbelief that welfare funds could be spent for such a purpose or with scornful dismissals that marriage is none of government's business."[92]

This lack of attention to marriage promotion changed on March 25, 2000, when in a "bold move," declared Horn, the governor of Oklahoma announced that he would designate $10 million of the state's TANF Federal Block Grant for the purpose of promoting marriage. Horn anticipated that the "floodgates for spending" on programs were opening, and Oklahoma was on the front line. The state has been one of the most visible trendsetters of the marriage movement, evidenced by titles to workshops at the Smart Marriages conference like "Oklahoma: Leading the Way." Oklahoma does not represent the diverse marriage promotion programs that have peppered the country in the last decade, which are often small and community based. The approach and strategy in Oklahoma, however, have been significant inspiration for the creation of programs, especially for statewide initiatives. I met representatives visiting from Florida who were looking to start a statewide initiative at one of the training workshops I attended. The Texas Healthy Marriage and Relationship Initiative, which in 2007 began to allocate 1 percent of the state's total TANF Federal Block Grant each year to healthy marriage activities, has a similar model to that of Oklahoma. In recent years, a series of research briefs for HHS/ACF has used Oklahoma as the longest-running marriage initiative in the nation to offer examples to other states and programs.

Embracing the adventure, I packed my truck with clothes, books, and equipment for my research, and I drove twenty hours in February 2004 to Oklahoma, which became my home for the next ten months. Once there, I was able to contact one of the women I'd met at the Smart Marriages conference, and I began to do participant observation of the marriage workshops right away and, over time, I conducted twenty in-depth interviews with participants (see Appendixes A and B for more details about the entire sample and methods). Workshops for the general public were free of charge, and engaged couples who attended the program together qualified for a $45 discount on their $50 Oklahoma marriage license. The workshops included large Sweethearts Weekends that occurred every few months and offered marriage education on a Friday evening and all day Saturday. Advertised on local radio stations and in the newspaper, each Sweethearts Weekends workshop had fifty or more couples on average. Weekly smaller workshops were advertised on the initiative's website and through local churches.[93]

In addition to the workshops for the general population, the statewide marriage initiative also targeted specific populations, and, after my initial fieldwork on workshops for the general public, I began to branch out to study these other programs. In April, one of the marriage initiative employees informed me about marriage education workshops that were being taught to welfare clients (not advertised on the website for the general public) and asked if I would like to observe these. I prioritized attending these for the next three months to study the population that is central to the debates over the antipoverty focus of marriage promotion. These workshops met twice a week, were built into the client's first week of orientation, and each comprised five to twenty-five participants—predominantly single mothers. One married couple and two single men participated during the weeks I attended. In addition, I attended an entire weeklong orientation (Monday through Friday) to assess what other materials and classes were offered. During lunch, I often remained onsite to talk with clients while we ate. Other times, I would go out for lunch with the workshop leaders when invited. I also attended a six-week marriage workshop that met twice a week and was held during a class for TANF participants to get their high school equivalency diploma (GED). All of these classes were mandatory in the sense that they were offered either as part of the required orientation or as part of the GED curriculum (see chapter 4). Toward the end of my fieldwork, I conducted three focus groups with volunteer participants during their lunch breaks, with each session lasting one hour. I brought in sandwiches or pizza for the clients to eat and told that them that participating was completely voluntary, an opportunity to chat about their experiences in the relationship class.[94] I also interviewed four of the workshop leaders and the supervisor of the TANF office.

Another marriage initiative activity that I prioritized were marriage education lessons taught through family and consumer science classes at high schools. Again, I viewed these classes as especially important to study because teenage pregnancy has been central to debates about poverty, marriage, and single motherhood.[95] I attended daily classes at two high schools: one in a largely white, suburban area for a month and the other in an urban high school with a predominantly African American and Latino population for almost two months. These classes incorporated into their program a curriculum designed by the marriage initiative that included a workbook for each student. The initiative provided the teacher training and workbooks. In these classes, I assisted as a sort of "teacher's aide" and was thus slotted into the role of an authority figure. However, I would sit with the students as they did their exercises, and they sometimes would share things that "the teacher wouldn't agree with," such as their feeling that cohabitation before marriage is okay. At the end of my fieldwork at each school, I interviewed the teachers.

The marriage initiative also provided services to the Chickasaw Nation and the prison population. I was able to attend a workshop with a curriculum that had been especially designed for employees of the Chickasaw Nation. Attendance earned extra points toward the employee's year-end monetary bonus, and in that year about fifty had attended the one-day workshop. Fifteen were present at the workshop I participated in. Afterward, I interviewed the director who had designed the curriculum and supervised the workshops. I was able to interview a prisoner and his wife who had participated in a marriage workshop in prison as well as the chaplain who taught the course (see Appendix A for discussion of the problems accessing this population).

Finally, during my stay in Oklahoma, I conducted fieldwork on the campaign to ban same-sex marriage. I attended rallies, news conferences, and fundraising events in favor of and against the ban. I attended the church of one of the pastors who was leading the campaign against same-sex marriage and alternatively an "accepting" church of lesbian and gay parishioners. Over time, I conducted interviews with two leaders of the campaign against same-sex marriage and five leaders who fought the ban. Both of the leaders of the ban against same-sex marriage were also leaders of the marriage initiative, and I asked to interview them in connection with this program and then also asked questions about the ban against same-sex marriage. I sat in on meetings with several gay and lesbian organizations that were fighting the ban, and I interviewed an organizer from a national lesbian and gay organization who had come to Oklahoma from New York to help fight against the ban.

My last two months in Oklahoma proved to be especially disheartening after the constitutional amendment to ban same-sex marriage passed with 76 percent of voters in favor. During the many months I spent in Oklahoma, I experienced firsthand the suffering, mental anguish, and material hardships that lesbians and gay men endured due to lack of legal protections of their basic civil and human rights. One particularly tragic story, chronicled in the documentary film *Tying the Knot*, was that of Sam Beaumont, whom I interviewed during his five-year legal battle to save his ranch in Bristow, Oklahoma, where he and his partner, Earl Meadows, had lived for twenty-four years. When Earl died in 2000, long-lost cousins appeared out of nowhere to legally evict Sam, despite Earl's notarized will that left Sam the estate but mistakenly recorded only one witness signature rather than the required two. In a travesty of justice, Oklahoma courts bestowed the estate to the distant cousins. It is my goal in this book to uncover the boundary work that supports such discriminatory institutional and everyday practice.

Overview of the Book

Traveling throughout Oklahoma to study its marriage initiative, I discovered a number of important revelations that I map out in the following pages. Chapter 1 sets the stage in presenting the ideological connections between campaigns against same-sex marriage and marriage promotion initiatives. These two phenomena connect in their shared perception of marriage as the "building block" of the nation and as an essential component of American identity. Chapters 2 and 3 examine the ways that the ideology of marriage promotion forms the basic strategies and determines the dissemination of services on the ground. Chapter 2 investigates in depth the boundary work of marriage promotion workshops offered to the general population, which rehearses ideas concerning hierarchical gender relations. By teaching about the "opposite sexes," these workshops organize knowledge that depends on homosexuality's omission, a boundary troubled by the presence of a lesbian couple in two workshops. Chapter 3 uncovers the marriage initiative's strategies to preserve a boundary of heterosexual marriage through practices that, in contrast to the stated goal of closing the marriage gap, paradoxically do more to sustain or widen it.

Chapters 4, 5, and 6 focus on the boundary work of marriage promotion among targeted populations. Chapter 4 focuses on the small number of marriage workshops directed both at poor single mothers in conjunction with receiving TANF benefits and at the prison population. My research reveals how marriage promotion reinforces the outsider status of poor single women, and also the strategies that both social workers and TANF clients use to resist this ideology that has little relevance to poor women's lives. Chapter 5 examines classes that used the state-sponsored marriage initiative curriculum to teach the "essentials" of marriage to students at two high schools, and chapter 6 looks at the marital politics among Native Americans as an example of the importance of race and culture to understanding marriage ideology.

Overall, the politics of marriage in Oklahoma provided an unprecedented opportunity to study the hopes and fears of a broad range of Americans concerning the symbol of marriage within the context of transforming gender, sexual, and family relations, of ideas about welfare, race, and inequality, and of shifting moral and religious beliefs in American society. This book tells the story of a particular time and place that reflects broad trends, including an entrenchment of market fundamentalist ideals with a focus on cultural solutions to social problems, a political shift to the right propelled by conservative Christian leaders, and the political divisiveness of marriage politics. Marriage promotion politics in Oklahoma represents the perfect entry to study the social consequences of these significant shifts in American culture.

Unite!

Marriage and American Identity

We're the first state in the union to propose to use some of our TANF funds for the purpose of strengthening marriage. . . . Welfare reform, which I think, as a governor, was one of the wisest things the Republican Congress has done, has permitted us to say, forcefully, but not in a mean-spirited way, you need to take individual responsibility, you are a human being, you are a special asset, you are a citizen. We together, you and I, should help each other to be independent and responsible.
—Frank Keating, former governor of Oklahoma[1]

This is not a Democrat or Republican issue. This is between right and wrong, and marriage between one man and one woman is right. Marriage between two men or two women is wrong in America. You're standing for what's right here today. Right now in America and in Oklahoma, we're under siege.
—U.S. Representative John Sullivan (R-OK)[2]

Former Oklahoma governor Frank Keating gave the quote above at a lecture for the conservative Heritage Foundation, an influential public policy research institute that promotes the principles of "free enterprise, limited government, individual freedom, traditional American values, and a strong national defense."[3] He describes how he was surprised by an economic report stressing that, along with the standard "recommendations on the economic ledger side," Oklahoma needed to combat divorce among families with children and its out-of-wedlock births to improve the state's prospects for economic growth. Keating decided to address these social issues by forming the marriage initiative. Its initial goals were to promote government intervention "to reduce the high number of divorces in Oklahoma by one-third, by the year 2010; to teach citizens about the many personal and societal benefits of marriage; and to encourage currently-cohabiting Oklahoma couples to marry."[4] Accordingly, he states, "It is in the interest of good citizenship to abate this high incidence of divorce, out-of-wedlock births, violence, and drug abuse."[5]

In March 2000, the former governor announced that he would finance his marriage initiative with 10 percent of the state's Temporary Assistance to Needy Families (TANF) reserve fund, which worked out to $10 million, and Public Strategies, a public relations/public affairs firm, was awarded a contract to manage it.[6] In his lecture to the Heritage Foundation, Keating states that his reason for instituting the marriage initiative is a way to "make our state rich. That simple. To try to do what we can to have people prepared for marriage, to survive a marriage relationship, and to be able to provide a strong economic base for that family unit."[7] With these words, he draws together family, market, and patriotic ideologies that have had appeal to conservatives, and particularly to conservative Christians and their embrace of capitalism as an essential component of God's plan for America.[8]

The sociologist Andrew Cherlin points to two ideologies that motivate marriage advocates like Keating. Some take a moral position that marriage provides the best kind of family, while others favor it because, according to them, research proves that children do better when their parents are married.[9] For those motivated more by moral justification, many also support and are active in efforts to ban the legalization of same-sex marriage. Political scientists have found that this issue is particularly amenable to a framework of a religiously based morality that defines it in an inflexible and polarizing fashion.[10] Members of the religious right perform some of the most explicit boundary work in seeking to ensure that marriage remains heterosexual. Their efforts also harmonize with the tenets of marriage promotion in the assertion that marriage is central to social order and a bedrock of civilization. In his book *The Future of Marriage*, David Blankenhorn cites marriage promotion to be the "most important domestic initiative of our time," and he describes the importance of renewing marriage as "our primary social institution."[11] Tying together the moral and research-based secular trends of marriage promotion, he argues that marriage must remain heterosexual because kids need both a mother and a father. Same-sex marriage doesn't offer this normative configuration, and is thus detrimental to society. James Dobson, a prominent religious right leader, articulates a more extreme position against same-sex marriage: "Marriage, when it functions as intended, is good for everyone—for men, for women, for children, for the community, for the nation, and for the world." He describes the "revolution" toward legalizing same-sex marriage as a "tidal wave that threatens to overwhelm anyone who stands in its way," quoting an editorial in the *Boston Globe* that decries how adopting same-sex marriage would mean turning our backs on the expectation that men and women are not interchangeable and that children need both a mother and a father.[12]

While marriage promotion and campaigns to ban same-sex marriage have a different organizational structure and distinctive goals, in this chapter I examine their emergence and growth in Oklahoma to uncover their shared ideology that relies on an ideal heterosexual family as a way to manage and organize the diverse and often contradictory threads of market fundamentalism, religion, and morality. At a rally, Mike Jestes told the audience: "The very foundation of our civilization—marriage between one man and one woman, joined together as a family for the upbringing of children—is now under serious attack by an activist judiciary and a militant minority. . . . Marriage has been around from the beginning. Every known human society has marriage between one man and one woman."

This moral understanding links the ideologies of leaders of the religious right and marriage advocates, especially those who embrace a moral position, in their fight to strengthen heterosexual marriage as a social good. The dominance of Christian morality in the United States bolsters the "truth" of the universal one-man, one-woman marriage, ignoring the historical complexities of family and kinship. Even as many marriage advocates endeavor to distance themselves from the same-sex marriage debate, their embrace of heterosexual marriage as the superlative family form to raise children and strengthen society is a shared rallying point.

Setting the Stage for Marriage Promotion

Oklahoma offers ripe conditions for the unique blend of market fundamentalism, religion, and morality that motivates the state's efforts to strengthen heterosexual marriage in society and to ban same-sex marriage. Oklahoma is renowned for its embrace of evangelical Protestantism as a "Bible Belt" state, a term loosely used to describe the Southern region of the United States where conservative evangelical Christianity is dominant.[13] Almost 60 percent of registered Oklahoma voters say they attend church regularly, compared to the national average of 40 percent. This makes the state the sixth highest in the nation for church attendance. Nearly two-thirds of those who attend church identify as born-again or evangelical.[14] One in five Oklahomans is affiliated with the Southern Baptist denomination, ranking its membership third in the nation. The state accommodates several large

Christian ministries, including Oral Roberts University and Rhema Church and Bible Training Center. The Oklahoma Family Policy Council, an associate of James Dobson's Focus on the Family, puts out an election year voter's guide that provides candidate responses to election issues of import to those who embrace "family values" (many democratic candidates do not respond to these surveys). The Baptist General Convention is also a vital religious player in Oklahoma politics, actively supporting or opposing state ballot initiatives and legislation. Journalists have noted the importance of churches and religious organizations in Oklahoma as a significant factor in getting out the vote and winning or defeating initiatives.

Oklahoma also has a long history of legislating against lesbians and gay men.[15] Back in 1978, the state passed a statute stating that any teacher who is "advocating, soliciting, imposing, encouraging, or promoting public or private homosexual activity" may be "rendered unfit for his position," a measure that was struck down by the U.S. Supreme Court in 1985.[16] Oklahoma legislators worked at the national and state level to pass the federal law to deny recognition of same-sex marriages performed in other states, the Defense of Marriage Act (DOMA), that was signed into law by President Clinton in 1996. Howard Hendrick, a Republican state senator, drafted a state version that was signed into law by former Governor Keating in the same year. Elizabeth Birch, the president of the Human Rights Campaign, said of the political climate when she visited the state: "Oklahoma representatives cost my organization a lot of money, because we have to spend a lot of money to fight against what they want to do. We need a better atmosphere in this state for gays and lesbians."[17] One of the state's more draconian laws was passed in 2004: it was a bill that required birth certificates that were issued to children adopted by same-sex couples outside the state to carry the name of only one parent. Lambda Legal, which worked to overturn the law, described it as so extreme that it might have meant that children adopted by same-sex couples in other states would be orphans in the eyes of the law when in Oklahoma.

The year 2004 also brought an escalated national debate over the rights of same-sex couples after legal victories in 2003 for lesbian and gay rights, including the U.S. Supreme Court case *Lawrence v. Texas* as well as the *Goodridge* decision in Massachusetts. The decision of officials to issue marriage licenses to same-sex couples in San Francisco and other counties in early 2004 became a call to arms among religious conservatives. In the first few months of 2004, Oklahoma legislators introduced ten measures to ban same-sex marriage. One bill presented by Representative Bill Graves (R-OK) sought to deny recognition of same-sex marriages or civil unions, declaring such relationships "shall be considered repugnant to the public policy of the state."[18] The sheer number of bills was perplexing, because Oklahoma had already legislated a state DOMA, which, in March 2004, was corroborated by Oklahoma's attorney general in its effectiveness to limit marriage to one man and one woman and to proscribe out-of-state same-sex marriages. Still, lawmakers argued that a constitutional prohibition was needed to guard against "activist judges" who might render DOMA unconstitutional.[19] A coalition of government officials, churches, and parachurch organizations joined together to campaign against same-sex marriage, and several rallies were held at the state Capitol. All of these bills were killed at the committee level. Several sympathetic House Democrats had attended an unprecedented meeting with lesbian and gay activists to discuss the need to keep a measure to ban same-sex marriage from leaving committee. They agreed that, if a bill did exit from committee, it would easily pass.

This assessment proved prophetic. In April, conservative legislators revised a measure ready for Senate vote that dealt with crimes relating to underage sex. Gutting this bill, they created the "Marriage Protection Act" as an amendment to the Oklahoma constitution to ban same-sex marriage. The bill passed in the Senate by 38–7.[20] With little discussion and no debate, the House voted 92–4 in favor of sending the constitutional amendment to voters. State Question 711 (SQ 711) read:

> This measure adds a new section of law to the Constitution. It adds Section 35 to Article 2. It defines marriage to be between one man and one woman. It prohibits giving the benefits of marriage to people who are not married. It provides that same-sex marriages in other states are not valid in this state. It makes issuing a marriage license in violation of this section a misdemeanor.

Analysts noted the ambiguity of the phrase "benefits of marriage." As worded, the proposed amendment might prevent the state from recognizing any legal status for common-law relationships, civil unions, and domestic partnerships between gay couples *and* between heterosexual couples. Oklahoma is one of ten states to recognize common-law marriage.

Activism in Oklahoma to ban same-sex marriage represents a snapshot of the broad battles that have ensued across the nation. In 2004, religious conservatives fought and won the passage of thirteen state constitutional amendments to preserve an exclusively heterosexual definition of marriage.

The issue of same-sex marriage has transformed the religious right by changing its agenda to prioritize marriage, facilitating ecumenical and interracial
coalitions, producing new state organizations, and stimulating electoral
activities among congregations.[21] Religious right groups, such as Focus on
the Family, worked together to organize special events, including "Protect
Marriage Sunday" and the "Mayday for Marriage" rally in Washington, D.C.
Several groups formed the Marriage Amendment Project, which seeks to
pass a federal constitutional amendment to ban same-sex marriage. This
activism brought forward a renewed focus on the relationship of marriage,
Christianity, and American identity.

Marriage and a Christian Nation

Religious conservatives embrace a few core values. The importance of the
family and the attendant norm of sex within heterosexual marriage are central. The religious historian David Watt argues that among religious conservatives (and especially evangelicals) the family has become so important as
to supplant expectations of the "second coming" as a main source of hope in
a world of sin.[22] Family is understood as a timeless institution at the foundation of civilization. Yet, representations of family, seemingly fixed in time,
often date back to the 1950s, such as within illustrations by Norman Rockwell that portray the "happy families and the safe neighborhoods, the homespun quality of simple American virtues, the innocence and predictability of
it all."[23] The executive director of the Oklahoma General Baptist Convention
described to me his love of Norman Rockwell's work as a longing for a time
when family life was stable, predictable, and based on commitment in comparison to the uncertainty of today's world:

> I'm a great Norman Rockwell fan, probably because it's a period of his-
> tory I relish. It reminds me of growing up in a small town as a little boy.
> You know, marriages weren't perfect then. My mom and dad's marriage
> wasn't perfect, but you know what, my mom and dad had the same com-
> mitment that Paula and I have. They had Christ and a love for one another.
> So, when things got tough, it went back to the source of their strength. I
> think that across American history that certainly, before the rebellion of
> the '60s, it was easier to have this kind of unswerving commitment, and
> historically divorce was much less in those days than it is today. I think we
> are in a time when everything's up for grabs; all of the mores and anchors
> we've held on to are being questioned today.

While the executive director acknowledges that "in reality" marriages weren't perfect in the 1950s, his words speak to a mythical past when the American family was "kinder, gentler."[24]

This desire to reinvent a mythical American identity speaks to another element of consensus among conservative evangelicals: a tendency toward a "fervent nationalism."[25] The demographer Tom Smith characterized this nationalism as "the idea that America's political troubles can be alleviated by bringing Christianity into the government."[26] In a 2004 survey, the political scientist Tom Green found that, while white evangelicals comprise about a fourth of the U.S. population, 12.6 percent are "traditionalist evangelicals" who espouse the values associated with the religious right and more than half disagree that "homosexuals should have the same rights as other Americans." Only 3 percent of traditionalists favor same-sex marriage, the lowest among all religious groups studied.[27] Religious right groups such as the evangelical empire of James Dobson, whose Focus on the Family has an eighty-one-acre campus with its own ZIP code in Colorado, argues for the connection between family values and our "great nation." In an interview with the *Boston Globe*, Dobson spoke of two "starkly contrasting worldviews that predominate today's moral and cultural debate. One side defends the traditional values that have made this nation great for more than 225 years; the other works to chisel away at that foundation."[28] Many traditionalists perceive a growing global secularism that threatens their values.

The religious right in Oklahoma held political rallies and events to confirm the importance of patriotism and morality to American identity and to condemn practices and behavior outside the boundaries of this definition. I was at times caught off-guard by the prevalence of language and rhetoric in public settings against homosexuality, such as t-shirts at rallies and events with the slogan "God Made Adam and Eve, Not Adam and Steve" donned by matronly women with silver-bouffant hairdos. While sometimes startled, I was quite familiar with the conservative Christian disapprobation against homosexuality. I remember complaints by members of my childhood church about how homosexuals had hijacked the word "gay" to describe their sinful lifestyle, and fears abounded that American culture was heading toward Gomorrah. The words of the executive director of the Baptist General Convention were then no surprise when he confirmed the need to take a stand against homosexuality: "I am very strong. I am uncompromising. I make no bones about it that it's a sin. In fact, the scripture calls it an abomination to God, and I believe that is so. He calls the sin the abomination, but the homosexual is no worse a person than I am." This hard-line position is softened by the idea that everyone sins and Christians should hate the sin and not the sinner. Yet this one sin galvanizes people in a way that many others do not.

For religious conservatives, the idea that lesbian and gay couples would be allowed to marry impinges on the centrality of marriage to the American nation. The executive director of the Baptist General Convention underscored this point:

> I think many who may not be passionate or take a strong stand at any other time take a stand here, because [marriage] is the foundation of our culture, and I believe that people in general see that when you have fractured the foundation by saying that homosexual marriage is the same as marriage between a man and a woman, it goes against everything—against history and the Bible. Where this has become the norm, it has been the breaking point of culture and society.

Thus, marriage is *fundamental* to what makes America a great nation. Having been raised in an environment that taught similar principles, I found myself nodding in agreement when I interviewed the director of the Family Policy Council as he argued for the importance of marriage as a Judeo-Christian value in the founding of our nation: "We believe that our country was founded on Judeo-Christian principles and we do everything we can to fortify these, such as marriage between one man and one woman." Conservative Christians view religion, marriage, and American values as being in a symbiotic relationship. Marriage, like the nation, is founded on God's principles to shine forth as an exemplar of democracy and freedom. For many on the religious right, America—once a beacon of hope to other nations—is now itself threatened with the conditions of secularism and "humanism" that wreak havoc on its identity and culture.

Thus, in regard to the future of America, religious right leaders signal a need to acknowledge marriage's unique relationship to democracy. At the "God and Country Rally" held at the Oklahoma State Capitol, Rick Scarborough was the featured speaker. Leaving his position as pastor of Pearland First Baptist Church in a Houston suburb in 2002, Scarborough founded Vision American, an organization dedicated to engaging "patriot pastors" to work to restore Judeo-Christian values to the moral and civic framework in their communities, states, and nation. At the rally, he told the audience of roughly a hundred believers huddled together on a cold, rainy day about a "patriot pastor" in Canada who expressed to him that "when the clouds gathered over the horizon, when the province of Nova Scotia where I live legalized the travesty called same-sex marriage—a contradiction in terms—I immediately revoked my government license for marriage administration." Scarborough informed us that this "travesty" in Canada accentuates the need to vote in the United States to fight against a similar scenario and that it is a "crime against our God" that so few Christians vote—only 24 percent who profess faith in Christ voted in the last election. He rallied the crowd, "As believers of the Lord Jesus Christ and as citizens of the United States, we have access to participate in freedoms that most of the world doesn't. . . . We must vote. I wish I had a banner I could put on my lapel that would simply remind us how would Jesus vote?"

A few weeks later, I attended the Oklahoma Family Policy Council's yearly First Things banquet honoring "Family, Faith, & Freedom." The keynote speaker, David Barton, has been a central figure in laying the groundwork for a Christian nationalist history. He is the founder and president of WallBuilders, a Texas-based organization whose purpose is to educate the public on the founding fathers' intention for "Christianity to be central to American government."[29] Barton began his "Let Freedom Ring Presentation" by responding to those who think our country is a secular nation. He made the case that the Christian basis of our nation has allowed it to exist as the longest constitutional republic in the world, whereas France has had fifteen forms of government, and Italy fifty-five. His next slide was a close-up of two men kissing, and the women at my table groaned in disgust. This, he declared, represents a major threat to our republic. Next, he gave statistics of other nations (specifically Scandinavia and the Netherlands) that have legalized same-sex marriage to make the case for a correlation between its legalization and marital decline, a theory discredited by demographers.[30] In Missouri, Barton told us, the initiative to ban same-sex marriage brought out more voters in their primary, and this must happen in Oklahoma for the November election. He concluded, "You Christians are accountable, whether you accept it or not."

In the United States, the legal and cultural aspects of heterosexual marriage generate a moral boundary in the construction of what it means to be American. Longing for an ideal past when heterosexual marriage was dominant, conservatives cling to a vision of America from the 1950s when Christian morals prevailed among white, middle-class families. "For many Americans—provided they were white, middle-class, Christian, and heterosexual—the decade probably *does* recall an innocent past."[31] Drawing on this mythology, a subtle form of racism emerges from several interviews with religious proponents of Judeo-Christian values. One Christian leader explained to me that these values are being diluted by other cultures and religious traditions: "Because we are a melting pot for many countries, a growing percentage of our people are not faith-based, and therefore that affects the decision-making process. They bring their own faith, culture, values to the table and we're a melting pot." For this leader, the melting pot and the interracial relationships that it implies represent an ethnic mixing that dilutes dominant cultural ideals based on Christian values. In our interview, he applied this worry about the diluting effect of outside forces to the case of Africa where his adult children work with orphaned teenagers to underscore the relationship between marriage and social order: "I know, such as in Africa, where my adult kids work, those orphaned teenagers have never experienced the value of marriage, and because of that they wouldn't know what a marriage looked like. Many of their parents weren't married and had multiple relationships. Children were the by-product. So we are dealing with a society of people like this that come forward." Here, the relationship among whiteness, Judeo-Christian values, and a middle-class orientation to the traditional family is evident. Those fighting to ban same-sex marriage consistently emphasize the superiority of marriage to a moral order that privileges virtuous (middle-class, white) values over those raised in broken (single-mother and coded black) families who perpetuate crime and a chain of more broken families.

Conservative religious leaders and politicians draw on depictions of outsiders to imply that lesbians and gay men are "other" to American society and wish to raze it by destroying marriage. A video distributed to over 6,000 churches across Oklahoma featured the state senator James A. Williamson, an author of the bill to ban same-sex marriage, and his wife, Sandra. Portraying an image of lesbians and gay men as a threat to the American family, Williamson addresses the camera: "I am Senator James Williamson and this is my wife Sandra, and we want to talk to you about an issue that concerns all conservative Christians in Oklahoma. The God-ordained concept of marriage between one man and one woman is under attack in the U.S. and in Oklahoma." In the apocalyptic tone of many conservative Christian leaders, Williamson suggests that legalizing same-sex marriage will lead down a slippery slope: "Homosexual marriage will quickly destroy the traditional family and will lead to polygamy and other alternatives to one-man, one-woman unions." He denounces lesbians and gay men as universally promiscuous and therefore unfit to parent: "Homosexuals are rarely monogamous, often having more than a hundred partners in a lifetime. The implications for children growing up in a world of constantly changing parents are profound." For Williamson, the moral argument is clear: "Judeo-Christian values have always been the basis for American law and culture." Thus, Williamson's argument draws a distinct boundary to demarcate Christian morality as integral to the definition of heterosexual marriage and American values.

I attended a conservative, nondenominational church that aired this video. The pastor gave an introduction drawing on fears of Muslim terrorists in a post-9/11 world. He urged his congregation to vote to fight against the "terror alert in all our homes. Terrorists are trying to get into your home and break up your family." After the video and sermon, the pastor announced Marriage Protection Week, a national week initiated by conservative religious leaders to fight against same-sex marriage. That day, they honored both sets of couples married for ten to twenty-five years and for twenty-five to forty-nine years with bronze medals. Roughly seventy-five predominantly white couples marched down the aisle to receive a medal while the organist played "Onward Christian Soldier." The medals, placed around each person's neck, included a large red, white, and blue ribbon. The merging of marriage, Christianity, and militarism offers a potent window into conservative Christian anxieties about the global as well as local forces that are producing multicultural, less "secure" societies. Behind this anxiety is the nostalgia for a past when the unquestioned norm of marriage ruled, a norm that was implicit to distinct boundaries of race, class, and sexuality. The loss of freedom that the threat of same-sex marriage implies represents a loss of the preeminence of the white, middle-class, heterosexual family in American culture. While this specific formation of anxiety around Christian identity and marriage may be more particular to conservative Christians, a general anxiety concerning the declining dominance of heterosexual marriage and its relation to American identity brings together the ideologies that motivate the fight against same-sex marriage and the need to promote heterosexual marriage.

Promoting Marriage to Restore America

Rather than concentrate on the threat of same-sex marriage, marriage advocates seek to alleviate America's problems by restoring a marriage culture in society. A 2004 report issued by the Institute for American Values states: "Why should law and public policy support marriage? A large body of social science evidence confirms that marriage is a wealth-creating institution." It continues, "A government and a society that actively supports marriage (in fair, reasonable, and prudent ways) is the goal, not marriage neutrality in public policy."[32] This perspective of promoting marriage for economic and social benefits complements the religious-moral framework embraced by the religious right in its focus on the importance of marriage to American identity. As quoted in the beginning of this chapter, Governor Keating attributes his motivation for launching the marriage initiative in Oklahoma to economics. As the marriage initiative emerged, factors driving it spoke to religious, market-capitalist, and nationalist concerns. Over time, the marriage initiative evolved to implement its programs based on what social scientific research says about marriage rather than on an overt religious-moral agenda. As I discuss below, however, some initiative leaders acknowledged the blurring of boundaries between religious and nonreligious activities on the ground.

In the initial stages, religious conservatives were highly influential in the creation of the marriage initiative and in shaping its focus on reaching out to religious communities. Jerry Regier, then-Cabinet Secretary for Oklahoma's Health and Human Services, had long been involved in conservative Christian politics. He had founded and served as the first president of the Family Research Council in 1983, a conservative Christian think tank in Washington, D.C., that has organized against lesbian and gay rights, feminism, abortion, and other issues. Influenced by Regier, Keating announced in his January 1999 State of the State Address that Oklahoma's high rate of divorce was a social problem, and four out of the seven goals he outlined focused on marriage promotion and strengthening: to reduce divorce and out-of-wedlock birth rates by one-third and to reduce drug abuse and child abuse and neglect by 50 percent by 2010. Taking steps to inaugurate the Oklahoma Marriage Initiative, Keating convened a First Lady and Governor's Conference on Marriage that was funded by the conservative "pro-family" Burbridge Foundation and the Baptist General Convention.[33] Speakers were prominent figures from conservative and centrist organizations, including Patrick Fagan, a senior researcher with the Heritage Foundation; Wade Horn, then president of the National Fatherhood Initiative; and David Blankenhorn, president of the centrist Institute for American Values. The conference also brought a self-identified liberal, Theodora Ooms of the Center for Law and Social Policy, who asserted that marriage promotion is neither liberal nor conservative but "everybody's issue."[34]

A key component involved churches and religious leaders as being crucial to renewing marriage. Regier states: "Churches will play a key role in this initiative, not just because of their moral mission, but because of their direct contact with those who seek to be married. Whether or not people regularly participate in a local church, most seek the guidance of a religious leader or express a desire to use a church facility when they make the decision to marry."[35] The executive director of the Oklahoma Family Policy Council, a nonprofit organization that is a central clearinghouse for antigay and lesbian campaigns in Oklahoma, was a representative of "family and faith" on the initial steering committee, and three of the initial six representatives were from conservative Christian churches or organizations. Churches spearheaded the Oklahoma initiative with an effort to promote marriage preparation.

One goal was to hold religious leaders responsible to disseminate the message of marriage's importance, culminating in the Oklahoma Marriage Covenant, a contract that asked pastors to make a commitment to set aside a "preparation period" of four to six months before performing a wedding, to require four to six marital preparation classes, and to encourage mentoring of the newly married. It reads: "I believe that marriage is a covenant intended by God to be a lifelong relationship between a man and a woman. I promise to God, to my family, and my community to encourage couples to remain steadfast in unconditional love, reconciliation, and sexual purity, while purposefully growing in their covenant marriage relationship."[36] Over 1,200 pastors are listed as signatories on the marriage initiative website. The wording of the covenant derives from the national Covenant Marriage Movement, which bills itself as "a movement of God to provide an avenue through which His people can boldly stand alongside thousands of other couples and congregations to affirm God's design for marriage as a covenant relationship."[37] Three states—Arizona, Louisiana, and Arkansas—have passed covenant marriage legislation to give couples an option of a more restrictive marital contract.[38] Similar legislation, introduced most recently in 2007, has not succeeded in Oklahoma.[39]

Conservative religious leaders traveled to cities across Oklahoma to set up a special event, a luncheon, or a speaking engagement to enable pastors to sign the covenant. The majority of those who made the commitment to offer marriage preparation were from conservative Christian denominations. On the marriage initiative's list of 1,200 signatories, only thirty-eight were from non-Protestant churches: twenty-six were Catholic, eight Episcopal, two Orthodox, one Jewish, and one Islamic. These figures are not surprising given the religious profile of Oklahoma. According to the Pew Research Center, 85 percent of Oklahomans who adhere to a religious faith are Christian, accounting for about 80 percent of the population. The percentage of Oklahomans affiliated with Catholicism is half the national average, while the percentage who identify as evangelical Protestants is more than twice the national average.[40]

In this early stage, the marriage initiative also appointed Drs. Les and Leslie Parrott to be "Marriage Ambassadors" in Oklahoma. Les Parrott, a professor of psychology, and his wife, Leslie Parrott, a marriage and family therapist, codirect the Center for Relationship Development at Seattle Pacific University, a Christian liberal arts college. They have written several books, including *Becoming Soul Mates,* which helps couples "not just to know God individually but to experience God together."[41] These ambassadors were paid a combined annual salary of $250,000 to serve as Scholars in Residence at Oklahoma State University, to travel the state speaking on college campuses, to train married couples as mentors for the newly married, and to write a short book, *Building Better Marriages in Oklahoma.*[42] All of these activities focused time and resources to gain the support of faith-based groups for the marriage initiative.

Early on, the novelty of the statewide marriage initiative propelled Oklahoma into the national media limelight as a pioneer of this new "anti-poverty strategy." To reach more Oklahomans, the initiative began to move beyond its initial focus on religious leaders as a strategy to offer marriage education workshops that used a skills-based curriculum. A federal government report on "Putting Marriage on the Agenda" points to the ways that Oklahoma sought to "gain credibility" by relying on social scientific research: "Oklahoma marriage supporters drew on research, and brought experts and advocates together to stimulate interest, address skeptics, and build awareness."[43] Another assessment of the marriage initiative in Oklahoma—"What If a Governor Decided to Address the M-Word"—again addresses the importance of research (over values) to then-governor Frank Keating's motivation for instituting the marriage initiative: "Marriage and divorce have traditionally been considered personal, private matters, the province of the religious community, not government. It was a bold step for a Governor to decide that strengthening marriage is government business. What were his reasons? Governor Keating's personal values and religious beliefs undoubtedly played a part, but it was research that provided the rationale."[44]

Over time, the marriage initiative embraced a multisector approach that offered marriage-related services through existing state systems in addition to the private sector (with its focus on churches) and designated a religious and secular track for its activities. Still, promoting marriage in the state blurred religious, legal, economic, and social dimensions. One supervisor described to me this diffusion:

There are several things kind of mixed up in this whole batch. Part of it is the whole move to faith-based initiatives. Now, to some degree, and in a lot of people's thinking, that's very separate. We've got lines of demarcation. But, in OMI [Oklahoma Marriage Initiative], things kind of float through that have a faith-based orientation, even with our TANF sessions [for welfare clients].

Created in the 1970s and 1980s, the federal government's faith-based initiative was significantly enhanced when former President Bush established the White House Office of Faith-Based and Community Initiatives (FBCI) in 2000. His goal was to expand the charitable choice provisions of the 1996 welfare reform law, to increase participation of religious organizations as social service providers by reducing alleged barriers to receiving federal funding, and to permit groups to maintain their religious identity. Religious organizations have long received funding to provide social services, but historically, to maintain church and state separation, they have been required to establish a separately incorporated organization and to use funds to pursue secular activities. New rules and regulations implemented by FBCI challenge this principle. According to a report issued by the Roundtable for Religion and Social Policy, the Bush administration's efforts "may have weakened longstanding walls preventing religious groups from inserting spiritual activities into secular services."[45]

Mary Myrick, the president of Public Strategies, told me that the marriage initiative is not part of FBCI. She said, "We have a faith component to our initiative and we have a faith coordinator who is developing that sector just like we have people developing the prison sector and other sectors. We like to say we don't discriminate against people because they are people of faith, but we are also not a faith-based initiative." Myrick argued that impacting people solely through their churches was not enough. When I asked her about issues of church and state separation, she was clear:

We believe that by law we could go much further than we have. We haven't gone nearly . . . we haven't gone very far. I mean, to the extent that we've gone is we fund faith leaders to be trained just like we fund counselors and others to be trained. So, we pay for that training for religious people, and they can deliver it in church; they can deliver it in public settings.

Yet the statement above about how "things kind of float through that have a faith-based orientation" suggests that the marriage initiative pushes the limits of the constitutionality of religious neutrality, as some volunteers who teach in government-funded TANF settings are evangelical Christians who openly discuss their faith (see chapter 4). While the marriage initiative is not funded through faith-based monies, it has benefited from FBCI policies to permit social service policy to mix with faith-based principles.

The initiative's strong faith-based component includes many religious leaders who were influential in the constitutional amendment to ban same-sex marriage. However, Myrick told me that the initiative sought to distance itself from the debate:

> We actually don't deal with it much. We are very clear about our mission. Our mission is to provide public information about what the research says about what works in relationships, and frankly, there's not a lot of long-term research about what happens with gay and lesbian couples. We don't really have much to speak to in that area. Our position is that we're a marriage initiative designed to encourage activities that lead to marriage, and our state has defined marriage as an act between a man and a woman and until the state defines it differently, we . . . it's really all defined for us. We don't get into the debate about it. We stay as far away from that in that it is for us a distraction from our mission, so we really work hard not to be in it.

The justification for focusing on heterosexual couples due to a lack of long-term research on same-sex relationships is inconsistent with its encouragement of "activities that lead to marriage" among other populations. For example, there is very little research on the effectiveness of marriage education workshops for poor, single mothers. Yet, the marriage initiative has provided workshops for them (see chapter 4). Likewise, there is little research on the effects of marriage education workshops on high school students, the prison population, and other groups, such as the Chickasaw Nation, targeted by the marriage initiative (see chapters 4, 5, and 6). Underlying Myrick's words is the assumption that these populations can be undisputed recipients of marriage education because of their presumed heterosexuality. Myrick informed me that the initiative wouldn't prohibit lesbians and gay men from receiving services. But this stance, I learned, was itself controversial.

A memo sent out by the federal government announced that government-funded marriage promotion services should not be afforded to lesbian and gay couples. One of the more progressive employees of the Oklahoma Department of Human Services (OKDHS), Deidre, expressed her dismay when she received this:

One of the things I noticed in a memo back in February or March of this year was from Wade Horn's desk. I don't remember the number on it because it made me so angry that I threw it away, but it was talking about marriage education services, not OMI in particular—and I don't remember how it came into the memo—but it was a real short sentence that said this will not be afforded to gay and lesbian couples because they are not recognized as legally married and blah, blah, blah.

One of her coworkers who had completed the marriage initiative training was planning to offer classes to the lesbian and gay community. This person had met with a group of lesbians and gay men who had been excited about the workshops. Then the memo arrived. Deidre explained,

> I went to her desk, and she told me, "I've had second thoughts about this as a DHS [Department of Human Services] employee." Especially since this memo had come out, she was concerned about putting DHS in a position. She is typically a person who will think beyond her personal stuff in thinking about how this is going to reflect on DHS—not overly loyal—but that's just the way she thinks. I said I respect that, but if you ever change your mind, you are a wonderful trainer, and I would love for you to continue this. Then I had to call this group to tell them that we can't provide the training above the radar, but I guess I am going to have to provide it under the radar.

Deidre said that as a social worker she felt she had ethical standards to meet that included providing services to people when they say they want them. "I'm not trying to kick up dust. I'm really concerned about when you are willing to discriminate against anybody, somebody is going to get hurt along the way." She went on to describe her efforts to ensure that the services would eventually get to "all Oklahomans," and not just heterosexuals.

In contrast to the stated goal of Mary Myrick to stay out of the same-sex marriage debate, religious right representatives of the marriage initiative were much more vocal about the need to ban same-sex couples from marrying to ensure heterosexuality's dominance in America. Mike Jestes, the director of the Oklahoma Family Policy Council, discussed the urgency of defending the one-man, one-woman marriage. At the statewide training I attended for instruction on the Christian curriculum, a marriage initiative employee introduced him: "Mike is involved in many things in this state, including abstinence and Christian marriage. He helps Christians find the tools to support the thoughts and framework of what God set down for marriage." Upon taking the stage, he urged the participants to vote for the ban against same-sex marriage in November. He told the audience,

> Who told our nation that marriage can be between two men or two women? Two men can't have a baby; two women can't have a baby! Every baby needs a mom and a dad. That is why the fabric of America is built on the relationship between one man and one woman. Our bodies teach us that we respond to the opposite sex differently.

This quote draws attention to the importance of heterosexuality and marriage in defining what it means to be American. He urged the audience to unite in "the culture war," telling us, "If you don't vote, you are not a good Christian. We are losing the battle in America because Christians think that they can just read the Bible."[46] I was amazed to hear this faith leader speak so frankly about his views on the moral vision of marriage at a state-sponsored training. Such instances of professing one's faith occurred in other state-sponsored settings and highlight the ways that the marriage initiative blurs the lines of religion and state. In addition, they demonstrate the ways that the marriage initiative brings together anxieties about changes in family and the boundary work that many feel compelled to perform to ensure that marriage remains exclusively heterosexual.

This chapter has shed light on the broad anxieties that motivate the fight against same-sex marriage and the goal of marriage promotion as a way to remedy the numerous social and moral ills that afflict American society. Wade Horn, one of the speakers at the First Lady and Governor's Conference, told participants that he cared about marriage because it is the best way "as a nation" to ensure children's well-being.[47] Marriage advocates and religious right leaders seek to promote (and protect) marriage against societal influences that bring fragmentation and challenge the social order, including globalization and a diversifying culture. Keating in his lecture to the Heritage Foundation summarized this idea succinctly: "We as a people recognize that strong families make a strong society; that intact families make for an intact, homogenous [sic] society."[48] Imperatives of the global economy have spurred unprecedented transnational movement of capital and workers across borders to make use of low-wage labor markets, have increased the demand for immigrants in the United States to work for minimum-wage, unskilled, and part-time jobs, and have pushed record numbers of women into the workforce to make up for the lagging male "breadwinner" wage.

Marriage advocates turn to marriage as the nation's best hope for renewing a "homogeneous" American identity to produce citizens who will nurture the ethos of a harmonious, unified nation. According to Keating, the problem of divorce and out-of-wedlock births "is not a Republican issue; [it] is an American issue" that raises "serious challenges to our future."[49] Regier elaborates on this theme of good citizenship: "The Marriage Initiative proposed by Governor Keating challenges Oklahomans to rise to our best. That pioneer spirit that has overcome odds has always served us well. . . . Together we will strengthen and honor marriage as an institution—for the good of all of us."[50] Pointing to the "pioneer spirit" to strengthen the institution of marriage, Regier speaks to a nationalist pride based on an ideology that upholds the middle-class, white, married, heterosexual family as the model of citizenship. In the next chapter, I provide an in-depth analysis of the boundary work of the marriage initiative on the ground that defends this model of family life and affirms the outsider status of lesbians and gay men through its embrace of traditional gender norms.

The Stakes of Gender
and Heterosexuality

"So they are no longer two, but one." Jesus Christ.
—Christian Prevention and Relationship
Enhancement Program (CPREP)[1]

The whole system of attribution and meaning that we call *gender* relies on and to a great extent derives from the structuring provided by marriage. Turning men and women into husbands and wives, marriage has designated the way both sexes act in the world.

—Nancy Cott, *Public Vows:*
A History of Marriage and the Nation[2]

As opposed to the sometimes bewildering fragmentation and vaunted diversity highlighted in American life, this era [the 1950s] invokes the homogeneity, the accord, the like-mindedness that are frequently the by-products of cultural cohesion. It suggests the orderliness and predictability of many a 1950s sitcom rerun, wherein Dad proclaims "Honey, I'm home!" and hangs up his hat.

—Mary Caputi, *A Kinder, Gentler America*[3]

On a dreary, rainy January day, I attended my first weekend marriage workshop at a church in Oklahoma City that I had located on the marriage initiative's website. After introducing myself as a researcher who was studying Oklahoma's efforts to strengthen marriage to the workshop leader and the two couples present, I was given a workbook. I sat down and tried to hide my astonishment as I read the cover: " 'So they are no longer two, but one.' Jesus Christ." This was the Christian version of the Prevention and Relationship Enhancement Program (CPREP). I had read about the secular curriculum before traveling to Oklahoma, but I hadn't realized that the marriage initiative had also adopted a Christian version. Matty, the workshop leader, began by telling the story of Adam and Eve, who were made aware of their nakedness after eating the forbidden fruit, and she continued to deliver a moral message about biblical marriage as part of a Christian curriculum.

Several weeks later, I met with a new surprise. Another rainy March evening at the end of the workday found couples arriving to attend the first of a six-week secular marriage workshop at a human service agency. Participants took seats around three tables arranged in a U-shape, as the two workshop leaders handed out "All About You" forms for participants to fill out. I counted thirteen couples, and during introductions I learned that ten were married, one engaged, one living together, and one had just begun dating. Four single women attended who—except for me—acted as coaches to the couples during the workshop exercises. The participants were predominantly white, with one interracial couple (African American/white). Just before the class was about to begin, two white women in their late fifties entered the room and took the last two seats across from me. Were they a couple, I wondered? No, I told myself, that's improbable. My speculations gave way as the two workshop leaders began the class. David, a white man in his late fifties, told us that he held a master's degree and had been married for thirty years. Randy, a bit younger and also white, introduced himself as an associate Baptist pastor at a church in town. We then proceeded in a circle, where the male partner at the opposite end of the room set the example by introducing himself and his wife. The two women were last, and the first didn't miss a beat as she said, "Hi, I'm Chris, and this is my life partner, Tammy." There was a moment of silence in the room, and then David mumbled a comment about the diversity of participants.

The presence of Tammy and Chris, along with an additional lesbian couple in the following workshop, troubled the generally seamless teachings on gender and sexuality that dominated the marriage classes. Workshops focused on conservative gender norms in relation to what it means to be a husband or a wife. Referencing the ideal nuclear family, they spoke to a conceptualization of gender that fits the theoretical perspective of the sociologist Talcott Parsons on male and female "roles" and their divergent social functions—the male role being "instrumental" and the female "expressive."[4] Conceptualizing these as complementary, Parsons argued for the necessity of "a clear separation of the sex roles such as to ensure that they do not come in competition with each other" to safeguard "family solidarity."[5]

In this chapter, I examine marriage workshops, attended by predominantly white, middle-class, heterosexual couples, that promote conservative gender norms and often emphasize the Christian principle of the one man and one woman marriage. Workshops focus on the problem of gender relations within an implicit and pervasive heterosexual imperative that is built on the absence of nonheterosexuals and the prohibition of their desire. This lack "haunts" marriage workshops as the unexamined backdrop for teaching about the "opposite sexes," and it organizes an epistemology whose internal logic depends on homosexuality's censure.[6] Workshops teach principles about marriage that rely on commonsense ideas of gender and heterosexuality, ideas that speak to a mythical gendered American family whose predictability is captured by the 1950s sitcom ethos when Dad, after a long day at work, hangs up his coat and proclaims "Honey, I'm home!" In contrast to this predictability, the presence of same-sex couples in the marriage workshops troubled easy assumptions, creating tension and a paradox. No longer an invisible backdrop, heterosexuality was made less stable. The reaction involved boundary work to reaffirm the heterosexual imperative.

Teaching Gender Hierarchy

As the marriage initiative evolved, the primary emphasis focused on facilitating marriage workshops by using the PREP curriculum and its Christian version throughout Oklahoma. The initiative offered PREP through existing state systems in addition to the private sector. Initiative leaders called this the "Service Delivery System," which targets three key public agencies: the State Department of Health, the Cooperative Extension Service at the Oklahoma State University, and the OKDHS. The goal has been to train volunteers and state employees to offer marriage workshops in the PREP curriculum (the following chapters offer in-depth accounts of why these workshops draw predominantly middle-class couples and how they are configured when other populations are targeted). The training is free on the condition that volunteers commit to teach four workshops, free of charge. By April 2004, the initiative reported training 1,072 workshop leaders and offering the workshops to 18,721 individuals.[7]

Leaders selected PREP as the curriculum for these workshops, because of "its strong grounding in research."[8] PREP helps partners "say what they need to say, get to the heart of problems, avoid standoffs and connect with each other instead of pushing each other away."[9] It emphasizes lowering risk factors such as poor communication and negative interaction and raising protective factors such as increasing a couple's awareness of commitment. While PREP's design is based on the tenets of marital therapy, the marriage initiative emphasizes that workshops are not marital counseling or therapy but "marriage education." Taking a PREP workshop involves "coaching very much like learning to play tennis or golf."[10] PREP teaches basic communication skills. Each person attending the workshop receives a "PREP Couples' Manual," a workbook that has writing assignments, blank space in which to take notes, and homework assignments.

The keystone of the curriculum is the "Speaker/Listener Technique," which provides a structure for safe and effective communication. At the back are two perforated squares called "The Floor" that provide the rules for the speaker: "Speak for yourself, don't mindread! Keep statements brief. Don't go on and on. Stop to let the listener paraphrase." For the listener: "Paraphrase what you hear. Focus on the speaker's message. Don't rebut." And for both: "The speaker has the floor. Speaker keeps the floor while the listener paraphrases. Share the floor." An awkward style of exchange that slows down the communication process, the technique involves passing the floor back and forth after each person has expressed her or his concerns and the other has paraphrased what they heard. Flipping through the pages of the workbook, one finds topics on filters that shape the way a message is received; hidden issues that are subjects or feelings not discussed openly; expectations that can either be "in the fog" or "in the clear"; problem-solving exercises that include agenda setting, brainstorming, and agreement and compromise; and forgiveness, a conscious decision not to pay another back for a wrong.

The Christian version of PREP combines moral principles with the secular version's therapeutic language.[11] In CPREP, each new communication or relational skill is followed by a Bible verse, and there is an emphasis throughout on God's design for marriage. The central theme is "Oneness" in marriage, which derives from a key biblical passage (Genesis 2:24) that conservative Christians regularly cite as theological proof of marriage's original union of one man and one woman: "For this reason a man will leave his father and mother and be united to his wife, and they will become one flesh."[12] Oneness involves mystery that is hard to define. It is about "blood kinship as well as spiritual, emotional, psychological, and sexual union between husband and wife." The curriculum explains that the "first marriage" represented an absolute, harmonious union of man and woman. In the beginning, Adam and Eve were "naked and unashamed" and there were no barriers to intimacy. The first thing they did after their sin was cover up: "They hid from each other and they hid from God. What had been great intimacy between man and woman, and with God, was shattered."[13] A section titled the "Theology of Marriage" suggests that because God designed marriage to be a perfect union of a man and a woman, marital problems can be traced to original sin. The CPREP curriculum points to an opportunity to achieve a pre-Fall innocence in marital, heterosexual relationships similar to the one possible with God—full of mystery and revelation.

While the Christian curriculum explicitly lays out the tenets of "opposite sex" marriage, it relates to a broader epistemology that equates natural (biological) gendered patterns of heterosexual behavior with what it means to be a husband or wife. The pop psychologist John Gray, the keynote speaker for the Saturday luncheon I attended at the Smart Marriages conference in 2004, offered a secular version of this epistemology. Presenting on "The Mars/Venus Solution," Gray has appeared as a keynote speaker at most of the annual conferences of the marriage movement to speak on his claim that women and men are so different in their communication and behavior that they might as well be from different planets.[14] Gray utilized the lens of biological essentialism—the idea that men and women are intrinsically different due to an internal, biological essence that differentiates them—to analyze what he sees as a decisive divergence of male and female desires, emotions, and behaviors. He explained these differences in terms of hormones: in contrast to male behavior that is driven by a need to preserve high levels of testosterone, female behavior seeks to raise oxytocin levels. Thus, men feel a need to be right and to be the hero, whereas women need to feel cared for and connected.

For Gray, these differences translate into a gendered hierarchy in marriage. He expressed,

We [men] just want [to be] our little master-of-my-own-kingdom. OK, I'm following everybody's orders at work, they want me to talk a certain amount, I'll do that. I have to wait in line at the airport. I have to follow other people's orders. The king is here, the king is here, the king is here! Give me one place where I'm king, just give me one moment, and that's what a man needs sometimes.

In this quote, Gray refers to the old axiom that "every man is king in his own house."[15] His words reflect nostalgia for a time when one of the main purposes of being a wife was to meet a husband's needs after a long day's work.[16] He illustrates this hierarchy by juxtaposing men's "innate" seriousness against women's "natural" frivolity. In a chapter from *Men Are from Mars, Women Are from Venus* on "Scoring Points with the Opposite Sex," Gray describes how men score for the big things—bringing home the bacon, whereas women score for the little things that husbands ignore—housework, emotional availability, and so forth. Gray argues that compromising on each other's scoring system is essential to a healthy relationship.

Gray's depiction of ways to harmonize the "opposite sexes" is illustrative of marriage workshops that naturalize and teach about gender hierarchy. I attended the three-day training for volunteers to learn the curriculum, which offered the secular and Christian versions. The creators of the curriculum, Howard Markman and Scott Stanley, along with Natalie Jenkins—the vice President of PREP, Inc.—instructed trainers at a Christian university in Oklahoma City. On the first and third day, everyone gathered together in a large auditorium for general instruction. The second day offered a choice to attend the PREP or the Christian PREP version of the training. I chose the CPREP training to learn more about the differences between this and the secular curriculum. Overall, the crowd appeared to be largely white, and many who were present were counselors and educators and were receiving Continuing Education Units for their participation. The three presenters were lively and upbeat, offering the material with lots of banter and jokes.

The first day, the presenters offered an overview of the state of marriage in the United States and in Oklahoma, providing many of the familiar statistics about divorce's negative effects on children. A good portion of the presentation focused on what men do versus women do. According to Stanley, one of the greatest barriers to restoring marriage in American society is the prevalence of cohabitation, which is especially bad for women. Arguing that cohabiting is not a good first step to test marriage, he cited the research of David Popenoe and Barbara Dafoe Whitehead showing that young men who live with their girlfriends tend to think she is *not* the "one," while the young women think just the opposite.[17] He lamented, "We have talked young people out of thinking that marriage matters, particularly young women. Women get the worse deal if men don't marry them." Practicing serial nonmonogamy hurts women because, Stanley suggested, marriage is the only means to ensure a man's commitment.

All three presenters emphasized the biological and cultural differences between men and women to provide a message about how to manage gender differences within heterosexual relationships. Stanley, for example, described how researchers have found a pattern that involves females pursuing an issue and males withdrawing. He attributed this to biological factors that cause males to be more physiologically reactive and females to be more aroused. Stanley admitted that these patterns of behavior are complex and that researchers have had difficulty deciding what is physiological and not.

But, he concluded, the pattern seems to reflect a greater need for men *not* to argue with their mates. Howard Markman presented one of the videos of a young African American couple who argue over the amount of time the husband spends watching sports. During the young man's explanation for why his sport watching is not excessive, Howard Markman stopped the video to point out the way he lifted his hands up and "gazes towards heaven." Markman called this the "beam me up Scotty response." He explained, "This really is an appeal to God. We have a special message to the women in the room. If your partner, husband, son has this response, you might mistakenly think that he is withdrawing, but he is having a spiritual moment." I laughed along with the rest of the audience, and I wrote in my notes that what made this statement funny is the assumption of men's essential difference from women. Because women cannot really understand the nature of men, this leads to the kind of exasperation shown in the video.

Throughout the presentation, Stanley, Markman, and Jenkins performed gender in a way that was just as important as the message they offered about gender difference within marital heterosexuality.[18] Their bantering constantly focused on the fundamental differences between men and women. For example, Markman told a joke about how many men it takes to change the toilet paper. The punch line: there is no scientific answer because it has never happened. A little later, he flipped the remote as if he were surfing television channels, distracting Natalie Jenkins's presentation. She told him to "sit," and she informed us that she forgot to take the batteries out of the men's toy. Next, she conveyed the reason she needed the two men is because she is not the most technologically advanced. As we watched a video of a couple fighting over the way the husband puts the laundry soap in the washer, Jenkins asserted that the woman is "missing the miracle. He's doing the laundry!" Later on, Jenkins discussed expectations and how, when she was first married, she wanted flowers because all her friends were getting them. She and her husband were having financial difficulties, so she found a 99-cent coupon for a dozen carnations. She put four quarters and the coupon on the fridge with a note saying, "Honey, if this coupon expires, so will you." He did not buy her flowers, thinking it was a joke.

All of this gender work solidified for the audience the differences between men and women. Men play with their toys; women want flowers. To make marriage work requires recognizing (and performing) these differences. As the presenters performed and instructed the normative expectations of gender, the program took on a "he said, she said" character that seemed to epitomize the nature of marriage. The three instructors taught about how gender motivates much of the friction in marital relationships, but they also just taught about gender. At heart was a lesson about how gender difference is the glue that brings and keeps two people of the "opposite" sex together. These differences are tied to understandings of bodies to establish a moral boundary of marriage. At one point in the PREP program, Stanley held up a picture of his two sons and told the audience that his younger boy asked him, "How do two bodies know when they are married? How does the woman's body know when to have the baby?" He observed that his son asked these questions in the context of marriage but will soon learn that this is not the way it goes in this culture.

Providing a moral vision of marriage through gender difference and its connection to bodies and heterosexuality was even more pronounced in the CPREP training. Scott Stanley, who led the training, told the audience how gender differences originate back to the Genesis passage that tells a man to leave his mother and father and unite with his wife. He explained,

> I think it is interesting that it says man [will leave his mother and father] and not man and woman. I have come to believe from science (and this is going to sound sexist) why males are called to a higher level of commitment and sacrifice, biologically and scripturally. Women are inherently made more vulnerable than men because they have babies. Males need to protect. Unfortunately, in our culture, we have gutted that, and women bear the most burden by the lack of a sacrificial ethic.

Stanley's words draw on the evangelical Protestant ideal of male leadership and authority that places the "burden" on men to spiritually guide and provide for their families.[19] Because God made men to be the stronger sex (Stanley seems to mean here physically stronger and emotionally more stoic), husbands need to take responsibility for making decisions for and protecting their families. For evangelical Protestants, this means a higher level of commitment and sacrifice because the husband is directly responsible to God for the well-being of the family, whereas the wife is responsible to the husband.[20] Women, in this worldview, have strong relational skills, which makes them less capable of heavy decision making.

Stanley described how the beauty and mystery of marriage is attained through the union of the two sexes when they become "one flesh." He read Galatians 3:26: "You are all sons of God through faith in Christ Jesus, for all of you who were baptized into Christ have clothed yourselves with Christ. There is neither Jew nor Greek, slave nor free, male nor female, for you are all one in Jesus Christ." Explaining how this passage struck him because it is about overcoming differences, he surmised, "It's not that differences don't matter, but it's that oneness trumps differences. The power of oneness trumps everything. That is a beautiful image for marriage." The ideal of oneness is only possible through the union of the "opposite sexes," thus preserving gender differences through a complementarity that honors the mystery of heterosexual marriage.

Stanley explained how Adam's reaction to Eve was "pretty strong." He asked the audience what nakedness without shame means. Audience members answered safe, proper, and then jokingly, proper temperature. Stanley pointed out that, when Adam and Eve recognized they were naked, they tried to cover their genitals with their hands. He said,

> God meant something when He specified that there should be male and female and what to do with bodies. I don't just mean sex and physical union, but I mean oneness. They covered up where they are most obviously different. We don't cover up where we are similar. We fear rejection in relationships because of the possibility of difference. Difference symbolizes physical union, which is now apparent to them.

Stanley summed up with the idea that CPREP speaks to deeper longings. There are some things that make it unsafe to be naked and unafraid, "to drop the fig leaf."

The teachings on CPREP promote a strong moral boundary of marriage that relies on a hierarchical divide based on women's vulnerability and essential physical and spiritual difference. Heterosexuality is an essential component not only in terms of sex but also as an institution created by God. The envisioned complementarity relies on male headship and authority to make men responsible for their families. Thus, to promote marriage from a conservative Christian perspective means to unite the difference of "oppositely" sexed bodies. The message of the two curricula is not only one of managing difference but of creating a superior relationship—marriage—that unites gender difference through legitimate heterosexuality. This moral boundary carried over to the marriage education workshops.

Marriage Promotion for Sweethearts

While the thirty public marriage workshops I attended presented a variety of presentation styles, there was a persistent emphasis on teaching about gender in marriage. Two of the Sweethearts Weekends I attended—highly publicized marriage workshops that brought in larger crowds and were taught on a Friday evening and all day Saturday—offered prime examples of the focus on conservative gender norms. The first took place in an educational center of a small town in the eastern part of the state. Although this town had a substantial Native American population, most of the twenty-nine couples who attended appeared to be white and middle class.[21] Roughly ten people with PREP training were present to coach couples in the techniques. The workshop was led by a white, married couple, Sarah and Jeff, both in their fifties who were lively presenters.

Similar to the training I attended, much of the jesting and examples focused on differences between men and women. In particular, the presenters described ways for men to manage women's emotions. Jeff and Sarah depicted women as excessively emotional and often consumed by frivolous ventures. In a discussion of the willingness to compromise, Jeff told the audience, "I don't mind going to a romantic movie, but can we at least have a little action? We went to the movie *Jersey Girl*. Boy, was that a chick flick! The popcorn was okay, and that's all I'll say." Later, they discussed hidden issues, which are the unconscious concerns or feelings of hurt that can motivate anger and resentment. Jeff said, "Every once in a while, she goes off like Old Faithful. That can't just be hormones!" The two performed gender to demonstrate how they deal with emotions. Sarah told us that when she is upset there are physiological changes, presenting to the audience how her breathing changes and her voice raises. In turn, Jeff described the method he used to alert her to these heightened emotions by saying, "It seems like you are upset," to signal she should calm herself down. He said this in such a deadpan voice that everyone laughed.

The assumption behind the skills being taught is that men are more rational, fun-loving, and easygoing, and women are more irrational, demanding, and at times petty. For example, the two discussed the problem of giving gifts that focused entirely on Sarah. Jeff decided to give Sarah an expensive coat that would combine her birthday and Christmas present together. He told the audience how she enjoyed her birthday present. At Christmas, she was waiting for her "big gift." He went to the closet, brought out the coat, and said, "Merry Christmas, honey." He continued, "What she did not say spoke volumes. How many think that Jeff wasn't at the store getting something for her on the 26th? It's not how much you spend; it's about pomp and circumstance." Sarah chimed in, "I said I didn't want anything for Valentine's Day. I didn't want any chocolates because I am on a diet." Jeff responded, "How many believe that Jeff didn't buy her something for Valentine's Day? How many believe that he will ever do that again?" The take-home message is that wives must be catered to because they do not know their own minds.

These vignettes reinforce a gendered boundary of emotional and household labor between women and men. Sarah related how she didn't do dishes on her birthday week, but that payback was tough when Jeff decided to go fishing and golfing on his. This description speaks to the expectation that doing dishes is women's work, while there is no expectation for the husband to do household labor. The gendered performances clearly place women as the helpmates of their husbands. At one point during the presentation, Sarah helped Jeff find his pointer in his pocket as he scrambled for it, and he informed the audience, "We all need a wife, guys!" Their performances also included instruction on men's leadership in marriage. They gave an example of a time when their son was using drugs and they had to apply tough love. Sarah said, "We told him he had to leave the house." Then Jeff told the audience, "Mom didn't want to take that step." And Sarah followed up with, "Jeff sat him down. My son needed to know that Jeff is the head of the house." Later on, Jeff brought up Arnold Schwarzenegger and Maria Shriver as an example of compromise: "Arnold Schwarzenegger is a Republican and his wife is a Democrat and she has chosen to walk with her husband. She is willing to support what he is doing. Her values tell her this." The message is that gender hierarchy in which wives support their husbands benefits a successful marriage. Unfortunately, this "exemplary model" has been shattered under the ultimate test of marital infidelity as Schwarzenegger joined the list of high-powered men who cheat. Shriver is no longer willing to compromise, and the couple is divorcing.

An ideology of gender hierarchy also translated into descriptions of sexual pleasure where the man's needs predominated. In a discussion of expectations, Sarah described Jeff's fantasy of her visiting him at work in a tight short dress and giving him a kiss. She said, "On the slowest day of the week, I showed up in the white dress. It really happened. That was an expectation he had." Sarah then introduced the "forty-eight-hour rule" a woman in her Bible study group used to keep her husband sexually satisfied. Because her husband wanted sex "all the time," she would never "let him go" without sex for more than forty-eight hours. There would be a sensual day when the husband did not bug her for sex, but he knew "tomorrow is coming." Sarah said, "She would start to think about how to make that experience more comfortable. Plan it. Wear something special. For her husband, it was a win-win situation. He never felt deprived. He understood that he had a higher sex drive, and they made a compromise." Sarah did not discuss possibilities for the husband to make the experience more comfortable (or pleasurable) for his wife.

Throughout the presentation, Jeff and Sarah made it clear that marriage encompasses a hierarchy based on the essential differences between men and women. The implicit emotional and physical frailty of women meant that the caring husband has to cater to his wife's expectation for romance and her unpredictable emotional states. She, on the other hand, as a caring wife must cater to his sexual needs and support his leadership role in the family. Their dialogue represented Sarah as being somewhat emotionally unstable and demanding. However, later in the presentation we learned that she manages the finances, balances the checkbook, and provides Jeff with enough money for the week. She said, "We decided that it is better for me to do the finances because I am the detailed business person." Jeff added that he and Sarah handled the finances "as a team, but we know who really handles them. Details elude me!" This brief narrative opened a new window on their relationship, complicating Jeff's and Sarah's earlier references to the evangelical concept of male headship. The sociologist Sally Gallagher demonstrates in her study of evangelical identity that, in practice, people who adhere to this belief mix together "symbolic headship" with "pragmatic egalitarianism" that allows for more flexible gendered behavior.[22] In this case, Sarah's handling of the finances appeared to constitute a leadership role in the family, but both agreed that Jeff is the head of the household, a "patriarchal bargain" that allowed Jeff to maintain his identity as the leader of the family.[23]

A subsequent Sweethearts Weekend held in a town outside Oklahoma City endorsed an even stronger moral boundary of marriage based on hierarchical gender differences. Stewart and Sally, a white couple in their early fifties, taught CPREP to about twenty-five predominantly white couples at a local community center. The leaders were licensed counselors who worked for a Christian counseling center. Although they volunteered to lead this workshop, they also charged money to teach CPREP workshops for up to $1,500 at churches and marriage retreats. This event was advertised on NPR, in newspapers, and Sally and Stewart did an interview with a local television station.

The leaders began the workshop by talking about Christian marriage and the compatibility of research and scripture. Sally read passages from the Bible about the oneness that takes place when a man leaves his father and mother and is united to his wife. She asked, "How many of you had that in your wedding ceremony?" A few couples raised their hands. She went on to say that oneness is inherently mysterious—echoing the language of Scott Stanley—but there are many barriers to the kind of openness that allows the husband and wife to unite before God. Sally told the audience that Adam and Eve covered up where they are most different. Sin is at the root of shame over nakedness. In reference to barriers to openness, Stewart told the audience, "Guys, I just learned three months ago, instead of saying, 'Honey, I'm going to do this,' I say, 'I am thinking about doing this. What do you think?'" Stewart's statement appears to assert a more gender egalitarian perspective than the one presented by Sarah and Jeff. Yet, as the workshop progressed, conservative gender norms again established a hierarchy.

After discussing the theology of Christian marriage, Sally and Stewart moved on to communication. They acted out a fight over a pair of expensive shoes that Sally bought when they were on a tight budget. A majority of their examples focused on women's love of shopping. At one point, Stewart exclaimed, "I'm going to rent someone to go shopping with you." Stewart later described how men don't need to try to fix everything all the time. He told the men in the room that sometimes women just want to be heard. Describing a day when Sally came home upset about her hairdresser leaving, he told us his reply: "Okay, we can find a new one." He told the audience that this wasn't what she wanted to hear. Instead, she wanted him to listen. A man near me raised his hand and said, "So, what you are saying is that women are illogical." Stewart smiled and said, "I am not going to agree with that if I want to sleep in bed tonight." As in the workshop with Sarah and Jeff, women were portrayed as overly emotional and frivolous.

The next day, quite a bit of time was spent talking about expectations. Sally told the audience that wives should not expect their mates to read their minds. She said, "Girls, this is for us. Sometimes we expect the guy to know what we want, and we feel that he doesn't care or that it doesn't feel as romantic if we have to tell them. This is a typical female attitude. Men are not women, thank God, and we have to help them understand us." PREP teaches the couple to express their criticisms in XYZ statements: When you do X in situation Y, I feel Z. Each couple was asked to write down a feeling they had about their spouses, and Stewart read some out loud. He recited, "I like it when you put your hand on my back to gently guide me through the door." His response: "Women like to feel safe and secure." Next, he read, "I like it when he puts his arms around me so I can cry. I like it when he pretends to be interested in my bargains from the garage sale." Stewart commented, "Women want to know that they are not just bimbos, a sex slave, just a beautiful body with no brains!" He continued, "I like it when he pulls out my chair for me."

Following this list of expectations that focused on women's emotionality, Stewart suggested that women can be manipulated to satisfy men's needs: "All women (guys put on your tape recorder) want to feel like a princess. If you make her feel like a princess, she will make you feel like a king, if you get my drift. . . ." Sally shot back, "You guys have your mind on only one thing!" Stewart addressed the men,

> Ladies, close your ears. I want to talk about sex. When you listen to your lady's heart, it has great sex appeal. God wired us to look at her pretty face and it does something to us. Being listened to does the same thing for her as vision does for us. If you are complaining that nothing is getting done around the house, then maybe you are not listening to her!

These workshops sent a clear message about heterosexual marriage: Men and women are wired differently so that women have a uniquely feminine need for protection and security.

Throughout the workshops I attended for the general population, the focus on hierarchical gendered patterns in marriage appeared unremarkable and beyond question. Over and over, the workshops demonstrated, subtly and at times overtly, that it is men who, as the stronger and more rational gender, must safeguard women who tend to be irrational and excessively emotional. Workshop leaders presented these ideas as taken-for-granted attributes of heterosexual marriage. However, the presence of a lesbian couple in two workshops I attended challenged this coherent gendered boundary. The resulting tensions uncover a more general anxiety concerning transformations in gender and family.

Marriage Boundary Work

Tammy and Chris were having serious problems in their relationship. They had been together, excluding a two-year break, since 1993. Chris, a sixty-three-year-old white woman, told me that she realized there was something different about her at age thirteen but she didn't know what it was. She grew up in the standard Oklahoma environment where she told me that you just keep your mouth shut. At fifteen years old, she met her husband who was nineteen and she quit school to get married. After having her daughter when she was twenty-six, she described realizing "who and what I was and thought now what do I do?" She made an unsuccessful attempt at suicide but stayed in the relationship for nineteen and a half years by "trying to be the best person I knew how to be." Tammy, a fifty-four-year-old white woman, was also married heterosexually for twenty-four years. At her oldest daughter's high school graduation, she thought to herself, "In two years, both of my daughters will be out of the nest and it will just be the two of us. I just got this sinking feeling in my gut." The two worked together and Tammy discussed the problems in her marriage with Chris. Then, one day she had an unexpected urge to kiss Chris in the elevator. After their romance budded and Tammy had divorced, they moved in together about a year later. As time passed, they found that they had a number of issues with communication. Tammy said, "As soon as we'd get crosswise, everything would just spiral, it would cascade."

Tammy felt they desperately needed to go to a communication class, and when she heard a blurb on television about the Sweethearts Weekend that was happening right after Valentine's Day, she jumped on the computer to sign them up. When she realized that the dates conflicted with her youngest daughter's bridal shower, she contacted a representative of the marriage initiative who told her about the six-week workshop. She enrolled herself and "a friend." She told me, "I wrote down friend, because I just didn't know if they would screen. I didn't know if I would get a note saying the class is full and whether there would be fallout or repercussions. I just put that down, and we showed up." Chris was a bit apprehensive, but she decided to give it a try since Tammy had been "banging a communication class on my head for ten years." She told Tammy,

They won't let you in, and if you get in, as soon as they see us, they will probably ask us to leave. . . . Is there anywhere on there that says gays and lesbians welcome? [Tammy] said 'No, but they won't have the guts to throw us out! I will stand up and make such a scene.' I said, 'You? Ha!' But then I just agreed to go. I figured we had a fifty-fifty chance of being allowed to stay.

They were pleasantly surprised that they were accepted in the class.

Similar to presenters at other marriage workshops, David and Randy—introduced at the beginning of this chapter—taught about gender hierarchy as a central feature of marriage. They incorporated sports analogies, for example, to get the men's attention. David introduced the first lesson by skimming over the statistics on divorce and the static and dynamic factors that put a marriage in danger, such as having parents who are divorced. He talked about the tendency for one person to withdraw in an argument, and said, "This is just what men do, withdraw." Randy asked why people withdraw and provided the analogy of playing baseball. When you get hit a few times, you tend to give up. He said this is the same with arguing: sometimes it just feels easier to give up or withdraw. Instead of giving up, what you need to do is practice. David piped in, "Can you do the same analogy with knitting?" and Randy came back with, "I can't, but I'm sure there are those in the audience who can!" Randy described how women have a whole life experience of communication that men don't have. This is why men are more likely to withdraw and avoid. When Randy introduced the listener-speaker technique, he told us that there is one person, usually the female, who wants to talk.

Throughout the workshop, Randy used the baseball analogy to highlight the fundamental principles of a healthy marriage. At the second workshop, he moved chairs to delineate four bases. First base, he told us, is managing the negative; second base is positive connections; third base is commitment and sacrifice; and home plate is feeling safe at home. He asked, "What happens to people when they get married? They get complacent and take each other for granted. Why does this happen when we commit to the other person? You may subconsciously devalue the other or you don't do things to let the other know they are appreciated."

He read a quote from *Fighting for Your Marriage*, written by the creators of the PREP curriculum: "A friend is someone who is happy to see you and doesn't have any vision for your future improvement." His message on the gendered aspect of heterosexual relationships: "With guys, hair on the back of the neck starts to stand up when someone tries to change us." He related how his wife asked what she could do to get him to take out the trash. His reply, "Pinch my butt and tell me how cute I am. Love them into change!" His advice suggests that a simple request is not good enough. When dealing with men, women must make the extra effort to cajole and flatter them. He related another story about a couple who were enjoying an evening in the hot tub until they got into an argument about taking their dog on vacation. Randy asked us what happened to their fun, and one of the men replied, "She became a social engineer."

Another lesson looked at filters or the things that get in the way of listening, one being inattention. Randy addressed the male partner of a younger couple, "When you are watching a game on television, what happens if your partner says something to you?" His wife responded for him, "He loses his mind." Randy conjectured that perhaps this happens with women and some television programs. A woman in the audience suggested soap operas, and Randy offered reality shows. He then told the women in the audience, "If you need to say something to your husband, you may need to take his head in your hands to get his attention." One of the men in the audience complained, "Can't it wait until third down?" Randy replied, "That's okay, but whose responsibility is it to ask for that?" Chris spoke up: "The person whose attention is occupied," disrupting the gendered assumption that inattention was a problem specifically relating to men. As it turned out, this had been an issue for Chris and Tammy.

The next lesson examined expectations in marriage. Randy explained that expectations are a problem when they are unconscious, unreasonable, or unspoken. Randy asked for some examples. A woman in the audience said she had an unreasonable expectation about cleanliness because she was a neat freak. One of the men told us that it is unreasonable to think your wife should be a mom. His wife retorted, "You must be really disappointed!" Another woman related that she expects her boyfriend to know when she is upset. Randy remarked, "Gals, if you can train us for twenty years, then maybe we will know. But, otherwise, you have to put it down on the table."

The smooth flow of these gendered illustrations was often disrupted when Tammy or Chris spoke up. Both were very vocal, and their questions and comments often acted as a monkey wrench in the assumptions being made about gender hierarchy and heterosexuality. In one session, David presented a lesson on making "I feel" statements. He described how his wife would yell at him from the other room and get angry when he didn't respond. He had his hearing checked and the physician told him he had some hearing loss but didn't need a hearing aid. He related how the physician told him, "Go to your wife, and tell her that when she has something important she wants to tell you, she should approach you and tell it to your face." At this point, Tammy made a snort and rolled her eyes, suggesting that this has happened with Chris. David continued talking about how it is important to work out these kinds of communication problems. When he finished, Chris said that in her defense, given all the "histrionics" going on next to her (Tammy's snort), "What if one person goes to tell the other something, and it is clear that person is busy and shoos you away." He replied, "Tell her you have something important to say, and it is up to her to listen." Tammy's and Chris's communication problems made the assumption of gendered communication appear incongruous.

The last class covered sensuality and sexuality. David was the presenter and he told the audience how Randy and one of the coaches, Susan, had exchanged emails several times with him about who should give this presentation. David became the default person. He asked, "Why is it we are so uncomfortable talking about sex?" Whereas the presence of the same-sex couple had been more muted by the focus on the emotive aspects of relationships, the topic of sexuality brought the issue of gender and heterosexuality to the forefront. David asked people to share about the way their families of origin dealt with sexuality. I was sitting at the end table with an older couple and Tammy and Chris. David asked the couple at the table opposite from us to begin. One woman said she grew up on a farm, so sexuality was just a fact of life. Another said her mother had given her the book *Our Bodies, Ourselves*, which had been very helpful. David continued around the room but ended with the last person at the table next to mine. Conveniently skipping the table where Tammy and Chris were seated, he related his own experience of how he had found a condom and neither of his parents would discuss it with him.

If the goal was to keep Tammy and Chris from discussing their sexuality, it did not work. When David asked about sensuality and touch, Tammy spoke up, "We assume that what we like the other person likes." Her words drew attention to the fact that her partner is a woman and not a man. While it is probably true that heterosexuals and nonheterosexuals alike make this kind of assumption, her statement stood in bold relief to the dominant message of managing difference in marital (heterosexual) relationships. During this last session on sexuality, Tammy put her arm around Chris. However, even as their presence and comments disrupted the heteronormativity of the marriage workshop, the workshop leaders and participants worked to reintroduce its dominance. Susan, who had declined leading the sexuality session, spoke up after David talked about getting out of ruts and keeping things fresh sexually. She shared what she thought to be a helpful example from Christian PREP— the story of Adam and Eve and their fig leaves. Taking off the leaves was a way to learn to trust each other, and having trust enabled the exploration of sexuality. A little later, David told us that men are from Mars and women are from Venus. Venusians tend to hold a grudge. He talked about how this may be a function of upbringing. Randy remarked that his wife sometimes needed him to understand just how deep the hurt is. He asked, "Is it a man/woman thing?" David responded that, in the case of his wife, he knows sometimes to steer clear because of her hormones. Tammy challenged him, "It is not just about biology or that a woman is on the rag!" Dead silence followed.

On the one hand, the boundary work that focuses on gender within the confines of marital heterosexuality meant an effort to render the same-sex couple's relationship invisible. As the workshop leaders presented the curriculum, no acknowledgment was made of any other relationship outside the heterosexual marriage model. On the other hand, even as the workshop leaders concentrated on the imperatives of gender hierarchy and heterosexuality, these discourses became awkward in the presence of Tammy and

Chris. The performance of gendered patterns of marital behavior intrinsic to institutionalized heterosexuality, a generally seamless aspect of the marriage workshops, was rendered more palpable and transparent. This paradox marks the ideological contradictions of what the sociologist Chrys Ingraham refers to as "thinking straight," which requires simultaneous affirmation and negation of same-sex sexuality, at once imbuing meaning to heterosexual identity while at the same time denying the threat of same-sex sexuality to the naturalness and universality of heterosexual desire.[24]

Lesbians Speak Out

While the official memo from the desk of Wade Horn, then the assistant secretary for Children and Families, provided guidelines to ban marriage education services to lesbians and gay men, employees of the marriage initiative told me that there had been instances where "homosexuals attended the workshops." Over time, marriage initiative officials took the position that "individuals of alternative lifestyles were welcome." During my participant observation within thirty workshops for the general public, only two included a same-sex couple. Because the form that the participants filled out did not ask about sexual orientation, there was no way to determine the frequency of lesbians and/or gay men in the workshops. My sense was that the majority of workshops did *not* attract same-sex couples. Rather than representing a generalizable phenomenon, the significance of their presence served to uncover the contradictory dynamics that sustained an epistemology based on conservative gender norms within marital heterosexuality, a dominant feature of the workshops. The fact that both of the same-sex couples were white lesbians is also significant, because being lesbian and white may have elicited a greater level of acceptance than if the couples had been gay men and/or racial minorities. Literature on homophobia consistently shows more prejudice in society against gay men than lesbians.[25] In the next workshop I attended, Amanda and Jennifer, also both white, expressed a similar feeling to that of Chris and Tammy of limited recognition but also frequent awkwardness.

Cynthia, who participated in the first workshop, had convinced her lesbian friend, Jennifer, and Jennifer's partner to attend the next six-week class. Jennifer told me, "Cynthia knew we had been fighting a lot and we couldn't agree on anything. A couple of times we'd blow up in front of her and would just go at each other. She was like, y'all should try this class!"

Jennifer and Amanda were younger, at thirty-five and twenty-four, respectively. At the initial class, they each introduced themselves separately and didn't make it clear they were a couple. It didn't take long, however, for people to figure it out. The two had one of the more tumultuous relationships in the class and required quite a bit of assistance from the coaches. They had met at the Metropolitan Community Church, and they'd been together for a year and a half. Jennifer was married at twenty-one, and her husband had been physically and emotionally abusive. She filed for divorce while he was in jail after he broke a restraining order and tried to break into her condo. She was able to file an emergency order due to the abuse and the divorce was final in ten days. She expressed, "I went through this intensive counseling process, and I realized that [dating women] was an option for me that hadn't really occurred to me before." She had been surprised when she developed a "huge crush" on her female counselor.

Amanda was about ten years Jennifer's junior and worked as a police officer. She had one previous relationship that lasted a year and a half. Being raised in a Southern Baptist family, the expectation was one day she would marry a man. Coming out was difficult for her, but her parents were eventually supportive. Three months before the workshop started, Jennifer sold her condo and moved in with Amanda. She was having health problems and couldn't work. Moving in together added more stress to their relationship. They both expressed a desire to make the relationship work but found themselves bickering almost constantly. After attending the first marriage workshop, Amanda told me that neither of them wanted to return, but she had borrowed a dollar from another participant to buy a coke that she needed to repay. They attended the second class and were hooked.

The dynamics of this workshop were similar to the first. Jennifer expressed frustration at the focus on gender hierarchy. When I asked whether anything in the workshop made her uncomfortable, she replied:

> Whenever Randy would say things about like it's the male's responsibility, it really infuriated me. He did it a lot. I think it was probably to try to get them on board and say hello, pay attention!
>
> Me: By "them," you mean men?
>
> Jennifer: Yeah, THEM! I think knowing that this was not for gender-diverse people, I was able to try to self-direct. . . . I don't know that he should change it, but I know that in our relationship there is not a male, so, hello, we were just sitting there going [she demonstrates confusion], that just makes us more confused! We're thinking each one of us should step up, you know. So, that was really almost stifling because I kind of resented him saying it the way he did.

Her reflection on gender diversity stressed the teachings on gender hierarchy and heterosexual marriage in the workshops that excluded them. Jennifer expressed: "So, that was the thing I really found offensive because they kind of gender stereotyped relationships, and I don't think that is completely appropriate if you're teaching gender-diverse people." Jennifer's statement reflects on the way being lesbian in a heterosexual marriage workshop made her and her partner visible as "not-women."[26] Being lesbian placed them outside the rigid gender binary that was fundamental to the training.

As was true of many aspects of their relationship, Amanda disagreed. She said,

> If [Randy] wants to say, the men usually do this, and the women usually do that, and this is specifically how men are, I don't find that particularly offensive. Jennifer made a couple of comments that she thought those statements excluded us, which I mean it is geared towards heterosexual couples. I mean, I'm going to get the same thing out of the class whether he says that or not.

But later in the interview she admitted that she probably would have felt more comfortable and open to discuss her relationship if the class had been geared to focus less on heterosexual couples. I asked her if she would encourage her friends to attend, and she replied, "If they don't feel uncomfortable in a heterosexual environment, and I'll tell them it is a heterosexual environment, but I'd definitely encourage anybody to go."

Amanda speculated that if others in the class had issues with their presence it would most likely be Randy, the associate Baptist minister:

> I think probably out of the whole group, he's probably the one who I'd point out who had a problem with it. He was the only one who would make comments about gender roles in relationships, where he'd say the men do this and the women do that. He'd say the man is usually the one who withdraws. It was usually an "us" men type of thing. I don't know.

Although Amanda was personally not offended by Randy's comments on gender and heterosexuality, she acknowledged that his emphasis on gender differences in heterosexual relationships may translate into homophobia or an aversion to same-sex relationships. As lesbians, she and Jennifer stood outside the boundary of the gender binary.

Chris and Tammy were also aware of the focus on conservative gender norms. They were especially annoyed by some of the comments made by David. In fact, Chris said that eventually they'd like to take the class again, but they would be sure that David was not the instructor: "I had a real problem with David. He made three or four comments, statements, remarks during those six weeks, and during that last day, the last one he made—that she's on the rag—I almost leaped out of my chair. So inappropriate!"

On the other hand, Chris expressed that she wanted to listen to everything Randy had to say because he was so open and honest. When I asked Tammy about whether she felt comfortable in the class, she responded:

> You know, it's one of those things that it's interesting to be in a minority group because you learn what you need to swallow. You just learn where to make waves and where to keep quiet. By the second or third week of class, I knew these people wouldn't have said anything to hurt anybody. The fact that they were using the term "marriage," well, that's basically who it was set up for. I did every time on the form, when we had the evaluation, the screening questions asked are you married, and every time, I said, well, what do you mean? Do you mean spiritually, emotionally, yes. Legally, no, of course not. We are not allowed. Maybe the form should be changed. Maybe the law should be changed.

Tammy felt that the heteronormativity displayed in the class didn't necessarily come from animus but more from insensitivity: "You see that when you are in a minority kind of relationship, you see the way the majority thinks differently than you do. It doesn't occur to them that it would be in some way exclusionary if not discrimination. I think it's just insensitive." Their participation made that insensitivity somewhat more visible, even as the workshop leaders and participants conducted themselves as if a lesbian couple were not present.

During our interview, Amanda discussed participating in the class as a form of activism. She told me that neither Jennifer nor she had signed up for the class to make a statement but because they wanted to learn better communication skills. However, she suspected that the relationship workshops were never meant to help a lesbian couple: "Even if the thought was, we are only going to help straight people get married or have better relationships, fine, you know. I'm picturing me flipping them off right now. Look at the benefit I got from the class. Ha!" Tammy also felt that she and Chris should be able to benefit from the class: "This thing was put on by the Oklahoma Marriage Initiative. I know it is about marriage, but it's a taxpayer thing. Shoot,

I'm a taxpayer!" Chris, Tammy, and Amanda all pointed out in the separate interviews that it was important for heterosexuals to take a class with a lesbian couple to change perceptions and attitudes. Amanda expressed,

> I don't know the personal story of all these people in our class, but if they never met a lesbian before, and now they do, now they see, and hear what I say in class, and don't think we are the devil now, you know, that's a goal in itself. I mean, people are ignorant, and they don't know. So just being open and honest about stuff and talking to people or just being a good person around them and knowing you are gay, it has a positive influence.

Amanda's words speak to research demonstrating greater acceptance of lesbians and gay men through interpersonal contact.[27] Interviews with participants in these classes offered some evidence in favor of a positive impact.

Making Homosexuality (In)visible

I interviewed twenty participants who had attended the workshops that included the lesbian couples who held a variety of ideological beliefs and responses to the presence of the two lesbian couples. On the most liberal end of the spectrum was Bettina, a white woman in her thirties and a self-identified feminist, who attended with her fiancé, Shaun. I asked her if there were any surprises for her in the class. She said:

> I was surprised at the lesbian couple who attended. I was shocked every time we came and they were still there! I was blown away. I was very happy to see that, especially because I thought stereotypically everybody is going to be pigeon-holed into male-female. I can't imagine what that put on them. Then to know that you've got a Baptist minister teaching the class, and your relationship is so important to the two of you that you are going to face all of us and him and come in here. I mean, I respect them immensely for that.

Bettina had a past romantic relationship with a woman and understood the stakes for a lesbian couple of attending a heterosexual marriage class.

Bettina was also aware of gender stereotyping. She said she noticed that Randy made more than one reference to the idea of "you're the man, so you pick up the slack." She described how in her own relationship she and Shaun alternated who took responsibility, and she disliked the idea of male leadership: "The idea that you're the man, you get to make the choice—really, I feel like it's such an excuse for letting me off the hook. Then I don't have to be accountable. Randy did that in a class a lot." I asked her if anything made her uncomfortable and she said,

> No, I don't remember it being . . . I *was* uncomfortable for the lesbian couple that was in there because [Randy] kept saying male/female. I mean, he was making definite lines. Guys do things this way. We all know that stereotypically guys do things this way, but I was kind of like, but why can't you say as humans we can also learn to blah, blah, blah. I wished that part was taken out of it. And for them, I was like we're not all guys and girls in here. Granted, as a religious leader, he probably would not even want to acknowledge that situation, but as a teacher in a classroom, you need to open your mind and teach all of us.

Bettina's statement points to the disruptive nature of same-sex relationships that challenged the idea of the meaning-constitutive tradition that situates the heterosexual, monogamous couple at the unmarked center of other relationships.[28]

In contrast to the liberalism of Bettina, Becky, a white woman in her thirties who was married to and had four children with Martin, embraced a more conservative view. She answered my question about whether anything had made her uncomfortable as follows:

> Mmm. I did feel uncomfortable with the fact that there were couples in there of the same sex, just because I feel strongly about family values and what the traditional family is. But I know it is something that is happening in the United States, and there is really nothing I can do about it. And, I mean, they *are* human. They have needs too. It doesn't mean that I agree with them.

I started to ask a question about her feeling of surprise, and Becky finished my sentence for me, "that there were so many couples in there that were of the same sex?" I was confused because in the workshop I attended with Becky there was only one lesbian couple. I queried, "Wasn't there only one? I think there was only one. Was I mistaken?" Becky ignored this and said, "I wasn't really surprised because I mean in the workplace and stuff, it is common." She worked part-time at a department store. I followed up, "But you decided to stay in the class even though that was uncomfortable?" Becky said, "Oh yeah! I mean it wasn't fun, but if that was the most uncomfortable thing, I mean, it wasn't *that* uncomfortable." For Becky, the presence of a same-sex couple in the workshop stood out so much that her memory multiplied the number of same-sex couples. She struggled with her distaste to suggest that lesbians are "human" and have needs too. But she disliked dealing with the increased visibility of same-sex relationships in society.

When I interviewed Becky's partner, Martin, an African American military chaplain who also had taught marriage workshops, I asked him about the presence of a same-sex couple and his thoughts on marriage. He replied, "I hadn't thought about it. I'm for marriage between a man and a woman; I'll have to tell you that quite frankly. That's more a statement from my beliefs and training. I hadn't thought about it. I haven't even prayed about it!" He changed the subject suddenly to recount an incident that occurred while he was in high school:

> I had a homosexual in the eleventh grade. If you think back to that time, if you ever went outside and played sports, you get a lot of butt patting— good shot! [He demonstrates.] Everybody else is high-fiving them, and then you hit them on the butt and keep moving. I made a move in basketball in the gym, not on the team but in the gym, and the guy was known to be gay. I was at an all-boys Catholic school, and it was a white guy. I made a good move, and he goes good job [Martin demonstrates the guy patting him on the butt]. And, all I remember was turning around, right crossing him, watching him hit the ground, and he was unconscious. And I could care less. You violated my privacy, homeboy, because I didn't touch you.

This story is striking for several reasons. It is completely unrelated to my question about the workshop. Further, in jumping into a detailed description of an incident in high school involving homophobia and violence, Martin remarks that this boy was gay *and* also that he was white. Being white and gay were important to Martin's violent reaction to a ritual he described as otherwise normal and ordinary—butt patting. Being gay placed his peer outside the hegemonic ritual of manhood.[29] Martin's comment that he could care less was articulated in the present tense, letting me know his feelings about the incident had not changed. His story suggested the intolerance he felt when faced with another man's sexuality that challenged his own. In contrast, he was tolerant of the presence of a lesbian couple as long as a clear demarcation remained between "us" and "them." He confirmed this later in the interview. "Okay, our couple that was in there, that's not an issue for me. Partners, you know. Be gay. Don't force it on me."

Norm, a white man in his sixties, similarly made a jump in discussing the great responses offered by men in the class. All of a sudden, he articulated his disapproval of homosexuality:

At first, the unknown [was uncomfortable]. When you go around and there is more and more interaction, I felt like there was a quality of responses and information given by the men in that class that usually doesn't happen. I thought that there was some very good information put out there. [Pause] I do consider homosexuality a sin, but I'm not here to judge that. I have a lot of patients that are gay, and they have a lifestyle I *do not* approve of. But I thought even the gay couple had a lot of good information to toss out.

Similar to other interviews, Norm brings up the issue of homosexuality in the context of being uncomfortable. Norm seems quite surprised that the gay couple also provided good information on relationships. His response provides some evidence of the positive effect that the visibility of same-sex couples might have in this environment. Norm described working with lesbians and gay men, but being in a marriage class with a same-sex couple was a completely different context for observing such a relationship. He told me about how he had chatted with Chris and Tammy, and they had mentioned a great place for a romantic getaway that they would try.

When we talked about same-sex marriage, Norm was more condemnatory and forceful:

I am just opposed to that word marriage. That's the contradiction. That they want to be a lifelong pair, that's their business. I don't like the fact that this is being thrown out at us. I don't think they have the right to push their lifestyle down our throats or try to tell us that it is acceptable. It's none of my business, and I'd just as soon they keep it none of my business.

Similar to Martin, Norm could be tolerant, even learn from, a same-sex couple when he didn't feel they were pushing "their lifestyle" down his throat. He viewed Chris and Tammy as simply trying to get help to better their relationship. But when it came to the issue of same-sex marriage, he drew a boundary. For Norm, legalizing marriage for lesbians and gay men would mean making their relationships legitimate and legally visible, which he found distressing. Marriage would make the relationships of same-sex couples his business, a statement that reflects the power many heterosexuals feel over nonheterosexuals as a result of their monopoly on marriage.

This chapter has considered the boundary work that took place in workshops over gender hierarchy and heteronormative understandings of marriage. Taken as a whole, the marriage workshops located same-sex couples as outsiders to what constitutes a romantic relationship and dominant conceptions of family. The presence of a lesbian couple palpably uncovered the work necessary to draw a moral boundary of heterosexual marriage based on an understanding of nonheterosexuals as outsiders. Responding to the heightened anxiety about sweeping gender changes of the last fifty years, marriage advocates do work to reaffirm the boundary between the public "male" sphere and the private (domestic) "female" sphere. While these actors often disavow a desire to move back the clock on gender equality, the marriage workshops reference a time past when gender "roles" were clearly defined and were viewed as offering stability to family and nation. Teaching about gender hierarchy in marital heterosexuality acts as a citation to normative conceptions of the white, middle-class, heterosexual family. Generally, marriage workshops rehearse more than ideals of conservative gender norms and marital heterosexuality but speak to an endeavor to define a boundary based on a definition of citizenship steeped in an ideology of family values and the (male) entrepreneurial, Horatio Alger spirit that influences American identity. The next chapter examines this ideology of family and citizenship, which has been central to the implementation of marriage promotion in Oklahoma and its redistribution of Temporary Assistance to Needy Families funds to offer workshops to white, middle-class couples.

Widening the Marriage Gap

The breakdown of marriage in the United States—which began about forty years ago as divorce and out-of-wedlock birthrates started to soar—threatens America's future. It is turning us into a nation of separate and unequal families.
—Kay S. Hymowitz, *Marriage and Caste in America*[1]

Oklahoma has rarely found itself at the vanguard of antipoverty thinking, but the class to which the two women were heading embodies a vigorous new idea—something known locally, and archly, as "the marriage cure."
—Katherine Boo, "The Marriage Cure"[2]

The cover of Kay Hymowitz's book *Marriage and Caste in America* presents a picture of a white nuclear family—husband, wife, daughter, and son—standing in a museumlike room with their backs to us as they gaze at three gilded photographs of single-mother black families from behind a roped partition. This representation is key to a central argument of marriage promotion: America has become a "nation of separate and unequal families." Marriage advocates argue that the cause of this inequality is the breakdown of marriage. The story for them begins in the late 1960s when the marriage rate began to fall and the divorce rate and unwed birth percentage increased. By the late 1980s the number of "broken homes" in America was at a historic high. Marriage advocates point to the "marriage gap" between differently educated segments of the population as a troubling new trend. Americans who are college educated—about 25 percent of the population—tend to have higher rates of marriage and lower rates of nonmarital births and divorce than their less educated counterparts.[3] Hymowitz explains the problem for low-income, single mothers who are unprepared to carry out "The Mission—the careful nurturing of their children's cognitive, emotional, and social development, which, if all goes according to plan, will lead to the honor roll and a spot on the high school debate team, which will in turn lead to a good college, then perhaps a graduate or professional degree, which will all lead eventually to a fulfilling career, a big house in a posh suburb, and a sense of meaningful accomplishment."[4] In contrast, she argues, young mothers who have children outside marriage condemn them to a life of perpetual poverty, locked outside the American dream.

Marriage advocates seek to close the marriage gap between poor and middle-class families, especially between black and white families. In an article appearing on the conservative Townhall.com website, Maggie Gallagher points to marriage as a reason behind the increasing income gap in America. She states, "When almost 70 percent of children in a given community are born outside of marriage (as among African-Americans today) that's a tsunami blocking the intergenerational accumulation of human and social capital."[5] Hymowitz tells the story of how the unraveling of the black family began in the 1960s with the rise of the out-of-wedlock birth rate and how this issue was brought to America's attention by Assistant Secretary of Labor Daniel Patrick Moynihan's 1965 report warning that "the ghetto family was in disarray."[6] Marriage advocates consider the report to be prescient of a troubling trend that has led to the emergence of a "second nation" in the United States, where "a child is raised by an unwed girl, lives in a neighborhood filled with many sexual men but few committed fathers, and finds gang life to be necessary for self-protection and valuable for self-advancement."[7]

A new antipoverty policy solution has been called the "marriage cure," shifting attention to marriage promotion rather than on other structural factors that perpetuate poverty. This thinking was central to the 1996 Welfare Reform Act, which focuses on marriage as a way to solve America's problems. The law begins: "*Marriage is the foundation of a successful society,*" and it spells out how the problem of unwed childbearing leads to poverty, delinquency, crime, and many other social ills, bearing the responsibility for "a crisis in our Nation."[8] Katherine Boo, a journalist who wrote about this cure in her award-winning 2003 *New Yorker* story, states: "Marriage is probably the most cost-efficient antipoverty instrument a society possesses."[9] She outlines how, for a very small initial investment, the government can offer marriage education classes for a poor single mother to hopefully marry so that the husband and wife's "combined income would remove both of them, in one fell act, from America's poverty rolls. Moreover, if they go on to have children, those children will be less likely than the children of unmarried parents to drop out of school, require public assistance, and become single parents themselves."[10] This reasoning places the responsibility on single mothers to pull themselves out of poverty through marriage. Boo, however, in her chronicle of the impact of marriage classes on the lives of two African American women from an Oklahoma housing project, also points to the limits of marriage promotion. She recounts how the structural and economic barriers the women faced were reminders that "there are many things besides being single that make it blisteringly difficult to bootstrap oneself up from places like Sooner Haven [a housing project]."[11]

The ideal of marriage as a means to "bootstrap" oneself out of poverty builds on America's love of rags-to-riches stories, such as the fiction of Horatio Alger whose protagonists persevere through poverty and misfortune to finally strike it rich. Of course, the fictional and real heroes of rag-to-riches stories are generally men and their success is not based on marrying up. The rags-to-riches story for poor women better parallels Cinderella being swept away by her charming prince. However, as Boo demonstrates in regard to the two women who live in Sooner Haven, the reality of racial barriers and discrimination in the United States makes Cinderella a poor analogy. The sociologist Chrys Ingraham, in her study of white weddings, documents how the ideology of romantic love unites images of whiteness, wealth, and weddings in the popular (heterosexual) imaginary.[12] The meaning-constitutive tradition of lifelong, internally stratified marriage also references whiteness as the standard for American families, as in Tom Tierney's "American Family Series" of paper dolls where families of all eras are represented as white.[13]

In this chapter, I examine how anxiety about trends in increased divorce and nonmarital childbearing rates for *white* families, as a parallel trajectory to the "tangle of pathology" Moynihan attributed to black ones, motivates marriage promotion. I uncover a key paradox in the marriage initiative's implementation that uses Temporary Assistance to Needy Families (TANF) money—ostensibly meant to help needy families—to strengthen marriage among white, middle-class couples. Even as the marriage initiative introduced an antipoverty agenda for poor women, it prioritized the more high-profile workshops offered to the general population that draw a predominantly white, middle-class crowd. In this chapter, I look explicitly at the racial, economic, and cultural boundaries that affirm a contested American identity battered by "the history of inequalities left unresolved in the economic and political domains."[14] I argue that this boundary work may actually widen the marriage gap between low-income and middle-class families.

A Brave, New Social Experiment

A few weeks after arriving in Oklahoma, I drove to a poor neighborhood on the outskirts of Oklahoma City to attend a marriage workshop at an Anglican church. The priest, Reverend Jones, needed to fulfill his obligation of teaching four classes and had contacted the marriage initiative about offering a workshop. Initiative employees put the class on the website and helped create a flyer that the priest posted on neighborhood apartment bulletin boards, mostly those within Section 8 Housing. The church was located in a white enclave bordering an impoverished largely African American neighborhood. Despite his hard work, even passing out flyers to people as they walked by, no one showed up for the workshop. Instead, he talked to me for the next two hours. After learning that the church's membership consisted of a very conservative, predominantly white congregation, I surmised that may be the possible reason individuals from the apartment complexes nearby might be disinclined to take the bait of a free marriage workshop. Most likely they assumed the workshop would be religious in nature and many would be disinclined to listen to a white priest discuss morality, marriage, and religion.

My conversation with Reverend Jones did not lead me to believe differently. He expressed frustration with the unbridled secularism in every walk of life, and he railed against those who lived together, expressing his belief that religious leaders need to take a moral stand in favor of marriage. Any couple that wants to marry in his church is required to participate in rigorous premarital counseling, and as in the Catholic Church divorce is forbidden. He was most vituperative against same-sex marriage, which would "make marriage a nothing." I did not get to experience his workshop, because the next week there was again no one but me to participate.

This example illuminates the struggle to reach low-income and African American Oklahomans. For example, during my ten months in the state, only one marriage workshop was specifically advertised for African American couples, and, although held in a poorer neighborhood, it drew only participants from wealthier parts of the city. The workshops I attended for the general population (advertised on the initiative's website) brought in predominantly white, middle-class, and heterosexual couples. Among those I interviewed, there was unanimity that they benefit from the workshops, and none questioned how the state is funding the free classes. As I observed the enthusiasm of marriage initiative staff and participants for the marriage promotion project, I struggled to reconcile my sense that these couples profit from learning communication and problem-solving skills with my perception of the injustice of using money allocated for needy families to fund the infrastructure of the marriage initiative and its focus on the middle class. This began a conversation with a variety of leaders and volunteers about why the target population is not welfare recipients when the money spent on the marriage initiative in Oklahoma comes from TANF funds.

With its initial emphasis on divorce reduction, initiative leaders view divorce as a central transmitter of poverty. They reason that improving the relationship skills of married as well as unmarried couples might avoid future divorce and therefore poverty. As I detailed in chapter 1, the early goal was to reduce the divorce rate by one-third by 2010, based on a philosophy that blends a mix of conservative economic interests, the commitment of religious right politicians and organizations, and the support of centrist liberals. In regard to divorce, Oklahoma's family demographics present an ostensible paradox. Oklahoma, in addition to other Bible Belt states—Tennessee, Arkansas, and Alabama— claimed in 1999 the highest frequency of divorce in the nation, roughly 50 percent above the national average according to research conducted by the Barna Research Group.[15] The state had the nation's second-highest divorce rate in 1990, 7.9 per 1,000 residents, according to the National Center for Health Statistics.[16] The research also found that conservative Protestant Christians, on average, have higher divorce rates than mainline Christians. However, this Bible Belt paradox is not so startling when one considers the broader demographic context. The high divorce rates in these states are correlated with low household incomes (Oklahoma ranks forty-sixth and Arkansas forty-seventh), and a tendency to marry at younger ages. Birth rates to unmarried women in Oklahoma are slightly higher than the national average, for example, and its teen birth rate is significantly higher.

In 2001, initiative leaders decided to gather statewide data on these trends and conducted a baseline survey on the attitudes and behavior concerning marriage and divorce.[17] The survey provides evidence that "Oklahoma is a marrying state" with 82 percent of Oklahomans having been married at one time compared to the national average of 73 percent. Oklahoma also has a higher divorce rate than the national average: 32 percent of adults are divorced in Oklahoma compared to 21 percent nationally. The data demonstrate that more married Oklahomans have considered divorce than the national average: 56 percent compared to 42 percent. The survey asked questions about policy and found general support—85 percent answered good or very good—to the idea of an initiative to promote marriage. Based on this data, Mary Myrick, the president of Public Strategies, and Theodora

Ooms, a senior policy analyst at CLASP, wrote a 2002 report regarding the unprecedented move by a governor to introduce strengthening marriage as "government business." His reasons, they argue, included his personal values and religious beliefs but most importantly "it was research that provided the rationale." In line with the national movement, Myrick and Ooms claim legitimacy for promoting marriage based on the "accumulating evidence of the negative effects of father-absence and single parenthood on children and on the benefits of marriage for children and for adults alike."[18]

There is debate among social scientists concerning demographic studies and their policy implications. While research indicates that, among heterosexual families, children who grow up in a single-parent family or stepfamily on average experience some disadvantage over those growing up in their two-parent, biological families—an increased likelihood of teenage pregnancy for girls, more chance of dropping out of high school, and reduced job prospects—most social scientists agree that the relationship between growing up in a single-parent family or stepfamily and undesirable outcomes for children is not a *causal* one.[19] Both factors might be attributed to other causes, such as poverty. Sara McLanahan and Gary Sandefur found that up to half of the disadvantage for children is attributable to poverty.[20] Scholars have also found that preexisting psychological and social factors can affect families and the outcomes of children. In a longitudinal study of children born in England in 1958, Andrew Cherlin and his colleagues found that some but not all of the harm experienced by children had to do with psychological distress and behavior patterns that were visible long before the divorce.[21]

Marriage advocates often suggest a causal relationship between family structure and childhood outcomes. A 2006 fact sheet from the Institute for American Values, for example, asked "What Is America's Most Serious Social Problem?" The answer offered is the weakening of marriage because this decline is "the problem that *drives* so many other problems."[22] The fact sheet then lists negative outcomes for children of being raised in a family other than an "intact marriage." Kay Hymowitz also makes this case: "It's common sense, backed up by plenty of research, that you'll have a better chance of fully 'developing' your children—that is, of fulfilling the Mission—if you have a husband around."[23] Statements such as these simplify a very complicated picture of how race, class, and other factors impact families. Causal arguments offered by marriage advocates—however misleading—seek to offer a strong political and moral case for marriage promotion. Specifically, they feed into moral anxieties about transformations in family life of the past decade to justify the need for government intervention.

Some initiative leaders embrace this oversimplified account of the causes and conditions of poverty, while a few are more wary. One Oklahoma Department of Human Services (OKDHS) supervisor who manages the contract with Public Strategies offers this evaluation: "The way Governor Keating attached lowering the divorce rate through a poverty-funded program, who are we blaming for the divorce rate? I mean that kind of message is real strong in my mind. I've got an education, so I was concerned about people living in poverty being blamed for the divorce rate and the state of families and that kind of thing." Attaching marriage promotion to TANF might shift attention away from transformations taking place among white, middle-class families to place it on poor ones, and specifically on what has become in the public imaginary the stereotypical poor, black single mother, the icon of welfare dependency.[24] At the same time, the ostensible goal is to decrease divorce in the general population, which means offering services to white, middle-class families rather than targeting low-income and racial minority families.

The initiative focused broadly on strengthening marriage in society by getting marriage education services to as many people as possible. Mary Myrick, the president of Public Strategies, the company that manages the initiative, told me that the initial goal of reducing the divorce rate shifted over time to focus on marriage-strengthening activities:

> The initiative really started out of a response to our high divorce rate. But as we began to think and plan and talk about what we wanted to do about that, it actually shifted some in its mission from sort of a divorce-intervention strategy to a marriage-strengthening activity. We began to see divorce as one of the outcomes that we might want to measure, but decided that there were some limitations to divorce as the only measure of our success. . . . We also became aware of just general family-formation issues that were equally causing stress on families—the lack of formed families, primarily, children born out of wedlock, which is another indicator that Oklahoma had that needed to be dealt with. So, we began to think about these marriage education services as services that could help on the front end and be an earlier intervention point.

Low-income couples became more of a concentration. On its website, the marriage initiative advertises its statewide Service Delivery System, which is designed to provide marriage workshops to couples. It states, "Low-income families, including TANF recipients, benefit from these relationship workshops as well." Many of the leaders and volunteers I interviewed believe that providing low-income families with relationship skills can help them get or stay out of poverty. One OKDHS employee told me: "We focus on low-income families. That is a target population because we want to build healthy and stronger families in relationships and to reduce teen pregnancies."

Data on participants from the marriage education workshops that the marriage initiative began to gather in 2003 reveal some diversity among those receiving services. The Bureau for Social Research at Oklahoma State University released a statistical analysis on May 19, 2004, of 2,037 forms completed by participants age eighteen or older. They found that 13 percent of participants are African Americans, 7 percent Latinos, and 10 percent Native Americans (less than 1 percent were Asian/Pacific Islanders). Given that Oklahoma's racial makeup from the 2000 U.S. Census stands at 7 percent, 5 percent, and 8 percent respectively, the former figures provide evidence of the services going to a fairly diverse range of the population. The data also show that 13 percent of the services are going to those with income before taxes below $5,000 and 13 percent to those with at least $5,000 but less than $15,000. The Census Bureau's poverty threshold in 2000 for one person under the age of 65 was $8,959, and 14.7 percent of Oklahomans lived below that threshold in 1999. Educational measures show that 13 percent have completed middle school and 43 percent have completed high school, so more than half of participants do not have a college education. Only 20.3 percent of Oklahomans overall receive a bachelor's degree or higher.[25]

The data demonstrate that a fair proportion, though still small, of the services is going to low-income populations. I was somewhat perplexed, because the figures did not match my experience of the thirty marriage workshops I attended. For example, all fourteen couples I interviewed from the general workshops made a salary higher than $35,000 and a majority of them were college educated. While I was not seeking a "representative" sample, I had attended enough workshops to get a good sense that they predominantly included a white, middle-class population. As I talked to marriage initiative leaders and employees, I learned that much of the diversity comes from workshops to families on military bases, and a more limited number from classes targeted to poor women through the Oklahoma State University Extension and one OKDHS office (see chapter 4). Even among workshops specifically meant to target low-income populations, such as through the Oklahoma State University Extension, they often do not draw participants from poorer and/or African American communities due to a lack of transportation. While I was in Oklahoma, the initiative was awarded a federal grant to initiate the "Transition to Parenthood" program that offers relationship workshops to fragile families on Medicaid having their first child. This new emphasis has no doubt increased the number of low-income clients that the initiative serves. Yet, with its funding by a separate grant from the federal government, this development does not help to solve the puzzle of why marriage-related services using TANF monies are not being targeted directly to TANF recipients.

Given the fact that unwed childbearing and multiple family transitions are more common among low-income populations, why not concentrate efforts in this area? An OKDHS manager explained: "Well, the initial directive from the standpoint we made in Oklahoma was we wanted all Oklahomans to be able to access this information period, regardless. To some extent, many of us breathed a sigh of relief because, otherwise we are talking about income standards, and we'd have to be looking at things to determine who is eligible and who is not." Although this manager was not part of the initial planning, she related what may have been a conscious decision to target the middle class:

I think there may have been some early discussions before I came into the picture that, if this was going to be successful, we've got to get the middle class to buy into it. That's how Social Security in 1935 became successful because of the middle class. They were the bigger users of it right off the bat. To some extent, I see that is how this is too.

This philosophy fits the historical legacy that has divided social insurance from public assistance programs and created the idea that some individuals are more worthy of government assistance than others. The white, middle-class majority is more likely to support government programs that are an entitlement to benefit their own group. Moreover, it is much easier to demonize services that are targeted to racial minority women.

The marriage initiative advertises its free marriage education workshops on its website and through local churches. Many of these workshops are not well attended, ranging from two to six couples and meeting at two-hour intervals for six weeks or for two all-day Saturdays. The higher-volume marriage workshops, also free, are called "Sweethearts Weekend."[26] These are highly publicized workshops that run on a Friday evening and all day on Saturday. An initiative employee sums them up:

They've got these huge Sweethearts Weekends. Those are more of the big PR events. I don't mean to say that in a negative sense, but some of these big events, like in Tulsa and Oklahoma City, do attract populations to see what's going on. If they don't get to the Sweethearts Weekend, they may go to the website and get information about local workshops where they get more meaningful ongoing stuff.

The initiative began to offer about one of these every couple months in cities throughout Oklahoma, and these attract some of the largest crowds. In its February 2005 newsletter, officials reported drawing a record five hundred people to the Community Sweethearts Weekend at the National Cowboy and Heritage Museum; this particular workshop was taught by Howard Markman and Scott Stanley. Both of the Sweethearts Weekends I attended brought in sixty to one hundred people. In addition to being advertised on the initiative website, these weekends are publicized on local radio stations and newspapers.

On the surface, providing services to the general population seems a democratic option to allow all Oklahomans free access. Yet, again, I asked myself, why use TANF monies toward funding an initiative that is not directed specifically to TANF recipients? Those most likely to hear about the classes, access them online, and attend are largely not those in need of public assistance and social support services. In this regard, the workshops represent an *un*democratic move to strengthen middle-class families at the expense of poor single mothers. Several people who worked in organizations that contracted with the marriage initiative expressed concern over who actually benefits from the marriage education workshops. The director of one of these agencies raised a concern about taking money away from poor women:

> I tell you that the amount of money that is spent on [the marriage initiative] really, really bothers me. I think it was $2 million this year! So, it was money that was taken away from poor women, and it hasn't been targeting poor women. In February on Valentine's weekend, there's a Sweethearts Getaway, and all these people come, and then you have the PREP [Prevention and Relationship Enhancement Program] spin-off for adopted couples and high school kids. Not that those things are not important, but they are being paid for with funds that were set aside for poor families.

In her critique of diverting funds from families in need, she offers Nancy, a single mother who can't make ends meet, as an example of the problem:

This is somebody who wants to make it. She doesn't want to be on welfare, and I think about the Nancys of this world, and I love Mary Myrick, okay, I am very fond of Mary, but she will probably end up a millionaire off the Oklahoma Marriage Initiative, and Nancy doesn't have enough support that she can keep a job long enough to earn medical leave. There's just something wrong with this picture. . . . It's just so much money that so far has been spent on so many middle-class people. That's my rub with it.[27]

Several staff expressed awareness of this problem and the need to get the services to the less privileged. One employee described to me the new program, Transition to Parenthood, and I responded enthusiastically that this seemed a positive direction, because it appeared to me that many of the current services were going to . . . , and she finished my sentence with "the middle class."

An OKDHS supervisor described a merging of the secular and religious. She told me,

It really took our team quite a while to really get to the low-income families. What we were trying to do was get it out there. Put some feet under it. A lot of people at first who were getting the services were in the middle class. The church groups, you know, the building of it was through the churches, and frankly mostly Protestant churches. The Catholics and Jews have already got it figured out about counseling and marriage education. . . . I kept thinking, well, this is more of a Protestant Oklahoma Marriage Initiative, but no one wanted to deal with that.

Many of the marriage education classes announced on the website are held in churches and, even among those that are not, the leaders are often pastors or individuals very active in church. As discussed in chapter 1, conservative Christian leaders were powerful actors in shaping the marriage initiative, and the strong conservative Protestant element is probably attributable to their influence. Yet equally important to the influence of the religious right has been the concentration of the initiative on research that points to what leaders believe might mean the disintegration of the white, middle-class family. In this way, the marriage initiative has focused a substantial amount of its resources on offering workshops to the general population. The ironic outcome is that these activities may actually *widen* the marriage gap between middle-class and poor families, the reverse goal of the one offered by marriage advocates like Kay Hymowitz.

Solidifying Race and Class Boundaries

Katherine Boo's 2003 *New Yorker* article, a highly ethnographic narrative that chronicles the impact of marriage classes on the lives of two African American women living in an Oklahoma housing project, propelled Oklahoma's notoriety as a leader in implementing the marriage cure. Boo followed the two women to a state-sponsored, three-day marriage education seminar taught by Pastor George Young, the African American pastor of Holy Temple Baptist Church. The friends, twenty-two-year-old Kim Henderson and forty-nine-year-old Corean Brothers, set out from their home at Sooner Haven, a housing project in one of the poorer, predominantly African American neighborhoods on the outskirts of Oklahoma City, to learn skills on how to get and stay married. Katherine Boo's reporting on marriage promotion drew attention to the racialized complexities of poverty. Kim, who tells Boo she wants "a healthy, wealthy, normal-lady life" that includes marriage, faces nearly insurmountable obstacles to obtain employment, let alone to marry. Trying to catch a bus home from the mall where she successfully secured an interview, the seventh bus that passed her by was the last back to her housing project, leaving her with a five-hour walk home. Fortunately, a black woman who was an assistant supervisor at a gift store in the mall pulled over to give her a ride, saying, "I know, I used to have to take the bus, too."

Reflecting national statistics, the poverty rate among African Americans in Oklahoma is significantly higher than for whites. In 2005, poverty rates for African Americans stood at 30 percent compared to whites at 14 percent.[28] Similar trends are found for Native Americans and Latinos. Whereas these two groups occupy a small percentage of the population in Oklahoma, they are significantly overrepresented among the poor. Moreover, poverty rates are much higher for African American, Native American, and Latina single-mother families than for those who are white and Asian American, both nationally and in Oklahoma. Almost half of all African American and Latina single-mother families in Oklahoma are living in poverty.[29]

In contrast to the marriage workshop described in Boo's article, the marriage initiative does not make providing workshops to the impoverished and predominantly African American districts in Oklahoma a main focus. George Young, who taught the class covered in the Boo article, explained: "I really only taught the one class that [Katherine Boo] sat in on at the church, but it was residents of Sooner Haven that were a part of it. We ran a bus over there to get them and pick them up, bring them over and fed them lunch."

He expressed that he would like to see more done to provide services in these communities, but he personally does not have the time. Working as an independent contractor for the marriage initiative, he travels across the country to talk with clergy and secular groups about forming healthy marriage initiatives in African American communities. The African American Healthy Marriage Initiative is a component of the federal Healthy Marriage Initiative, mainly a clearinghouse for information on impacting healthy marriages in black communities. Pastor Young has been involved in the efforts to deliver information about healthy black marriages. Between speaking engagements, pastoral duties, and family, little time is left to teach marriage workshops. The marriage initiative has not hired another person. Thus, the marriage initiative has paid Pastor Young to speak across the country about healthy black marriages even as little has been done to provide services to poor black communities in Oklahoma itself.

When I asked Pastor Young why racial minorities are not more of a focus for the marriage initiative, he replied, "They just didn't think about it. I think they were thinking about the larger problem about how the divorce rate was so high in Oklahoma, not in the African American community." He speculated, "I think they came to the conclusion a long time ago to make a broad effort on the whole state and not focus in on one particular segment." Pastor Young expressed a wish that the 2001 baseline survey had focused more on African Americans to be able to separate out that data: "I don't know how much of an effort was made to make sure that people who were contacted, how many were of African American descent. I can't say. I just don't think it was many." Direct discussions of impacting the African American community have been largely absent. Pastor Young described a lack of awareness or color blindness: "The lack of attention to certain particular areas or demographics always has a sense of some racial motivation behind it, in that even if you don't think about it, that's racially motivated because y'all didn't think about it! You ought to think about it." He clarified his thoughts on the motivations of the marriage initiative leaders: "I don't think it's an evil thing. I just think it is a lack of—hey, this is something we really need to look at if we want to impact the problem of marriage in Oklahoma."

To my knowledge, Pastor Young is the only African American among the roughly fifteen staff at the marriage initiative. During the year I spent in Oklahoma, no full-time salaried person was designated to work with the African American community. In contrast, the initiative did have a full-time staff member to work with religious communities. Pastor Young said,

Obviously, I don't have time to do what really needs to be done. I think probably, looking at it from hindsight, it would not have hurt to have had a full-time person who dealt directly with the African American community. . . . I think it would have been financially feasible to have someone do it in hindsight. The thought may have been they are bringing George Young on, so that would happen.

I asked him about my marriage initiative puzzle: the use of TANF funds to provide services that are not being directed toward TANF recipients. He agreed this was a problem but then clarified:

If you've got a divorce rate that is so high, you ought to have a state-wide initiative. So, do you have a statewide initiative *and*—I think the *and* is the operative word here—have a person that deals with the African American community or do we just have a statewide initiative and as a by-product let's look at these other communities that are having serious problems? I think that's the attitude they've taken. Good, bad, mean, evil. I don't perceive it that way. I wouldn't agree with it because I'm black. . . . And you're right, you are using TANF funds, well, why wouldn't you have a program that is really geared and focused on TANF recipients?

Pastor Young confirmed what many other marriage initiative employees articulated to me: the main thrust of the marriage initiative is to get services to "as many folk as we can," a goal that has had a significant impact on who benefits from the classes.

The practice of applying TANF funds for purposes other than helping needy families has made African American religious leaders in Oklahoma suspicious. Pastor Young described the difficulty he has had getting other African American pastors and church members involved: "There are some who are politically astute enough to have concerns with the fact that the money for the Oklahoma Marriage Initiative came out of TANF funding. They raised the concern: why are we taking money away from direct services to do marriage stuff? And good question!"

He had an answer: "I come back with, I think it is important. We need to start talking about this. You keep doing direct services but not do anything to change folk's minds and behavior, and to change folk's ideas and thoughts, you are going down the same road forever." His words raise the question of *whose* minds the marriage initiative wants to influence.

After my interview with Pastor Young, he and I discussed the possibility of interviewing members from his church to obtain some in-depth data on African American attitudes toward marriage and their views on government efforts to strengthen the institution. None of the church members in his congregation had participated in the marriage education workshops, and he expressed to me that many are wary of the marriage initiative as another project that might marginalize African Americans by portraying their families as dysfunctional. I began attending Pastor Young's church, and he introduced me as someone who was connected to the marriage initiative. As a white woman attending an African American church, there was little doubt that I stood out. I realized quickly that the congregants most likely associated me with the agenda of the marriage initiative, and the mistrust they felt of the initiative's program would most likely be transferred to how they viewed me. Over time, I was able to make a few contacts and gathered a couple of numbers. When I called, people were polite, but they were always too busy to meet.

Like the rest of the country, churches in Oklahoma are segregated by race (and to a lesser extent by class), and most of the initiative's efforts to reach out to religious leaders and churches have accessed white, middle-class Protestants who tend to offer more support for the idea of promoting marriage. As Pastor Young described, most African American pastors have kept their distance from marriage promotion, suspicious of the use of TANF money for this purpose. Two Latino pastors were beginning to target the growing Latino community in Oklahoma. But, again, the success of these efforts seemed based solely on their own efforts, as was the case for Pastor Young. Demographically, a majority of the churches that are involved in the initiative have predominantly white, middle-class congregations. Evangelical Christians, who in the past were associated more with the working class, have become increasingly middle-class after World War II when Protestant evangelicalism largely disengaged from more fringe, fundamentalist beliefs and moved into suburban neighborhoods.[30] Thus, conservative Protestant churches play a strong role in concentrating the marriage services on middle-class, white communities.

Marriage promotion follows a striking historical pattern that has systemically disenfranchised poor people, particularly poor women of color who from the very beginning of public assistance have been deemed unworthy of welfare benefits. In the next section, I provide a brief outline of this history to contextualize the import of marriage promotion in producing race and class inequalities. This history marks the links among women, poverty, the state, and the meaning of citizenship. Principally, welfare has served to control the boundary of citizenship along the lines of race, class, and gender as poor women of color have been deemed "undeserving" of benefits.[31] Laws and policies concerning the social stigma of "illegitimacy" have been a central mechanism in drawing these lines. The boundary of marriage therefore has been of critical importance in welfare politics to ensure the governability of the poor. In the current context, using welfare funds to provide marriage services to the public builds on the historical divide between worthy and unworthy citizens: white, middle-class marriages are normalized as the standard for "deviant" families.

Racialized Backlash

Demarcating race and class boundaries have long been central to the political and policy agendas regarding poor single mothers and their children in the United States. At the turn of the twentieth century, no federal or state public assistance programs existed to aid poor families. Reformers, who advocated "mothers' pensions," drew on maternalist rhetoric to argue their case that "deserving" single mothers needed to raise their children at home. In reality, mothers were forced to work to supplement the meager funds they received. By 1934, forty-six states of the then forty-eight passed such laws. Mothers' pensions functioned under the logic of the "marriage ethic"—the expectation that women would get and remain married. Juvenile court judges and social workers applied "suitable home" and "fit mother" regulations to bar unwed, divorced, or separated mothers from receiving aid, which meant that "deserving" white widows almost exclusively received assistance. These trends remained in place with the passage of the New Deal legislation that became Aid to Dependent Children. It wasn't until after World War II when federal welfare officials began to compel states to employ a less discriminatory application process that welfare expanded to include unwed white mothers and women of color.[32]

On the heels of welfare's expansion arose a backlash at the state level in the 1940s that valorized the stay-at-home mother.[33] The principal childrearing philosophy of the time argued that children's physical and mental health was predicated on the attention of a full-time mother and that maternal employment led to social problems and delinquency.[34] This philosophy, disseminated through the mass media, spurred a sizeable increase in marriage rates into the 1950s, and postwar economic prosperity, bolstered by federal home loans for veterans, made it possible for white, middle-class families to become avid consumers.[35] Increased economic security was not the norm for black men and women who faced multiple levels of discrimination like zoning in housing, restrictive covenants, and redlining by banks and insurance companies.[36] An increasing rate of joblessness among black men meant that, while rates of marriage increased for white women between the ages of twenty and twenty-four, it decreased for black women.[37] The fact that unwed childbearing was more predominant among black than white women spurred state officials to push "suitable home" policies as a form of racial exclusion.[38]

Alarm over the rise of unwed motherhood in the late 1940s and again in the 1960s onward set the stage for focusing welfare reform on work and marriage promotion. Aid to Dependent Children (ADC) was renamed Aid to Families of Dependent Children (AFDC) in 1962 and was specifically designed to enhance the family wage system to help poor single mothers raise their children at home, replacing the breadwinning father with the paternal state. The 1960s witnessed a number of victories for the rights of poor families; these gains were prompted by the civil rights movement, the grassroots welfare movement, and liberal electoral strength. A series of legal victories eradicated the restrictive policies that barred many poor women, and particularly poor women of color, from receiving benefits, and welfare to poor women experienced dramatic growth.[39] During this period, public concern began to grow over the increase in female-headed households that many pointed to as proof of the dysfunctional nature of black families.

Daniel Patrick Moynihan's 1965 report shifted public attention away from the arguments concerning civil rights and economic justice—the report was leaked to the press just days after the urban riots in Los Angeles's Watts on August 11, 1965—and onto the "tangle of pathology" of the black family. Moynihan's statement that "at the heart of the deterioration of the fabric of Negro society is the deterioration of the Negro family" foreshadowed the words of Vice President Dan Quayle during the 1992 campaign concerning the Los Angeles uprising that followed the Rodney King verdict: "I believe the lawless social anarchy which we saw is directly related to the breakdown of family structure, personal responsibility and social order in too many areas of our society."[40] Whereas Moynihan, a Democrat, focused his report on a liberal agenda to fight against rising rates of black male unemployment, Quayle, a Republican, sought to push a conservative strategy to dismantle welfare as the system that encourages "dependency and subsidizes broken families." Quayle's speech became infamous for his comments on Murphy Brown, a sitcom character played by Candice Bergen who as a *white* single professional decides to have a baby as a single mother. He castigates the sitcom character for "mocking the importance of fathers, by bearing a child alone, and calling it just another 'lifestyle choice.' "[41] His words mark an important shift in the discourse on the "pathology" of black families to concerns over the "breakdown" of white families.

Throughout the history of welfare, concerns about out-of-wedlock childbearing have focused on the improper heterosexual behavior of black women and men as a means to exclude unwed mothers from aid, and later to cut benefits or abolish welfare altogether. Two contemporary figures are Charles Murray and Lawrence Mead. In *Losing Ground: American Social Policy, 1950–1980*, Murray, who served as a former fellow at the conservative Heritage Foundation, focused his critique of welfare almost exclusively on the "bad" behavior of black men and women. He argued vigorously for the end of welfare because he felt that it encouraged unwed motherhood in this population. Rather than abolish welfare, Mead advocated stringent rules for welfare recipients and drew on racial arguments for justification, because "the worldview of blacks makes them uniquely prone to attitudes contrary to work, and thus vulnerable to poverty and dependency." Mead was one of a number of policy advocates who embraced what they called the "New Paternalism," the idea of conditioning the distribution of benefits on mothers' efforts to behave according to "dominant" American values and norms (i.e., those promoted by the state). New Paternalism often linked the idea of dependency to people of color.[42]

The cultural arguments of Murray, Mead, and others rely on a form of social Darwinism that views welfare as the corrupting force for poor women. Scholars have demonstrated the faulty logic of this reasoning, because there is little correlation between the size of welfare benefits, welfare usage, and rates of single parenting.[43] Yet these cultural explanations resonate with a large percentage of the U.S. population and feed into racial stereotypes that portray welfare recipients as lazy, irresponsible, promiscuous, and having bad values. One of the most pervasive racialized stereotypes is the "welfare queen," used by Ronald Reagan in 1975 to describe a Chicago welfare recipient whom he characterized as living in a wildly extravagant manner off her welfare check, driving a Cadillac and earning over $150,000 a year (he grossly exaggerated her fraudulent activities, which were more in the range of $8,000). Politicians and public officials have linked "race" to "welfare" for so long that just the mention of welfare brings to mind negative stereotypes about black single mothers. Policy analysts and state actors have frequently alternated the term "poor" with the racialized idiom of an "urban underclass" to suggest that poverty is found exclusively in the inner-city ghetto and to call into question the citizenship of poor people of color.

Marriage Promotion

The mid-1990s marked a new development in the discussion of poverty, welfare, and single parenting. After his 1992 speech in Los Angeles, the media castigated Dan Quayle for his remarks on Murphy Brown as being fogyish and unprogressive. The following year, the social historian Barbara Dafoe Whitehead published her widely read article titled "Dan Quayle Was Right" in the April 1993 edition of the *Atlantic Monthly*. Whitehead garnered social-scientific evidence to argue that unwed childbearing and divorce bring about disastrous consequences for children.[44] This article changed the public conversation in two ways. First, Whitehead offered justification for Dan Quayle's thesis that "marriage is the best antipoverty strategy of all" by marshaling social-scientific research to make a case that unwed childbearing *causes* intergenerational poverty, a problematic claim from most social scientists' perspective. While Quayle offered a specifically moral message about marriage and a commitment to Christian values to appeal to conservative Christian voters, Whitehead's argument focused on secular social science. Her article pioneered this new "revisionist" trend that puts prominent family scholars in conversation with conservative religious leaders and organizations to promote marriage.[45]

Second, Whitehead's article focused public concern and attention on the crisis of white families. Discussing the impact of "intergenerational poverty" on family life, Whitehead states, "Nor is the intergenerational impact of single motherhood limited to African Americans, as many people seem to believe. Among white families, daughters of single parents are 53 percent more likely to marry as teenagers, 111 percent more likely to have children as teenagers, 164 percent more likely to have a premarital birth, and 92 percent more likely to dissolve their own marriages."[46]

Picking up on Whitehead's assessment of single-parent white families, Charles Murray wrote a newspaper essay that calls the "black story" old news. The new trend, according to Murray, that "threatens the U.S. is white illegitimacy" and the emergence of a "white underclass" in which whites now account for the most people living in poverty, the most unwed childbearing, and the most women on welfare. He summarized that "the brutal truth is that American society as a whole could survive when illegitimacy became epidemic within a comparatively small ethnic minority. It cannot survive the same epidemic among whites."[47] As is true of the majority of Murray's thinking, his depiction of a white underclass relies on racialized codes meant to place poor white families in the realm of black deviancy. His words, however, also provide a window into anxieties driving marriage promotion politics: a fundamental unease over the future of *white* families and the blurring boundary that once clearly demarcated the "deviancy" of blacks from whites. These anxieties threaten a core sense of American identity.

In 1996, President Clinton signed the Personal Responsibility and Work Opportunity Reconciliation Act (PRWORA) into law in spite of reservations and protest from top staff advisors. He agreed with many of its provisions, including time limits and strict job requirements for welfare recipients but he also supported the creation of new job-training programs and better health care and child care to bolster employment. These latter measures were eliminated in the final bill that he signed to appease the Republican majority in Congress and to make good on his promise to "end welfare as we know it."[48] The final bill also included a provision to deny the right of legal immigrants to receive benefits, which was inspired by nativist fears of immigrants pawning off the system.

The logic of using welfare money to strengthen the norm of the white, middle-class family is written into PRWORA. The first goal specifies providing "assistance to *needy families* so that children may be cared for in their own homes," while the last goal seeks to "encourage the formation and maintenance of two-parent families," a provision that might apply to the general population.[49] With this wording, the welfare reform law implicitly sanctions the redistribution of resources from poor families to the middle and upper classes, as is occurring with the marriage initiative in Oklahoma. This practice is becoming more widespread. Other marriage promotion programs have modeled themselves on Oklahoma's blueprint as a pioneer and are similarly delivering a number of marriage services to the middle class.[50] One marriage initiative representative in Oklahoma gave me an estimate that not more than 5 percent of the services were actually going to TANF recipients. To get a sense of the economic impact of this redistribution on poor single mothers' lives, by April 2004, the marriage initiative reported training 1,072 workshop leaders and offering the workshops to 18,721 individuals. At 10 million TANF dollars (the amount of money used by 2004), the cost works out to approximately $500 per person (including the trainers). If just 5 percent of services are going to TANF recipients, this represents a significant amount of money being diverted. This estimate is more alarming when one considers the TANF cash assistance stipend for recipients of a family of three per month, which is under $300 in Oklahoma.[51]

Fear over the declining significance of the nuclear family has spurred the marriage initiative in Oklahoma to offer marriage education to the public as a mechanism to reinstitutionalize marriage. As one report put it, the strategy of the marriage initiative is to provide marriage education services to all Oklahomans to effect "specific behavior change at the individual level" and to "restore support for the institution of marriage as a valued social good."[52] When I interviewed the OKDHS director, he described being enlightened by reading Barbara Dafoe Whitehead's article: "You know, the *New Yorker* [sic] got a lot of heat over that article, and they are a left of center magazine saying that Dan Quayle was right. But it was very well-documented, and I think based on that you begin to see that there is a lot of social capital in marriage."[53] As Kay Hymowitz asserts, educating the young to be "self-reliant" members of a democratic society is the mission of white, middle-class families and that poor black parents are not "simply middle-class parents *manqué*; they have their own culture of child-rearing, and—not to mince words—that culture is a recipe for more poverty."[54] This philosophy harks back to nation-building principles that analogize marriage and the state as a necessary form of governance to produce worthy (white, middle-class) citizens.

This chapter has considered the paradox of the marriage initiative in redistributing TANF funds to families that have already achieved social capital. The ultimate goal that motivates national and local marriage promotion activities is to draw a boundary to elevate the married, two-parent, heterosexual family above all other family forms. A publication of the Institute for American Values summarizes this philosophy in a section titled "Protect the boundaries of marriage." It states:

> For marriage to function as a social institution, the community must know who is married. To support marriage, laws and policies must distinguish married couples from other family and friendship units so that people and communities can tell who is married and who is not. . . . The harder it is to distinguish married couples from other kinds of relationships, the harder it is for communities to reinforce norms of marital behavior, the harder it is for couples to identify the meaning of their own relationship, and the more difficult it is for marriage to fulfill its function as a social institution.[55]

This chapter has uncovered the boundary work of this philosophy and its demarcation of a failed citizenship for those unable or unwilling to exercise the proper "self-sufficiency" or "responsibility" to get and stay married. The goal of marriage promotion feeds a moral divide between the married, whose sexual relations are legitimate, and the unmarried, whose sexual relations, whether heterosexual or nonheterosexual, are not. While sexual mores and attitudes have changed radically in the last century as the boundaries of marriage are "redrawn," marital discourses still hold power to create a divide between "us" and "them."[56] The next chapter examines marriage workshops that are targeted to one population on the other side of the moral divide: welfare recipients.

Teaching Marriage to Single Mothers and Inmates

Marriage is a fragile institution. Unless you enforce it by social mechanisms including shame for not being married, stigma for having a child out of wedlock, then we will see marriage continue to suffer.

—James Q. Wilson, interview on *Frontline*[1]

Marriage per se is too simplistic a solution to the complex problems of the poor. Marrying a low-income, unmarried mother to her child's father will not magically raise the family out of poverty when the parents often have no skills, no jobs, and terrible housing, and may be struggling with depression, substance abuse, or domestic violence.

—Theodora Ooms, "Marriage Plus"[2]

Some high-profile marriage advocates aim to restore a time when there was greater stigma for divorce or unwed childbearing. The political scientist James Q. Wilson differentiates stigma from prejudice, where prejudice is about mistakenly imputing group traits on individuals and stigma is blaming an individual for immoral or dishonorable behavior such as lying, cheating, or extramarital sex. Prejudice causes discrimination and stigma causes shame: "Shame once inhibited women from having children without marrying and men from abandoning wives for trophy alternatives."[3] Wilson laments that society has "stigmatized stigma" so much that it no longer blames people for "immoral behavior." Those who view the marriage problem in this way assert that resurrecting marriage will take policies and actions that "*privilege* married, childrearing couples rather than [are] neutral to them."[4] They recognize that some will take offense by what might be deemed discrimination against single mothers and gay men and lesbians who cannot legally marry. But they believe a more uncompromising stance is necessary because the biological two-parent family is the "source of much of our moral nature and the foundation of social organization."[5]

All marriage advocates do not share these views. On the more liberal end of marriage promotion are those involved in poverty research, such as researchers at the Brookings Institution and the Center for Law and Social Policy (CLASP). These advocates tend to recognize that marriage promotion by itself cannot solve the problem of poverty. They emphasize that changing behavior and culture will have an effect but they also consider the structural barriers to marriage—lack of education and job training, a high prevalence of domestic violence, mental health and substance abuse, transportation, and access to affordable, high-quality child care.[6] Advocates and scholars have used the term "fragile families" to indicate that "unmarried couples and their children are, in fact, families," and that, while low-income, unmarried parents are at greater risk of poverty, economic insecurity, and family dissolution, marriage is not a panacea to these problems.[7] The Fragile Families and Child Wellbeing Study, a longitudinal survey of low-income, unmarried parents and their children, has shown that many unwed parents are in committed relationships, but they face numerous barriers to marriage, including low education, income below the poverty line, and health issues.[8]

Although low-income women value marriage and see it as part of "making it" or fulfilling the American dream, they strongly desire children and often don't marry the fathers of their children due to the men's financial instability.[9] Many avoid marriage out of fear of divorce, which can leave a mother more destitute than before marrying.[10] Marriage advocates also recognize a lack of "marriageable men" as another reason many poor women, and especially poor African American women, do not marry.[11] The economist Robert Lerman assesses the problem: "One reason for the low rate of married-couple minority families is that the unstable employment and inadequate wages of many low-income minority males reduce their marriageability. With few marriageable men available, minority women have less incentive to delay childbearing or marry the father of their child."[12]

While viewing marriage as a possible solution, this faction offers a number of solutions that include education and job training. The "marriage-plus" strategy, put forward by Theodora Ooms, "acknowledges that married and unmarried parents, mothers and fathers, may need both economic resources and noneconomic supports to increase the likelihood of stable, healthy marriages and better co-parenting relationships."[13] In this regard, services have targeted not only poor single mothers, but also men in prison.[14]

In this chapter, I examine efforts to promote marriage at the local level among single mothers and in prisons, uncovering vastly different strategies and responses. While marriage advocates seek to redraw a definitive boundary to compel marriage as a moral and social good, some are more willing to recognize the obstacles to marriage for low-income individuals and prioritize a number of relationship- and work-related services. On the one hand, workshops that emphasized moral and religious beliefs concerning marriage were met with resentment and aggravation. In contrast, workshops were more successful when they concentrated on the actual relationships that participants had with boyfriends, children, parents, and employers. The latter, however, went so far in downplaying marriage that they actually, in some cases, did more to affirm diverse relationships, an outcome that is contrary to the stated goal of marriage promotion.

Tying the Welfare and Marriage Knot

My time spent in Oklahoma uncovered a number of ironies. One was the goal to promote marriage in the context of a rather punitive state welfare system. Three years after unveiling the marriage initiative, a 2002 study by the National Campaign for Jobs and Income Support, a Washington-based organization involving over a thousand grassroots antipoverty groups, ranked Oklahoma number three in a list of the "worst welfare states" in the nation.[15] The report cited an incongruity between Oklahoma's marriage promotion initiative and its Temporary Assistance to Needy Families (TANF) rules that discriminate against low-income, two-parent households by requiring stricter work history mandates, as most states did at that time. The report was released in anticipation of the National Governors Association meeting to draw attention to states that have adopted particularly punitive policies. George Johnson, an Oklahoma Department of Human Services (OKDHS) spokesperson, told a journalist that the state can be proud of its kinship with the nine other "sister" states on the report's worst welfare list: Idaho, Wisconsin, Oregon, Wyoming, Arizona, Mississippi, South Dakota, Texas, and Utah. He stated, "We believe that taxpayers in this state do not want to support individuals who are not willing to work or participate in activities that will lead to work."[16]

Oklahoma ranks in the lowest states in its cash assistance provisions, and the sixty-month time-limit clock is strictly enforced whether or not there are stoppages or sanctions in receipt of benefits. In 2003, a family of three could receive a maximum benefit of $292 a month.[17] Howard Hendrick informed me that, while cash assistance is low, the state does pay a fairly "rich" work support benefit that, put together with cash benefits, "will take care of your costs, but you're not going to get out of poverty with it." The state also has a substantial child-care subsidy. According to Director Hendrick, at the height of the old welfare system, Oklahoma was spending $13 million a month on cash assistance. In 2004, this was reduced to $3 million. Before welfare reform, it was spending $40 million to $60 million in child-care subsidies, whereas in 2004 it spent $140 million. While the state has a strong child-support program, it does not give poor single mothers money from collected child support nor does it disregard the amount of child support that the family can keep without lowering TANF benefits. Director Hendrick stated: "People need to realize that we really are going to enforce child support, that there are consequences to choosing to have children and not be responsible for them." According to the sociologist Sharon Hays, this is a way of disciplining poor single mothers (and fathers) who are forced to disclose the biological father's identity to receive assistance and receive no financial gain from support collected.[18] The political theorist Anna Marie Smith studied the ways that the scope and structure of the child support enforcement measures, along with other directives like marriage promotion, contribute to a system of sexual regulation of poor families.[19]

Like most states, Oklahoma experienced a drastic decline in its welfare rolls after welfare reform, which the state precipitated before the 1996 law by instituting stricter work requirements. From 1993 to 2000, the number of participants on the welfare rolls declined from 140,000 to 55,000. Many eligible clients are dropped for noncompliance or do not even bother to apply. For those who do, after the first sanction, the family is terminated until they can prove they've fully met the required terms. One OKDHS supervisor told me that a large number of eligible clients turn to more dangerous means to make ends meet. He characterized the drop in the welfare rolls as a disaster:

> The official criterion is whether people are being self-sufficient. Self-sufficient can mean I'm now supporting my family with prostitution, drug sales. I'm now supporting my family by being in a violent domestic arrangement where I'm not safe. It can even mean living in a very extended family situation where you have up to five generations in the same home and everybody living off one person's income or one person's disability, and the standard of living is horribly low.

For those who are able to jump through the hoops and receive benefits, there are strict work requirements after twenty-four months, which neither post-secondary training nor education can fill.

Blended into this larger picture of a rather punitive state welfare policy is the marriage initiative. To disseminate services to a low-income population, the marriage initiative trains employees of the Department of Health, the Cooperative Extension Service at OSU, and OKDHS to teach workshops and make referrals to their clients. In the first two years of the program (beginning in 2001), the Department of Health agreed to meet a quota of workshops offered by staff members trained in the Prevention and Relationship Enhancement Program (PREP), with each conducting at least four workshops. I interviewed the OKDHS marriage initiative coordinator, who told me that about fifty-five staff members were trained. She said, "It was a program that was blessed at the state level, and everyone was encouraged to participate in it. So, there were staff who chose not to do the training. They backed out of it at some point." She explained that the Health Department was able to meet its quota because there were a few staff members who conducted numerous workshops. For those who had not completed the required four, "There were a lot of issues. Some of them felt like they were pushed into the training, you know, and that wasn't something that they would have done. Others just said that in recruiting to have the workshops, they had lots of issues, especially in rural areas, to get groups together to teach." Mary Myrick and Theodora Ooms acknowledged that many of the public agency administrators and staff members were skeptical and expressed concerns over the relevance of marriage to the predominantly single-parent, low-income population they served.[20]

The marriage initiative coordinator described a push in 2003 to "really work on the TANF population, since the monies for the marriage initiative are coming from TANF dollars." In October 2003, the marriage initiative began teaching PREP to TANF clients at one OKDHS office as part of its weekly orientation. The social services specialist who helped implement the workshops in his office described how he received an invitation to participate at an informational meeting in 2001. He had been pretty skeptical about offering marriage workshops to his clientele at first, but after talking with a representative from the Brookings Institution he began to change his mind. In 2003, a marriage initiative staff person visited the office to ask for help with referrals to a local day-care center that was providing PREP. The supervisor said he found out there was a nonfaith-based version of PREP and discussed its appropriateness for welfare clients.

The county office made the jump to incorporate PREP into its weekly orientations. The supervisor said:

> We felt that including this, the first goal would be to have better personal relationships. But we also had an aspect of self-interest in that if they got along better with their personal relationships, maybe they would get along better with their social workers too and even more important their employers. Of course, job hopping, for whatever reason, is our number one problem with our clients. Relationship hopping is another, so we felt our clients would be better armed to keep jobs, to keep relationships, to get along with their children, and improve their family.

This language underscores the increasing emergence of strategies of control, wherein contemporary welfare reform programs prioritize "the ethical reconstruction of the welfare recipient."[21] The sociologist Stanley Cohen argued that these technologies of control blur the boundaries between "inside" and "outside" the system to rely on other preventative institutions—families, schools, neighborhoods, and workplaces—to intensify surveillance.[22] In this light, relationship classes are used to modify the behavior of TANF recipients to become supple and compliant workers and citizens. The supervisor explained the main concern of OKDHS: "The big resistance to the marriage initiative rather than a relationship class is the word 'marriage' really triggers some things for people who have had bad marriages or are divorced parents. That's why the county office didn't want anything to do with it, because it was called the marriage initiative." Instead of marriage, the county office called it PREP Relationship. The OKDHS office was the first to embrace PREP "with any kind of open arms," said the supervisor.

PREP Relationship was integrated into the first week of orientation for new TANF clients called the "Steps to Employment Program." During the orientation week, clients took several tests: the Test for Adult Basic Education that measures reading and math levels, the Career Ability Placement Survey, the Career Occupational Preference System Interest Inventory, the Career Orientation Placement and Evaluation Survey about areas for career guidance, and the Substance Abuse Subtle Screening Inventory to help identify substance abuse problems. The week also brought speakers from job-training programs and community colleges to provide information on possibilities for education, as well as speakers on parenting skills, nutrition, and sexual and reproductive health. Two of the five days, Wednesday and Friday, were devoted to PREP Relationship. Every client must attend all thirty hours of the orientation during the week—from 9 A.M. to 3 P.M.—to meet the eligibility requirements.

The PREP class is mandatory in the sense that clients must participate in the week's orientation to fulfill their TANF eligibility. Marriage advocates disavow the existence of compulsory marriage education classes for TANF recipients, and leaders of the marriage initiative in Oklahoma have maintained that the classes are completely voluntary.[23] Nationally, Wade Horn advocates a public-health model for marriage initiatives similar to tobacco and good parenting: Educate but not mandate.[24] Diane Sollee on her Smart Marriages listserv discussed an August 2005 NPR story about marriage workshops for TANF clients: "This is wonderful and will help us get the news about Marriage Education to the country, though the opening line 'Oklahoma requires that some women on welfare take a marriage education course' is going to give the Oklahoma Marriage Initiative folks an aneurism [*sic*]. No one is REQUIRED to take a marriage education class—it's AN OPTION."[25] Sollee's assertion contradicts a discussion I had with a marriage initiative official who told me: "[The clients] are supposed to be meeting the participation rate of thirty hours a week. So, we have clients who will sign off on an employability plan with a PREP class in the orientation. And it has a mandatory nature about it."

A big concern over making workshops mandatory is the issue of domestic violence. The marriage initiative involved a domestic violence agency early on to present at the PREP trainings and offer, as the director put it, "our little—and that's as much time as we get—spiel to give people an awareness that domestic violence is out there." When I asked her about collaborating with the marriage initiative, she amended the meaning of the word "collaboration":

> It's a partnership—a cooperative relationship. Frankly, the reason we got involved was because they are going to do it with or without us, and it has been done more without us than it has been done with us, but we have to put in whatever protections we can to protect victimized women. I know that sounds negative, but we are just trying to make sure that women are safe.

She described how the coalition was ostracized in front of a national meeting because of its willingness to participate in the marriage initiative. She had been involved in presenting information about the marriage initiative to the regional hub office for the federal Department of Health and Human Services. She said, "Some of the women were so opposed to it that they just shut their minds, and they were unwilling to work with it. They said they would be selling out. I told them that I think I'm selling out the victims if I'm not involved in the process to be a voice for them." The agency's cooperation has proved beneficial. It worked with Scott Stanley and Howard Markman, the creators of the PREP curriculum, to produce an informational page on the circumstances under which people should consider not participating. Titled "Getting More Help When There Are Serious Problems," the sheet offered information on financial problems; serious marital or other family problems; substance abuse, addictions, and other compulsive behaviors; mental health problems; and domestic violence. It also provided hotline numbers for domestic violence, mental health/substance abuse, and suicide.

As is true across the nation, domestic violence is a substantial problem in Oklahoma. A 1999 survey conducted by the Oklahoma Department of Mental Health and Substance Abuse Services found that 17.4 percent of Oklahoma women over the age of eighteen who were married or in a relationship reported being abused in the prior twelve months. Among these women, 77 percent reported emotional abuse with no physical abuse, 5 percent reported being physically abused, and 17.7 percent reported both emotional and physical abuse.[26] In 2006, 24,105 domestic violence cases were reported; domestic abuse reports increased 4.4 percent between 1997 and 2006; and the state currently ranks tenth nationally in the number of females murdered by their intimate spouses.[27] The director described the domestic violence demographics: "We know that domestic violence crosses all boundaries, but the reality is that poor women are overrepresented in the reporting of domestic violence, and we are a very poor state. Housing is a horrible, horrible issue for women in this state, and it's one of the things that can keep them where they are, locked in sometimes." The problem is particularly acute in rural Oklahoma, and lack of funding is a major barrier to getting services into rural communities.

The services and funds directed at poor single mothers often end up penalizing rather than helping. OKDHS spends quite a bit of money assessing and providing services to poor women on their substance abuse issues, a much smaller percentage than on domestic violence issues. The director told me it does not support services around domestic violence. She described the situation for women whose children have been taken from them, especially in rural areas:

These mothers are in a shelter because they are trying to get their kids back, but there is no way that TANF is doing anything to help provide services to those women to help get them in a position that TANF thinks they are ready to have their kids back. Any given day in this state, there are several women who are in shelters because Child Protective Services said go to the shelter with that kid or I'm taking the kid with me. They have to leave their home, which is not necessarily a bad thing because they are leaving their abuser, but they are leaving their home and going to live in a shelter and DHS does nothing to support that participation.

The director described a punitive bureaucratic system that put poor single mothers who face domestic violence into double jeopardy by demanding they leave abusers but not providing the resources to enable the women to make ends meet. Due to this lack of support, the director was against using TANF dollars for marriage promotion, as she felt strongly that there were better ways to spend this money.

The director described a "classic example" of a client, Matilda, who came from a small town and had tried to make a bad marriage work. The man was abusive, and they eventually divorced. She was raised in a lower middle-class family and had aspirations, completing a couple years of college. Even though she did find a decent job working in a doctor's office, it was for minimum wage, and she was forced to receive some assistance from the state—food stamps and Section 8 Housing. In the end, she wasn't able to keep the job, because she was never able to work long enough to accumulate leave to stay home when her kids were sick. Her father had molested her as a child, so she couldn't leave the kids with him. The director lamented,

> Boy, there is a lot of money spent on the marriage initiative when we have so many poor people that we could provide . . . Matilda doesn't need . . . probably a little marriage initiative and work training wouldn't hurt Matilda, but it is not, for many of these women, the number one thing they need at this point in their lives. They need a safe home; they need to insure their car. And then they [politicians and policymakers] wonder why these women can't rise above the system!

Her criticisms reflect the assessments made by scholars and other antipoverty and antidomestic violence advocates.[28]

Although concerned about the money spent on the marriage initiative, the director told me that she hadn't felt domestic violence to be an issue because the marriage initiative had focused on middle-class communities and made the workshops voluntary: "Everything we've done pretty much up to this point has been expensive. It has been an expenditure that in my opinion should not have been, but it hasn't been harmful or dangerous." She felt the marriage initiative took the issue of domestic violence seriously: "In the grand scheme of the initiative, domestic violence is a small piece. I do believe that the marriage initiative has taken that responsibility seriously. Mary Myrick has really been inclusive to try to let us know what they are up to. She listens when we are concerned about what we hear. I really do give her credit." Nonetheless, she was worried about putting poor women at risk with the increased focus on the TANF population. She told me she was absolutely opposed to mandatory participation:

> My fear—I know the initiative has been working at the county office in eastern Oklahoma to offer PREP—is that these women (sometimes it's men, but mostly it's women) will not understand that they have the right not to participate. What's going to happen if they think they have to bring their abuser with them? There are some relationships where the classes are a really good thing, but what happens when we find a woman in an abusive relationship that is "encouraged to participate"? That was the language the OMI staff used at the advisory council meeting.

One meeting with marriage initiative staff had addressed the problem of domestic violence in implementing the program with TANF clients. A high-level staff member told the group that everything but the most minor domestic violence cases would be screened out. The director described how she had spoken up and said, "Wait a minute! The deal was we wouldn't be doing domestic violence cases." It was a difficult conversation in which the staff member ended up in tears. The director made it clear that you can't force women, especially those in violent relationships, to do this with their abusers. When the marriage initiative staff person said that the women could always say no, the director described the comment of the gentleman sitting next to her: "So you will just gently twist their arm up behind their back rather than by doing it with force. Just gently recommend that they participate."

In regard to screening out domestic violence cases, one problem for the marriage initiative has been to find qualified volunteer instructors. After the initial push to get OKDHS staff trained, the agency no longer required employees to lead workshops. A few volunteer to do lots of workshops and most others none. Every week, the marriage initiative schedules a volunteer for the orientation, including clinicians and social workers who conduct the workshops as part of their job. Volunteers also include students and retired family therapists or social workers. If all else fails, marriage initiative staff members will teach. The goal is to find volunteers with some experience teaching low-income populations and instruct them to focus on communication skills that are useful to all kinds of relationships. Some accomplish this goal better than others. Overall, I found the workshops that emphasized marriage lost the interest of the clients who resented the class for disciplining them as single mothers.

The Penalties of "Bad Behavior"

Ruthie, a white woman in her early seventies and a retired family therapist, had taught PREP to couples at her Baptist church but had two more workshops to fulfill her obligation. When an initiative staff person contacted her, she agreed to teach the class for the TANF orientation. Two students, Terry and Mandy, from a Baptist college, were completing prerequisites for the marriage and family therapy license program and volunteered to coach. There were five women in the orientation: four were white—Jane, Cindy, Patricia, Kelly—and one was African American—Tanya. While chatting before the start of class, Ruthie told me that she was going to focus on relationships and not marriage because most of these women are not married. Her good intentions, however, did not pan out as she relied heavily on the curriculum. She started off on a positive note by telling the women that the things she was teaching might be helpful in the workplace. But things went downhill quickly when she followed up with, "You are young and hopefully will get married one day." Ruthie used overhead materials provided by the PREP curriculum and provided statistics about the high probability of divorce for young couples marrying for the first time, which was roughly 40 percent. As she discussed the factors associated with "future divorce and/ or marital distress," one of the women whispered rather loudly to no one in particular, "We are screwed!" This comment was made seemingly because of frustration with the information being presented.

Although perhaps not intentional, Ruthie tended to talk down to the women, and her life experience provided few pointers on how to relate to them. In particular, Ruthie failed to address the issues that impacted these women's lives. All were in very difficult situations. Tanya's son was involved in a severe accident at eleven months old and part of his brain had been subsequently removed. Of Kelly's three sons, one had a speech and learning disability, and she was having problems finding adequate child care. Patricia, a mother of four, shared how her three-year-old boy had witnessed her ex-husband stab her with a screwdriver. She remarked there are some memories that just can't be erased. Her son had at one time tried to stab his brother. Cindy related how her baby's father is an alcoholic. As the day progressed, the clients displayed body language signals of boredom, and Ruthie had difficulty getting them to participate.

Instead of connecting the material to the women's lives, Ruthie emphasized her religious beliefs about marriage and taught about traditional gender expectations. She told the women that she had married at a young age and was in her fiftieth year of marriage to a "macho man." She had to teach her husband how to fight because he didn't have the skills to argue well, and this caused quite a bit of conflict over the years. Her comments made it clear that her husband was no romantic. When talking about expectations of marriage, she told the women, "If you expect roses every day, you might get disappointed. You would at my house. He's not that kind of man." In contrast to her pastor, a romantic who brought flowers to his wife every week, her husband wouldn't do that in a million years. Ruthie suggested that their shared religious values had made it possible to work through these kinds of disappointments.

As in the PREP courses for the general population, Ruthie taught about conservative gender expectations in marriage. She asserted that men had to learn how to calm women down: "Men were built, created, and developed to solve conflicts by fighting. In caveman days, that's what they had to do." When a man gets home from work, she told us, it is important to spend the first thirty minutes with him. This way the kids know they are not the center of the universe. Later on, Ruthie conveyed a story about a woman whose husband cheated on her and said, "He is the man. He has to take responsibility for his actions. He needs to say, 'Please forgive me.'" At one point, Ruthie asked about expectations of who is supposed to be the breadwinner. Kelly spoke up, "I just do it all myself. I tell my kids that their daddy has his house, and I have my own." Ruthie asked what her expectation had been before she had children with him, and she answered that she had expected him to take care of her and the kids. Rather judgmentally, Ruthie rejoined that Kelly's expectation was a form of dependency. This was an interesting response, considering that Ruthie had been married to and "depended" on a man for fifty years. Her language reflects the dominant thinking about welfare, which is seen to create dependency in welfare recipients.

Women in the class expressed skepticism concerning marriage. Kelly, for example, said she didn't want a relationship in the future, and others in the class agreed. When Ruthie said it was important to consider whether a relationship was forever, Jane blurted out, "No way!" At another point, Cindy told the class that it's better not to have a relationship if the man was going to get in the way of taking care of themselves and their children. The women felt that the speaker-listener technique was an unrealistic tool to use with the men they knew. Tanya commented that the men she had been involved with would never do this. After Ruthie talked about the technique, she gave us time to practice. I practiced with Kelly, a young white woman with two kids who was very shy and had no desire to participate. We ended up chatting instead about her goal to run her own day-care business out of her home. She confessed to me that the class was really boring and wasn't useful to her. "Who needs a man anyway? They just want to move from place to place. Men will get in the way of reaching my goals," she asserted. The women in the orientations I attended had a great deal on their plate. Most were having trouble with basics like paying the rent, securing transportation, finding decent child care, and jumping through all the hoops to receive TANF benefits. Some had just extricated themselves from bad relationships and were trying to make it on their own two feet. From this perspective, the prospect of a new romantic relationship and/or marriage would rank very low.

The attitudes of the women may also have been a negative reaction to feeling singled out for not having a husband. When I went to lunch with Ruthie and the two coaches, they made judgmental comments about the clients. Ruthie exclaimed that she couldn't understand "how these women got themselves into this situation. Three kids without a husband!" One of the coaches disclosed that she and her husband once received food stamps but that she "had done it right." She used public assistance to help get an education and now she was getting a master's degree. Her comment suggests a moral judgment about not doing it right. This undercurrent did not mix well with all the frustrations of a grueling week of orientation. On Friday, Kelly told me the day before had been difficult, because they had unannounced drug testing. Jane, who had been placed in rehabilitation, expressed her disgust about the class. She yawned loudly and declared, "This woman is going to put me to sleep." During a video, several of the women chatted through it.

After all the participants left on the last day, Ruthie remarked that she wouldn't do another class at OKDHS. Like Ruthie, a staff volunteer who had taught the class on several occasions decided to discontinue. She said,

> Well, my main thing was that they [OKDHS] did it during orientation, and I don't think that is a good time to be trying to teach people anything, because they've got more basic needs they are trying to get addressed. There are a lot of distractions. . . . They've got things they are trying to accomplish,

like they have to get drug-tested or they have to meet with the counselor or decide what work they are going to do. They have a lot of hoops to jump through, and their minds are more often in that place, obviously.

She suggested that the women would have been more receptive to a class during a different period of their lives. Other reasons I found for being unreceptive result from a focus on marriage and lack of attention paid to the clients' circumstances and needs.

Ruthie's class elicited one of the worst responses during the relationship workshops I attended. Other workshops taught by two women in their early twenties who were both married also elicited negative responses. During my first focus group, the five participants stressed their frustration with the teachings on marriage and a lack of sensitivity to their needs. Denise, an African American woman in her early thirties with two children, said, "I'm not trying to be mean, but today I found the class to be really boring. To me, it's not related to stuff." Sally, a twenty-seven-year-old white woman with one child, elaborated,

They haven't given any of their life situations that pertain to any of ours. They're like, well I have no kids. I haven't heard either one of them even once say a situation that happened in their household that they can relate to ours, but they want for us to pretty much have some type of feedback on what they're saying. But you're not saying anything we can relate to!

Not only was the instruction unrelated to their lives, but the participants felt that learning the speaker-listener technique was not useful. Melinda, a divorced thirty-nine-year-old African American mother of three, said that she didn't have anyone to practice with: "You know, there are a lot of us like that. You know, some are in prison for drugs, others just disappeared." Mary, a thirty-year-old white woman with two children, assessed the experience of the entire week: "I found it very agitating. I won't lie to you. Most of us aren't in a relationship and those of us who are, weren't ready to think forever." Melinda added, "Especially if we've been divorced, we're not ready to jump back in the saddle again."

I asked the five women about their perceptions of why PREP Relationship was part of the week orientation. Rachel, a divorced mother of two, said,

I think it is because, obviously, we are all single parents now, and there's a reason why we're single parents. Another thing, though, is that all of our cases are different. I think if they are going to do these kinds of classes, they need to address our reasons for being here. Mine is different than Melinda's, and Melinda's is different than Sally's, so it makes a difference. Whereas, we are all sitting here bored because it's not within whatever we're doing.

Rachel followed the perceived justification for marriage promotion with an argument against the tendency to lump single mothers in a one-size-fits-all box. The participants felt that the relationship class just added to a string of humiliations. They felt demeaned by the substance-abuse testing and the personal questions that were asked of them. Melinda talked about how she went home and cried after being asked all kinds of questions about drug use from when she was a teenager. Sally affirmed, "Yeah, they point the finger at you." Melinda continued, "If you miss one day or you're late, they're going to drop you from the program. Last night when I went home, I didn't care. I was to that point. I didn't want to come back. The money—$200 a month—is not worth the mental anguish!" She did show up though because, in truth, she needed the money.

The women also expressed frustration with the workshop leaders' middle-class perspective. Rachel described how one leader talked about fighting with her husband over leaving a dirty sock on the floor. She said, "Girl, that's just a part of life! There's a sock on the floor at my house all of the time. That's neither here nor there." Sally added,

> They act like we are real dumb. I am certain that we were all raised in different environments and have different religions, you know. We even have different times to go to sleep. . . . We all have different problems. [She points to Melinda.] Her mate is incarcerated, mine might have been domestic violence, Rachel is a disagreement with a child. We haven't hit any of those notes in this class.

The complexity of their lives was unrecognized in the workshops. Melinda expressed exasperation: "What they say is just petty stuff that people bitch and gripe about." Sally chimed in, "Exactly!" And Melinda continued,

> We just wish that was on our plate. Last night, my mom came and picked up my son at 10:30 P.M. I heard something at the door. I stupidly got up and opened the door without saying who is it because I thought it was a family member. I look out and my house is surrounded by cops! This is part of my life. I go through stuff [the workshop leaders] don't know anything about.

The women expressed that the difficult problems they faced would not be solved simply by being better communicators or by marrying a man. As they discussed the week they'd spent in orientation, one point came across loud and clear. They felt angry and resentful about participating in activities that they perceived to be a waste of time.

Dodging Domestic Violence

While the marriage initiative sought to address the issue of domestic violence early on and worked closely with a local agency to provide information and preventive measures, I found the issue to be an ongoing concern that was unevenly addressed in the workshops for TANF clients. Many TANF clients were sensitive to the issue in a way that was not true of the general population, and they made comments that often went unaddressed. During one workshop in which we watched a PREP video of a white couple fighting—involving raised voices and swear words, several of the women pointed out that the man was "obviously violent because he threw the screwdriver." I had watched the video dozens of times in workshops for the general population and not once did anyone mention the question of violence. In another case when Patricia told the class about how her ex-husband stabbed her with a screwdriver, I was surprised when Ruthie completely ignored her and just continued on with the curriculum.

In the following class, Sandra, a thirty-one-year-old white mother of eleven-year-old twins and a three-year-old boy, openly recounted to me during lunch her abusive marriage. She had been living in Texas with her husband and his biological son. Her two girls from a previous relationship were living with their grandparents, and she expressed how thankful she was that "they didn't have to experience that." She escaped to a shelter, and her son stayed in a day-care center while she attended therapy, finally moving to Oklahoma City to get away from her ex. We didn't get a chance to discuss this in the workshop, because the instructor, Cindy, taught by the book and didn't give the participants much chance to talk about the problems in their lives. She didn't address the issue of domestic violence. Sandra expressed her reluctance to attend the PREP Relationship workshop, and it became a very uncomfortable week as Sandra struggled with the curriculum. For example, during the section on forgiveness, Cindy was talking about how to get past anger when Sandra spoke up and said sometimes forgiving is itself the problem: "I did so much forgiving in my relationship that he took it for granted." Again, Cindy did not address the issue. A little later, Sandra told about her ex cheating on her: "They keep on doing it and doing it. They make it look like you have brain damage. He told me that I wanted him to cheat on me. I replied that if I wanted that I would have brought a woman home for him to get with! You blame yourself. You let it go on, and they just keep doing it!" Cindy ignored this as well. Sandra told me she felt the class to be a waste of time because she was not in a relationship, and her goal was to get a good job, not a man. A few weeks later, another situation occurred with a client who was involved in a physically abusive relationship while she attended the PREP class.

Nella, a white twenty-seven-year-old mother of two boys, had followed the father of her older fifteen-month-old baby to Oklahoma from Florida, and she had been residing with him outside Oklahoma City for four months. Her youngest son, three months old, had a different father. She had reunited with her first baby's father while pregnant with her second son. That week's volunteer, Janice, was a clinical social worker for the Health Department and also a white, single mother. She had been married for eleven years to an abusive man. After extricating herself from the marriage, she decided to volunteer at a domestic violence shelter. Fortunately for Nella, Janice's experience made her more sensitive to the issue, and her teaching style opened a space for the five women to bring in their personal experiences. During the discussion, Nella's history began to unfold. She told the group about her boyfriend, characterizing him as an unmotivated "piece of shit." Kaneasha, a thirty-year-old African American mother of three, challenged Nella as to why she stayed with him if he treated her badly. Kaneasha had been with an abusive man before marrying someone else. She told Nella that if she is not happy, it is not a healthy relationship. Nella began to cry as she asked, "How do you leave?" She told the group that her boyfriend had been abusive for the first time two weeks earlier and had beat her up pretty badly. She'd been holding the baby while he hit her. The police arrested him and put him in jail, then released him on probation with the stipulation of attending alcohol recovery. Nella asked, "How can I get him to understand this is my house?" Janice told her that he knows your weaknesses. She explained about getting a Victims Protective Order.

By this time, the class had turned into a rap session. Janice discussed danger signs in a relationship, and Nella asked a question about how to do the time-out. Janice replied, "How do you get him to talk about it? The most important thing is he needs to get some counseling. He could take this class. If he is not willing to do that, you need to ask yourself is this the kind of relationship I want to be in? In the meantime, it would be good for you to get individual counseling." Bringing her abuser to a PREP class didn't seem like the best advice, but, as Janice told me later, she felt somewhat constrained in what she could say as the teacher of the class. Nella told the class that she didn't want to hurt her boyfriend's feelings, and Kaneasha opined, "Who is most important? You've got to make up your mind that you are number one! He doesn't care about your feelings or he would never have hit you. He is trying to steal your thunder!" At this moment, Janice interjected to say, "To be fair, it is very complex. I've seen men struggle. If he didn't learn how to be a man, not to hit a woman, and how to have respect, the guy needs help. If a man hits a woman, he probably should be by himself." As the day wore on, Nella continued to seek advice on what to do. At the end of the day, Janice told Nella, "I just want to say that I don't want you to feel so empowered by all this that you go home and get hurt! You need to get your plan in place." After the clients left, she told me her greatest fear was that Nella would be battered and she would feel responsible. She said how difficult it was to teach under these circumstances, and that if she were counseling Nella, she would have handled the situation very differently, asking Nella questions to get her to come to her own conclusions. In this environment, she felt limited by the structure of the class and was especially uncomfortable with the way Kaneasha kept telling Nella what to do.

Nella's presence in the class put Janice in a difficult predicament of juggling her role as a PREP instructor and providing guidance as a counselor and an advocate against domestic violence. She seemed unsure about how much guidance she should give in this type of classroom environment. The other students sat through the class as it revolved more and more around Nella's situation. Interestingly, Janice didn't see it as appropriate to discuss the situation with Nella's social worker to try to ensure that Nella would get the counseling she needed. Janice expressed worrying that sharing this information might be read as a betrayal, especially since Nella was living with her boyfriend, which might have jeopardized her eligibility for TANF. Clearly, OKDHS did not have an adequate system for screening out women who were in or had been in abusive relationships. In almost every class I attended, there was a least one woman who told me about former experiences of abuse, and there were probably many more who did not speak up. For the ones who did, the experience was often far enough in the past that they might benefit from a class that taught about better communication and healthy relationships. Still, many expressed frustration that they were being taught relationship skills when their focus was on getting more education and job-training skills to move forward in their lives.

Communicate, Not Marry

Over and over, I heard from OKDHS staff who volunteered that one of the more difficult challenges to teaching poor single mothers was using a curriculum geared for middle-class married couples. Karen, a Department of Health employee who had conducted numerous workshops, felt PREP to be a great curriculum to support couples who are married, engaged, dating, or thinking about marriage. She noted, "When the whole thing started, it was about recognizing that most people in Oklahoma value marriage; even though they might not have been successful, they wanted to get married and they wanted to have healthy marriages. And PREP was a great curriculum to support that." Focusing the workshops on TANF recipients was a new experiment:

> I would say clinicians in my agency have struggled with taking a program that was designed for one thing and the research was based on using it for one population, and now being told that this was a program that would be used with a very different population than what it was intended for. That's been a real struggle—an ethical struggle, a clinical struggle, a logistical struggle. If we had been told that we were going to be working with TANF recipients, I would say, personally, I don't know if I would have chosen PREP.

The clinicians who had worked with this population on parenting issues were concerned that there were aspects of the curriculum that didn't fit and things that weren't addressed that needed to be. The problem was no current program on marriage was geared toward this population.

Many of the clinicians worked hard to modify the curriculum to provide a fit for TANF recipients. Karen said the most important modification was deemphasizing marriage: "Either they are not in a relationship or they've had a really bad experience in a relationship, and they are trying to focus on themselves right now and their children. Maybe they don't have access to healthy people to become married to even if they wanted to be." She said it was important not to insert her own values or beliefs about marriage: "I don't think I should bring in what I think about whether it is right or wrong to be married. I try to keep that separate." Susan, a clinician who often cotaught with Karen, introduced the topic of same-sex relationships as another reason to refrain from inserting beliefs and values about marriage:

In this workforce group that I was with yesterday, one of the women is in a lesbian relationship and they both have children and are living together. It was real obvious she was gay when I saw her. When I was done talking, the director pulled me aside and asked what did I think of that. Did I think it was okay for them to have children involved? It was real interesting that her personal beliefs and values were right there so open in an agency where they shouldn't be. . . . I just kind of laid it on the line for her that I am perfectly comfortable with her being in the class. She's a parent and has children to raise, and [I can teach] this is what you do that is appropriate and not appropriate regardless of the gender of each person.

The issue of boundaries again arose in this situation where one of the mothers was stereotyped as gay—Susan didn't express whether there was evidence to confirm what she believed to be "obvious." The director suggested that, since it might not be "okay" to have children involved, the lesbian mother might be excluded from the relationship workshop. Unlike the marriage workshops for the general population, this social worker was cognizant of the need to modify the curriculum to make it appropriate "regardless of gender."

As social workers, these staff members were committed to providing services that would be beneficial, which meant a particular sensitivity to the clients they taught. In what might be a direct response to the complaints of the participants in my first focus group, Susan told me,

I think it is important to adopt language that could apply to any relationship, because we don't know all of their situations. . . . Everybody is in some type of relationship. Even if you want everyone to be married, if you take that approach, you would lose a lot of your audience. You would prevent them from gaining really good skills with their kids, coworkers, friends, family. If they reject you completely, you know it was because you weren't relating to where they were at.

These two women adopted a style of teaching PREP that was quite successful because it didn't focus on marriage. Another volunteer, a white retired case manager in her late seventies, also modified and related the curriculum to the clients' everyday lives.

During the week I attended Sylvia's workshop, the tone was markedly different from the previous classes that focused on marriage. She told the clients that she was using a curriculum that had been prepared for couples who were either married or in long-term relationships, and she explained that she would expand the parts that used marriage or couples to include all relationships. I asked her about this, and she replied, "OMI is for the married couples or the couples about to be married—committed couples to the relationship. I'm taking their material and I'm expanding it to everybody— your children, your parents, your brothers and sisters, your friends, your boss, your coworkers, because that's what they need. Surprisingly enough, the feedback has been very positive."

Expanding the curriculum to address the needs of the clients, Sylvia was not judgmental in the way other volunteers had been, and she expressed her admiration for the clients' hard work to change their circumstances. Taking a very different approach to teaching about commitment and marriage, she told the participants that a breakup in a long-term relationship—whether married or not—is traumatic for children. The important thing is not automatically to marry but to be committed, she advised. Clearly, this advice promoted a goal contrary to that of marriage advocates who want to reinstitute the importance of marriage in these women's lives.

During my second focus group at the end of Sylvia's workshop, the women expressed strong approval for the relationship workshop. Sarah, thirty-one and a white mother of three, said, "We deal with our kids on a daily basis. We don't deal with a man most of the time. Sylvia helps us see how we can apply this to our children." The other four nodded. Erica, a twenty-two-year-old African American mother of one, discussed how the parenting class, also part of the week orientation, complemented what they learned from the PREP workshop:

Yesterday, she was telling us how to speak to our children and what to say. One of my downfalls was my daughter would try to tell me what she was doing for the day, and I would tell her to tell me later on. Yesterday, from hearing her say you need to give your child more attention or they feel like you are ignoring them, I made myself pull away from the TV and listen. I learned that.

Sarah told the group that the week of orientation had really helped her think about how to be a better parent. She shared a story about returning a U-Haul the morning before and using the speaker-listener technique on her kids when they acted up. While she was inside the rental store, her three sons got into the car and the oldest called dibs to play games on the cell phone. The next youngest tried to snatch it from him, and the older one popped him in the mouth. All three came into the store trying to tell the story at once. Sarah recounted how she listened to each one separately and repeated back what each said.

Crystal, a white mother of three, had attended one day of the PREP workshop a few weeks earlier with two workshop leaders and discussed the difference:

> The difference was that they tried to make you sit with someone you absolutely do not know and practice the technique that was totally . . . it was just demeaning and awkward. I felt like it was totally ridiculous, whereas Sylvia here is seventy-eight years old and has a lot more experience! I'd rather hear from her than somebody who is here because they have to be. She's not getting paid, you know what I mean? Someone will listen to her a little more.

She observed that they are required to be in the class to get assistance: "With the other presenters, I was being forced to be there, basically. They were locked into the material, and they were delivering the material, which was not applicable to me at that time as far as the way they were presenting it." She described blocking out the information. Her boyfriend was out of state working for the government: "You know, I don't have a man to deal with that kind of stuff, and automatically I'm, like, stop! I don't have a man at home. I don't need to hear this right now. I have kids, so teach me something about my kids. I mentally put the barrier up there." Her words echoed those of the women in my first focus group who also felt frustrated about sitting through a class unconnected to their reality. But when the information was presented not to focus on having a man at home, the women were more receptive.

Karen and Susan taught successful PREP workshops through an educational GED program. The class met twice a week for two hours over a three-week period. This arrangement had the advantage of more time to teach and practice the skills, as well as the opportunity to build relationships with the students over a longer period of time. Similar to Sylvia's method of instruction, Karen's and Susan's focus made it clear that the workshop was about relationships and not marriage. Susan, for example, introduced the idea of filters as roadblocks to communication. One is inattention. She described how if you are tired and have had a long day, you probably won't be fully able to give your attention as the kids attack you at the door. She offered suggestions for handling this, such as "mommy needs ten minutes before she can fully pay attention to what you need to tell me." Karen and Susan elicited and integrated examples from the clients' lives. When Susan brought up how alcohol and drugs can be disastrous to relationships, Kathy, a thirty-five-year-old African American mother of three, told the class about her friend who was involved with a man who uses. Susan asked, "Who can you change?" and several of the women responded, "Yourself!" Later, Karen discussed the difference between events and issues and how they can affect relationships. She asked about events that can cause stress in a relationship, and the students all piped up with examples: an extra bill, a cutoff notice, running out of diapers, and so on.

In modifying the curriculum, Karen put together a number of handouts in addition to the PREP booklet each student received. They included topics such as "communication patterns," "repairing trust," and "five ways to really know someone." One of the main additions was a session about how to create a "healthy long-term relationship." The material for this was taken from a marriage program popularly known as "How to Avoid Marrying a Jerk," developed by John Van Epp and delivered every year at the Smart Marriages conference.[29] Again, Karen made sure that the focus was on relationships rather than on marriage. She pointed out that people often spend more time choosing a cell phone than a partner and pointed to the handout on getting to *really* know someone: through their family dynamics and background; through their attitudes and actions of maturity, according to compatibility potential; from previous friendships or relationship patterns; and from their relationship skills. Karen said that it is possible to get in trouble with relationships when you compromise too early, don't get enough information, ignore your inner voice, and let lust get in the way. To this last point, one of the women exclaimed, "That's it 99 percent of the time!"

In the third focus group I conducted, most agreed that they had felt suspicious of the class at first. I asked whether attending was voluntary. Rebecca, a thirty-year-old white mother of two, said that they had a choice to take the class or just to study their work, but Tanisha, a twenty-four-year-old African American mother of one, said she thought they had to attend. Makiah, who was twenty-nine, African American, and had two children, tried to clarify the discrepancy: "It's like most things here. You have a choice to be paid or you have a choice, you know [to not be paid]. I think that's kind of how they deal with it." A couple of women expressed their negative feelings about being in a marriage class. Kathy told the group, "I thought it was just for couples—for married people, you know. I was like, blah! Then once the course started, I was like . . . you can take it instead of being your partner towards your kids or your grandparents or anybody." I asked how they would have felt if the class had focused on marriage. Tanisha said, "Probably wouldn't want to attend. It would have been nonproductive. I would have been just sitting there and just say, okay, it don't pertain to me. I don't care." Rebecca disagreed, "I would have still attended because I've been married before, and so I still would like to know what was needed. Maybe he will thank me in my next marriage."

Overall, the clients felt that the information they received was useful. Makiah told the group that she had been going over her papers to see what she'd learned:

> I feel that because of the class, now I can scan and look for a better mate. It's not worth taking someone less than I'm worth. I need it too. I don't have to be in a relationship just to prove to nobody that I need to help somebody. I need to be in a relationship because I really care, and it's where I put my 100 percent.

Several of the women agreed. Kelly, a white twenty-eight-year-old mother of two, said, "We had that one paper of what you expected out of a relationship. I took that home and he and I talked about it and went over it. It was kind of interesting to hear what he thought and for him to listen to what I thought." The women also recognized the usefulness of the information for nonromantic relationships. In response to my question of whether they had practiced any of the skills, Tanisha told the group,

> I tried it with my daughter. I did stuff that I usually don't do. The other day I went outside and I didn't have the money . . . or the gas to go to the park. I just took a bucket out of the house, got a little ball, and went out in the backyard and tried to see if we could get the ball in the bucket. She said, "Mommy, that was fun!" That's something you can do to have fellowship with each other.

Kathy agreed: "This can help you with a lot of things. Not just with relationships with your partner, your friend, your teacher, but with the outside world period." They all felt that the class had opened their eyes to a new way of looking at relationships. Kathy exclaimed, "I mean even if you don't think it means nothing now, but it will later on down the road."

The tone changed a bit when I asked them their opinion of why they were required to take the class. Kathy said, "Most of us are single mothers." Tanisha interrupted, "I'm kind of getting irritated a bit about how society always . . . I mean, I think men need training. I think they need to be disciplined. People should go out and teach them how to treat women, how to live and be responsible!" Tanisha's statement shows that, although she felt the class to be useful, she understood that requiring single mothers to take a relationship class has a gendered and disciplinary element to it, blaming poor women more than men for having children outside marriage. Kathy stated that the government should require the class in men's prisons, and I replied that the class was taught in many prisons but that it was voluntary. Tanisha responded that it should be mandatory: "It doesn't have to be prison, but I'm just saying that would be a good place for them to be taught free in prison. I mean the ones that are incarcerated, and then the ones that are out, it should be offered to them, say they are receiving food stamps like we do." Rebecca agreed, "I think a lot of stress or problems would be avoided if we had programs for men on how to improve their relationships."

The conversation turned to a discussion of men's deficiencies, and the women became more animated. Patricia, a twenty-seven-year-old Latina mother of two, offered her assessment: "Society has trained [men] not to show their feelings. You can't cry; you can't feel pain." Makiah agreed: "I just feel that men need to learn how to express themselves more better instead of using . . . you, know, trying to . . . [exasperated], I just can't explain it!" According to Kathy, "There are a few good men out there, but most men are—you know what I'm saying—they're just dogs! Most men. That's why I'm single now." Tanisha, however, pointed out, "But the reason that they are is because they have no training. They are not educated." The women expressed resentment that they were singled out as the ones in need of marriage classes and made it clear that, even though they had learned skills for considering what's important in a mate, it was not going to be easy to find a man who could hold up his end of the bargain—being able to communicate and listen.

Prison PREP

Indeed, I had discovered that incarcerated men are being taught PREP communication skills. The summer of 2002 witnessed the implementation of the workshops that became known as Prison PREP. After its initial pilot, the Oklahoma Department of Corrections (DOC) adopted PREP as an official program, "meaning that state-wide implementation would be supported from the top down."[30] By the end of 2007, all chaplains had been trained, and more than two thousand inmates had participated in Prison PREP offered to couples and individuals three times a year (including female inmates who make up 10 percent of the prison population in Oklahoma).[31] All inmates are deemed eligible despite marital status (except for sex offenders, inmates in mental units, and those who had no possibility of parole). However, a 2009 research brief of the U.S. Department of Human and Health Services claims that the DOC made a decision to focus on services to married inmates, because "married inmates experience a very high rate of divorce during incarceration."[32] The brief notes that, different from the marriage promotion policy for poor single mothers, it is *not* DOC policy to promote marriage among inmates because of the high dissolution rate. Prison PREP is voluntary, except in the case of inmates who wish to be married while serving their sentence. The chaplain explained that most of the men who are married get married while in prison.

Due to restrictions on gaining access, I was only able to interview one chaplain and a married couple who had participated in his workshop. I met the wife of a prisoner at a workshop for TANF clients who told me that together the two of them had taken Prison PREP. I interviewed her first and then contacted the chaplain who had taught the class. Through the chaplain, I gained clearance to interview him and the inmate at a medium-security prison outside Oklahoma City. Sandy, a white woman in her fifties, met Daryl, an African American man also in his early fifties, through a prison pen-pal program in 1995. Sandy described how they had written very simple letters to one another until Daryl suggested they speak on the phone. She described the change: "As soon as he heard my voice, he just—his whole letters changed, his whole demeanor changed." Sandy had been married twice before. Her first marriage ended after the birth of her first child and her husband committed suicide. She married again and had two more children. Fifteen years into the marriage, she was diagnosed with cancer, and her husband left her. Daryl had never been married. After five years of correspondence and Sunday visits, Daryl said that his feelings pushed him to ask "for her hand in marriage." At first, Sandy told him that she would rather wait until after he was released. He had been charged as an accomplice to murder and was seeking parole. He had been in prison since he was eighteen years old. Eventually, she changed her mind, and they were married in 2002. She said,

> One day I just woke up and it just hit me, "Yeah, it's time to get married." So, I went and got my bishop and we went out there and he married us out there. And it was kind of surprising to him because he really didn't think I would. And our relationship did a 180 after we were married. He became incredibly open to me, told me a lot of things that had happened to him while he was in there that he never shared before. We've grown extremely close.

Even as they have grown closer, they have not consummated their marriage. Oklahoma, like most states, does not allow conjugal visits. Sandy called herself a "born-again virgin," and reminded me, "This is the Bible Belt, you know." We both had a good laugh.

Daryl had been very enthusiastic about taking Prison PREP with Sandy— it was his first serious relationship and one that he wanted to last. The two were among the first few couples to take the workshop in 2002 that was held after visiting hours for six consecutive Sundays. Daryl felt that he and Sandy gained some valuable skills: "What we came away with was the skill in how to talk about something uncomfortable, controversial or her view versus my view without anything escalating." Sandy discussed how the chaplain made the curriculum apply to their particular situation. Similar to the TANF work- shops that modify PREP to fit the needs of single mothers, the chaplain makes efforts to adjust the curriculum to fit the special needs of the incarcerated. He described needing to expand on parts of the curriculum dealing with safety: "Most people involved in prison don't know what a safe relationship is, have no clue, never seen it modeled." He remembered one case in particular:

> One of the couples that was here taking it—she had come from an abusive relationship in regard to previous marriages. She had been molested and raped by her uncle and other family members. Now, he knew that, but he didn't know all the details of it. Well, once the structure got safe, she felt safe in telling him, and made her feel safe to say—because this guy was in here for murder—"And when you get out," and he will get out, "How will I know you're not going to handle your anger like that now?" And, before, he probably would have said, "Well okay, if that's the way you think about me, fine," and just walk off. But now he can stop and say, "I see your fear. I see your concern."

Corresponding to the TANF workshops that are more like a rap session for solving problems in the women's everyday lives, the chaplain seeks to pro- vide a space for the couples to discuss their particular circumstances that could create tension and misunderstanding.

One aspect of prison life that offered a particular challenge to teaching PREP is sex. The chaplain explained that same-sex sexuality is integral to the culture of prison life but doesn't necessarily define the men's sexuality: "There are certain men in prison that provide those services for the nonhomosexual men. If a guy in prison is a heterosexual, he may have him a boyfriend in here. That does not make him a homosexual in this environment. Okay?"

I asked about the men who have relationships outside prison whether the women knew of their sexual relationships in prison. The chaplain replied: "Oh, most of the time no, because I've sat in visiting rooms—would she be hugging and kissing on him if she knew who he's got celled up with him and why he's celled up with him? Probably not. But the excuse is, 'Well I have to take care of this someway and this is the way we do it and this is acceptable.'" He described how the men viewed their relationships with men inside prison not as some secret they were keeping but as part of survival in prison. While PREP teaches about open and honest communication, same-sex sexuality is not an aspect of prison life to be discussed openly. There is a hidden side that, in the words of the PREP curriculum, must stay "in the dark."

I asked the chaplain about how he dealt with the lesson on sexuality in the PREP curriculum, and he provided another glimpse into prison life. He described how, when wives or girlfriends come to visit, often they would find a way to have sex: "There are some visiting yards you can go on and if you know how to look at most any given moment somebody is having sex in there. You may not recognize that, but they are. They've become very creative." In teaching PREP, the chaplain said that he would address the issue head-on:

> But when we address it in PREP, I don't try to back away from it because it's an issue that they've got to talk about. Like, I tell them here, I said, "Intimacy is extremely important in marriage. Intimacy does not always have to equate with sex. Now you guys, you think it's one and the same, but you've got to understand that it isn't. Because you know yourself if you get caught having sex, you're going to lose your visits, you're going to get written up and she can't come in for a year. It's not worth it. And then have you honored that female? I don't think so, not by having sex with her in a room with a bunch of other people." And I think all men have a problem processing that, I really do.

As apparent from the chaplain's remarks, teaching Prison PREP requires boundary work. On the one hand, same-sex relationships remain hidden and in the background, much like the situation for the two lesbians in the marriage workshops whose sexuality remained an invisible backdrop. Heterosexual sex, however, can be directly discussed to inform the men that it doesn't "honor the female" to have sex in a room with a bunch of other people. This kind of boundary work makes the discussions of sexuality appear transparent, even as a deeper undercurrent concerning sexuality is left unaddressed.

Prison PREP is also taught to individual men who are not in relationships with women outside prison. The 2009 OKDHS research brief points to findings that are similar to those I discovered in the PREP Relationship classes for TANF clients. According to the report:

> The curriculum is designed for use with couples, and some [inmates] felt that the concepts were confusing since they were not currently in relationships, and may never have been married. . . . The single men thus felt that adapting the curriculum to make it more relevant to other types of relationships would be useful. . . . They also suggested that using terms like "communication skills" may be a better way to advertise the class rather than "marriage skills."[33]

Prison PREP is also taught at the sole female correctional facility in Oklahoma. The 2009 report offers an interesting glimpse into how the marriage initiative has rethought promoting marriage among female inmates *and* poor single mothers: "Eventually, they found its focus on sustaining marriage off-target for their inmates, who needed instead to address unhealthy or abusive relationships. Leaders of the OMI received the same message from local welfare offices that began offering PREP to Temporary Assistance for Needy Families (TANF) recipients, the vast majority of whom were single."[34]

The marriage initiative worked with the creators of PREP to produce a modified version of the curriculum called "Within My Reach," which teaches "individuals how to identify, stabilize, and sustain good relationships; identify and safely exit from dangerous relationships; and make good relationship choices in the future."[35] An overview of the curriculum states that the goal is to help individuals attain relationship success for themselves and their children, helping those in a viable relationship "stabilize" their unions, those in a "damaging" relationship leave, and those desiring a romantic relationship choose one wisely.[36] Marriage is mentioned as an advantageous outcome only if the participants desire it. Moreover, Within My Reach offers skills that may benefit participants on the job, in their communities, and with their children. This curriculum is now being used to teach PREP to TANF clients as well as to inmates.[37]

Overall, the more uncompromising approach to marriage promotion that seeks to redraw a strict boundary of marriage and stigmatize those who have children out of wedlock is not effective when working with TANF clients and female inmates. Social workers teaching the classes recognize that marriage is often not a viable or a desirable option for TANF participants, and their modifications to the curriculum ultimately resulted in a new curriculum that deemphasizes marriage and, instead, focuses on the actual relationships that are important for these women to strengthen, including relationships with their children and with their employers. The curriculum even guided women on how to exit bad or dangerous partnerships. Modified workshops also deemphasize the gendered boundary work that was so common in the workshops for the general population.

This chapter has examined the boundary work involved in PREP workshops offered to TANF recipients and to the prison population that either stresses or downplays the importance of marriage, a strategy that either makes or breaks their success. The fact that it is the *marriage* initiative that oversees these workshops has the potential to reinstate a moral message about marriage that some instructors seek to disseminate. Classes that are most successful, however, focus on communication skills, and TANF clients in my focus groups related the benefits from the classes when they taught about these skills with others rather than just a romantic partner. All the social workers I interviewed felt it important to address the diverse needs of the clients, even in the case of a lesbian mother who was taking the workshop. That said, homosexuality continued to remain a hidden backdrop to the assumption that relationships are always heterosexual, a boundary that became even more important to maintain in the case of Prison PREP. The workshops thus organized an understanding of marriage based on the boundary of heterosexuality, even as they challenged the ideal of marriage promotion. In the next chapter, I examine the consequences of boundary work in PREP classes for secondary education.

Marriage Recitals in High School

Teenagers today grow up in a world that bears little resem-
blance to the world their parents grew up in. Almost from the
cradle, today's young people are bombarded with sexual come-
ons and appeals. . . . Even though some media outlets portray
the issues of sex, love, relationships, and marriage responsibly,
it's also the case that a pornographic aesthetic pervades much of
the music, fashion, video games and cable television shows that
teens now enjoy.
—Barbara Dafoe Whitehead and Marline Pearson,
Making a Love Connection[1]

Perhaps it is a sign of the decay of courtship customs (if we
mean by courtship not simply dating, but the conscious, for-
mal process of mate selection) that only one curriculum [out of
ten] broaches the subject of teen dating as a rehearsal for mate
selection and marriage, or urges premarital sexual abstinence
of teens.
—Dana Mack, "Educating for Marriage, Sort Of"[2]

In May 2009, Diane Sollee posted on the Smart Marriages listserv coverage of a recent documentary, "Oral Sex Is the New Goodnight Kiss," and she
lamented, "Why we need to focus on youth: Read it and shudder."[3] Interestingly, the documentary examines not American but Canadian middle-class,
white girls who describe oral sex as a common activity among their peers.
A few depict partaking in sex for trade such as selling their virginity or performing oral sex for a designer handbag. The story was picked up by *Good
Morning America*, which included a discussion with a group of American
girls who verified the common practice of oral sex among youth. While the
filmmaker interviewed a relatively small number of girls whom school officials found were involved in sexual activity with groups of boys (including
a prostitution ring), the media coverage suggested that oral sex and "casual

prostitution" are becoming the new (American) norm.[4] Such depictions are deceptive. A 2007 Guttmacher Institute study found that slightly over half of 15- to 19-year-olds have engaged in heterosexual oral sex, half in vaginal sex, and 11 percent in anal sex, and that the prevalence of both vaginal and oral sex among adolescents has remained steady over the past decade.[5] Teen birth, abortion, and pregnancy rates have all dropped in the past ten years as teens are now *more* likely to abstain from sex or to use contraception during their first sexual experience.[6] Generalizing isolated cases to the overall population of teenagers fuels moral panic surrounding the issue of sexuality and youth that, since the 1980s, has focused on promiscuity, teenage pregnancy, and a declining moral code.

Panic over youth and sexuality is nothing new, but it attests to the difficulty for Americans of coming to terms with deep-seated transformations that occurred in sexual behavior since the 1970s. The sociologist Kristen Luker explains that the real "epidemic" in teenage pregnancy occurred back in the "golden days" of family life when rates peaked in 1957. Since then, rates have drifted back to earlier levels and have remained somewhat constant or have declined since 1975.[7] Societal norms, however, have transformed unalterably since the 1950s when women married younger and, in cases of pregnancy outside marriage, usually submitted to shotgun weddings. Luker describes how the national obsession with teenage pregnancy helped Americans to explain "a number of dismaying social phenomena, such as spreading signs of poverty, persistent racial inequalities, freer sexual mores, and new family structures."[8] It concentrated fears that a rising illegitimacy rate among white unmarried teenagers would bring to fruition a "white underclass," as Charles Murray termed it, alongside historically disadvantaged African Americans.[9] Many came to believe that fixing the problem of teenage pregnancy—which conservatives formulated as a crisis of sexual abstinence and marriage—would fix many other problems in American society.

The question of marriage is central to the battles over sex education and abstinence. Access to contraception and abortion has allowed women to pursue their dreams before marriage, pushing the median age of marriage up from 20.1 and 22.5 for women and men, respectively, in 1956, to 25.3 and 27.1 in 2003.[10] In her recent book *When Sex Goes to School*, Luker uncovers how people view marriage differently whether they favor comprehensive sex or abstinence education. Those who support comprehensive sex education prefer their children marry later (late twenties) and do not see it as feasible that young adults will abstain from sex until marriage. Favoring abstinence-only education usually comes with a philosophy that marriage is the only option and any kind of sexuality outside marriage results in youth who are "'damaged goods,' hardened and jaded and closed off from the miracle of true emotional and physical intimacy that a happy marriage can bring."[11] As Luker points out, one of the fundamental frustrations for conservatives who fight against sex education in schools is the devaluing of the esteemed institution of marriage in the classroom, meaning that teachings on sexuality do not provide a moral code to tell students that sex outside marriage is wrong.[12]

The marriage movement has focused on bringing marriage education into the classroom not necessarily to teach sexual abstinence (although this may also be a goal for some), but to provide students with the "necessary knowledge, skills, and strategies" to give them a roadmap to "build healthy relationships during their teen years and later, for those who choose it, a healthy marriage."[13] By focusing on marriage education and "healthy relationships" for teens, the marriage movement appears to sidestep the shrill debates over the benefits of abstinence-only versus comprehensive sex education. However, there is a tension inherent to bringing marriage education into middle and high schools: the ideal of promoting heterosexual sex solely within the bounds of marriage presents a problem for marriage advocates to deal with changing attitudes and practices of family and marriage, such as how to deal with the increasing length between adolescence and entry of marriage, rising rates of cohabitation, and the growing visibility of lesbian and gay families. Is it reasonable to ask young people to wait until marriage to have sex? Where does teaching about contraception fit in? How do you challenge the changing attitudes of young people who look more favorably on cohabitation than older generations did? Most important, how do you teach about the purpose and meaning of sexuality within marriage (the goal of marriage promotion) in the presence of "out" lesbian and gay youth when marriage is banned for same-sex couples? Similar to tensions present in the broader politics of marriage, I examine here the boundary work and contradictions of promoting marriage in high school.

Sex, Lies, and Debate

Despite the at times overblown representations of the "sexual revolution" of the sixties, the term does acknowledge a significant transformation in Euro-American sexual cultures. As the sociologist Janice Irvine argues, "The increasing commercialization of sex, greater media explicitness, and diverse shifts in attitudes and behavior all marked the transition from the midcentury's sexual liberalism to a more sexualized society."[14] Irvine, in her book *Talk about Sex*, maps how conflicts over sex education facilitated a shift to the right in American politics that has meant the decline of comprehensive sex education, an increase in attention to abstinence-only programs, and a boundary for acceptable discourses concerning sex in the classroom. For the pro-family movement, America is veering from a righteous past to one of moral turpitude where youth are taught sexually explicit material. For example, a fundraising letter written by Jerry Falwell of the Moral Majority declares on its front page: "Is Our Grand Old Flag Going down the Drain?" The response is "YES! . . . Just look at what's happening here in America" and he goes on to outline fears of gay teachers and pornography in schools.[15] Irvine notes that while not all sex education opponents are fundamentalists or evangelicals, this kind of rhetoric has become pervasive and eventually has culminated in new energy toward abstinence-only sex education.

During the 1990s, the prevalence of abstinence-only instruction increased significantly. A study by the Alan Guttmacher Institute found that in 1988 only 2 percent of teachers taught abstinence as the sole way to prevent pregnancy and sexually transmitted diseases; by 1999, this figure had grown to 23 percent.[16] Increased federal funding for abstinence-only sex education was attached to the Welfare Reform Act of 1996, which, along with its focus on marriage promotion, offered states matching money for school programs that teach youth to wait until marriage to initiate sexual activity and that did not offer instruction on contraception.

There is some evidence that the embrace of abstinence has a short-term effect on delaying the first sexual experience among youth. A study involving 12,000 teenagers found that those taking virginity pledges had sex eighteen months later on average than those who had not taken the pledge. It also found that 88 percent of pledgers *still* had sex before marriage and were *less* likely to use contraception when they did have sex—only 40 percent used condoms, compared with 59 percent of the nonpledgers.[17] A troubling report prepared for Rep. Henry A. Waxman (D-CA) in 2004 found that over 80 percent of the curricula funded to teach abstinence-only education offered "false, misleading, or distorted information" about the effectiveness of contraceptives and the risks of abortion.[18] Over $1 billion in federal aid has been spent on state-run abstinence-only programs since 1998; California, Maine, and Pennsylvania are the only states to refuse federal funding tied to abstinence.[19] While the Obama administration eliminated funding for it in the 2010 budget, the "abstinence-only sex education industry" is well established in its grassroots organizational structure.[20]

Marriage promotion curricula for middle and high school students seek to avert the political quagmire of abstinence-only versus comprehensive sex education by seeking a "middle ground."[21] Marline Pearson, the creator of one popular curriculum *Love U2: Getting Smarter About Relationships, Sex, Babies and Marriage*, asserts that American society has "separated sex from relationship development and made it a health issue."[22] She terms her approach "heart-based," and her curriculum focuses on the social and emotional issues of sexuality: how to deal with infatuation, how to gauge whether a relationship is healthy, and what it means to be sexually active. Pearson's depiction of the middle ground, however, doesn't address the fact that most abstinence-only and sex education programs already deal with relationship education, in the former case within the context of abstinence and the dangers of teenage sexual behavior and in the latter within the context of intimacy, identity, and reproductive health.[23]

The nuance in the curriculum, according to the publisher's website, is that it is "unapologetically pro-abstinence for teens, but not for reasons that have to do with religion, ideology, or politics. It strongly encourages teens to wait on sex because it is concerned about the emotional and social well-being of teens."[24] The focus on social science research and health provides a justification for teaching abstinence; yet the reasoning that Pearson applies is also ideological. To prepare youth for successful marriages, the curriculum teaches "what earlier generations took for granted: a normative sequence for the timing of sex, marriage and parenthood. Today's teens struggle in a culture that no longer tells them how these three events should be sequenced, or what the optimal sequence might be."[25] The idea of a "normative sequence for timing" refers to a past in which sexual activity outside marriage was resolutely stigmatized. Suggesting that sex outside marriage is dangerous and perhaps shameful, the curriculum moves beyond simply empowering teens to say no to sex, pushing them to "change course" to avoid "getting pregnant or an ugly STD."[26] The curriculum treats relationships as unquestioningly heterosexual.

Marriage advocates want to teach youth that marriage is a distinctive institution, and they are upset when textbooks or educators portray it as a "type" of family life in American society. In a 2000 report, Dana Mack, who was the director of the Childhood and Adolescent Project at the Institute for American Values (IAV), criticizes most of the ten curricula she reviewed for focusing on building "relationship skills" that treat marriage just as "a form of relationship." She laments that many of the programs are unwilling to even use the word "marriage," and those that do use it offer "dismal warnings to teenagers on the 'risks' of marriage."[27] According to Mack, marriage needs to be taught as "a spiritual, moral, and civic vocation, a universal institution deeply rooted in culture and human instinct, not just one among many relationships."[28] A subsequent IAV newsletter explains that in defense of the publishers who "would welcome a focus on marriage," it was local school officials who do not accept course materials that seemed to endorse the institution. The newsletter asks, "Is this dispute over vocabulary really important? It is all-important. Nothing matters more. If we lose the word 'marriage,' we lose marriage."[29]

The sociologist Norval Glenn outlines in more depth the ideology behind such criticisms. In his report to the nation on college textbooks, he decries the portrayal of marriage as one of several equally acceptable relationships: "An anthropologist from Mars who knew nothing about American families but what was contained in [college family] textbooks would come away with several basic beliefs. First, in America, marriage is just one of many equally acceptable and equally productive adult relationships. These various relationships include cohabiting couples, divorced non-couples, stepfamilies, and gay and lesbian families."[30]

The "anthropologist from Mars" reference suggests an objective stance not present in the textbooks in question. Glenn criticizes them for failing to explicate the "social functions" of marriage, "the role of marriage historically and currently in the biological and cultural reproduction of populations and societies."[31] His statement assumes that there is a universal role that marriage has played throughout history in regard to reproducing populations (through sex). However, historians and sociologists have shown that the history of marriage is quite complex, drawing on shifting and multiple roles historically. For example, the historian Nancy Cott offers a thorough analysis of shifts in the public role of marriage in American history.[32] Glenn further reproaches the texts for their focus on social justice issues, such as reducing prejudice, defending the welfare system, and promoting gay rights, which "may be worthy objectives" in themselves, but "when they become a major focus of textbooks ostensibly devoted to disseminating social science's understanding of marriage and the family as institutions, they undermine these books' capacity to carry out their core educational mission."[33] While many of Glenn's criticisms of omissions and misattributions of scholarship in these textbooks appear well founded, his analysis fails to outline the debate over marriage between a conservative vision that views marriage as the spiritual and moral foundation of society in contrast to a progressive one that would more readily focus on social justice issues. *His* omission allows the request for better textbooks to appear objective in the face of the ideology he suggests is offered in the textbooks.

These debates make teaching marriage education fraught with questions of the place of morality in the public school system and *whose* values are being taught. The approach of marriage advocates is similar to the founders of the nation who, as Nancy Cott outlines, had a "political theory of marriage" so embedded in the commonsense of Christian morality that its assumptions were rarely articulated.[34] Thus, it is possible to justify marriage education by referring to social science data without referring to deeper political and moral theory. Nonetheless, public school educators and officials are keenly aware of issues relating to values, particularly in relation to debates over abstinence education and same-sex marriage.[35] There has been some support for marriage instruction; as of 2001, experts estimated that more than two thousand public schools nationwide were offering some kind of instruction on marriage and relationship skills.[36] Marriage advocates assume that all students can benefit from learning skills that will help those who marry make marriages work and avoid divorce. Diane Sollee summarizes the theory: "This isn't rocket science; it's more like driver's ed. It's about teaching kids the basic communication skills they need for a healthy marriage."[37]

Legislators in Florida raised red flags concerning the "whose values" question when the state mandated marriage education. In 1998, it became the first and only state to pass legislation requiring marriage and relationship education to be taught to all public-school children. Critics of this move questioned the concept of marriage education in schools, arguing that it is an area best left to churches and community groups, not for "high-school students working through a crowded curriculum that too often fails to cover basic academic skills."[38] Debate over marriage education in high schools has been further fueled following news coverage of a mock church wedding performed in New Jersey as part of a high school marriage and family class. It read: "For weeks these Butler High School students have planned everything, down to the favors on the reception tables. They have consulted a wedding planner, sent out invitations, baked three-tier cakes and created their vows with a minister's guidance. Guests will pack the pews as the high school seniors walk away from the altar with rings on their fingers."[39]

The mock wedding was the final event after weeks of relationship and communication training, and the idea is to get students to recognize that marriage is work. Critics, however, question the practice of holding a public school class in a religious building, potentially raising separation of church and state issues. Catherine Lugg, an education professor, speculates: "There may be gay and lesbian students, so are they going to discuss gay and lesbian partnerships? If not, it could be profoundly alienating."[40]

Oklahoma has not mandated marriage and relationship classes for schoolchildren, but it does fund statewide abstinence-only and marriage education programs. Abstinence-only programs began in 1999, funded with grants authorized under Title V of the Social Security Act.[41] In 2006, Oklahoma's birth rate among girls ages fifteen to nineteen shot up 10 percent to 59.6 births per 1,000, making it the sixth highest in the nation. From 1991 to 2005, its rate had fallen 25 percent to 54.2 births per 1,000, compared to the 1991 rate of 72.1.[42] Oklahoma's rates have consistently hovered above the national average. The picture of teenage pregnancy in Oklahoma is complex, involving culture, poverty, socioeconomics, and racial demographics, a picture true in other states with higher rates of teenage pregnancy, such as Mississippi, New Mexico, and Texas. These statistics bring to the fore questions concerning the benefits of abstinence-only and marriage education taught in public schools. What is the most effective way to help young people avoid early sexual activity, pregnancy, abortion, and sexually transmitted diseases, along with their economic and societal consequences? In light of a recent survey where 95 percent of Americans reported having had premarital sex, what is the place of abstinence and marriage education in public schools? Are these teaching "public" values?

As a state, Oklahoma has embraced a "yes" to the value of marriage education in public schools. Its marriage initiative funds a program for elective Marriage and Family Life courses, which most schools offer under the rubric of Family and Consumer Sciences (FACS). Once known as home economics, the field of Family and Consumer Sciences has changed radically since the 1960s, when home economics classes were populated completely by women who learned skills such as sewing and baking. Today, classes tend to include a diversity of students and are up to 40 percent male. Also different from classes in the early 1960s are FACS programs for teenage parents to help them earn their diplomas. The content has changed dramatically as well, such as teaching students how to use spreadsheets to analyze a nutritious diet.[43] In Oklahoma, the FACS program is supported by the state's career and technology education system, and each course has to meet state-approved standards. Teachers, however, have some say in the course's design, giving the marriage initiative flexibility to introduce a new curriculum.

The initiative chose the *Connections* curriculum, developed by Charlene Kamper, a California-based high school teacher, with its focus on skills-based education and information about relationships and marriage. Inviting the authors of *Connections* and PREP (Prevention and Relationship Enhancement Program, the curriculum used in the statewide classes) to work together to add instruction on communication and conflict-management skills, the initiative introduced *Connections+PREP*, which provides instruction for younger and older adolescents. The first workbook, "Dating and Emotions," targets grades 8–12 and instructs on "healthy dating," including how to handle jealousy and anger, determine whether a relationship is working, and how to end it. The second workbook, "Relationships and Marriage," is for grades 11–12 with an emphasis on teaching what it means to form and sustain a "healthy marriage," including participation in a mock marriage where students pair up, plan their wedding, decide on household duties, create a family album, figure out their finances, and work through a crisis together.[44] Implementation of the curriculum began in 2002 when the initiative trained twenty-four teachers in a pilot program. Next, the initiative made the curriculum available free of charge to any interested FACS teacher and offered a one- to two-hour overview. In the past few years, the initiative began sponsoring an annual training on the curriculum. By 2007, over three hundred FACS teachers in the state had received training, which was being offered in 90 percent of Oklahoma high schools with a FACS program.

While I was in Oklahoma during 2004, I attended the Marriage and Family Life course at two different high schools. The first, Red Earth High School, is located in a middle-class suburb with a predominantly white student population (75 percent compared to a state average of 58 percent).[45] The racial minority population is 5 percent black, 1 percent Asian, 3 percent Latino, and 16 percent Native American.[46] The poverty rate for the area hovers around 6 percent compared to a state average of 15 percent, and only 32 percent of students are deemed eligible for free/reduced lunch compared to 56 percent statewide. The second, Monroe High School, is located in an urban area with a much higher racial diversity: 19 percent white, 21 percent black, 1 percent Asian, 54 percent Latino, and 6 percent Native American. It is also a much poorer area with a poverty rate of 22 percent, and 93 percent of students are eligible for free/reduced lunch. The four-year dropout rate at Monroe High is 30 percent compared to 11 percent at Red Earth High. The racial makeup of the Marriage and Family Life classes I attended also reflected the differences between the two schools: out of thirty students at Red Earth, twenty-two were white, two were black, one was Latino, and five were Native American; out of thirty-one students at Monroe, seven were white, fifteen were black, eight were Latino, and one was Native American. At Red Earth, there were twenty-four girls and six boys, and, at Monroe, there were twenty girls and eleven boys. In both classes, the students were in the tenth- to twelfth-grade levels. In conjunction with the dissimilar demographic compositions, the teachers in the FACS classes I attended also had very different approaches to teaching marriage education. In the following, I offer a comparison of these two classes as a way to answer the question of "whose values" and to analyze the boundary work involved in teaching marriage education classes.

"Whose Values"?

At Red Earth High, the students taking FACS classes were not among the more elite, university-bound students who take Advanced Placement (AP) classes. In fact, none of the students in the Marriage and Family Life class I attended were in AP classes. Maria Bailey, the FACS teacher who was a white woman in her early fifties, told me during our interview:

> The classes are open to everybody, but it's a scheduling conflict for AP students. It is a scheduling conflict for some of the sports people. So the majority of my classes are people that are not in band, choir, sports, or AP classes. I have a high percentage of special needs kids. They could be academic needs; they could be emotional, development problems. Of people that are pretty much not able to be successful in other classes or if they've already had art, which is one of their elective choices they have.

Offering marriage education in this context allows the marriage initiative to target some of the more vulnerable students who come from poor and/or minority families. According to Maria, a high number of her kids "are in foster homes, kids that come to me from juvenile detention, living with aunt, uncle, grandparents, best friends because of the situation at home. I have a very disrupted bunch of students."

Due to the at-risk background of her students, Maria felt it necessary to spend extra time getting to know them. She described how she would "spend time with them, observe them, listen to their conversations, allow some freedom to talk so I kind of know their maturity level and their emotional level. Then, I can move them to the next step." Her approach to teaching marriage and relationship skills concentrates on sex education and abstinence:

> The most critical thing for my kids is how do I teach them to wait about having sex. They think . . . they are fifteen years old, and they think sex is entertainment, and everybody is doing it, and they either don't understand

the dangers or they have a really short-term analysis of the world that the most dangerous thing that could happen to me is I get caught today, and that's the part that's the most critical for me. How do you fit in and not be like everybody else?

I asked her whether she covered this issue using the *Connections* curriculum. She replied that the curriculum only indirectly addresses the issue, on teaching "personal standards and those kinds of things." She supplemented these teachings with the Red Cross STD book to inform students about some of the myths that they believe in, such as "you can't catch a sexually transmitted disease if you have only oral sex or if the guy looks pretty clean and all that kind of thing, he can't possibly have anything."

Maria's perspective on abstinence and sex education highlights the complexity of teaching students who come from at-risk backgrounds and those who see having sex as a way to "be cool" and fit in. I asked Maria about teaching abstinence, and she replied that the Red Cross book covers it by saying that the ultimate, safest method of protection is abstinence. However, she felt that this message might present a somewhat unrealistic expectation:

MARIA: The fact that there are so many of them sexually active [that it] is so hard for them to become unactive.

MELANIE: Do you think it would be very realistic?

MARIA: Once it fits their lifestyle and patterns of thoughts or whatever, it takes . . . I don't know, a major life-changing event to decide to do something different.

Her response reflects an ambivalence about "whose values" to teach and how best to help students. In our discussion of the problem of early marriage in Oklahoma—Oklahomans marry on average two and a half years younger than other Americans, increasing their risk of divorce—she explained the difficulty of making blanket statements about early marriage:

The problem is so much bigger than early marriage but I don't know how to fix it. Of the five girls that I had that married before they got out of high school, four out of five married because they left an abusive home. They went to somebody kinder to just start over. I can't tell them that that is a bad reason to get married. So, early marriage is not necessarily a problem. The problem is they might not have a home to stay in any longer.

She suggested that statistics do not capture the complexity of the lives of her at-risk students, where early marriage might be the best option available.

I also asked whether she addressed cohabitation, a topic of particular interest among marriage advocates. A number of studies have shown that those who enter into cohabitation before or instead of marriage tend to have more fragile relationships at a higher risk of dissolution. Youth are more likely to favor cohabitation before marriage than the older generation. Again, selection factors are involved, including the experiences, characteristics, attitudes, and values of both young people and their parents.[47] Concerning the issue of cohabitation, she expressed the desire to leave out her own values:

> Do I address that? Ummmm. Not directly. My main objective is for them to have healthy, safe relationships. Now whether or not it is legal or not is more of a value issue for me as a teacher. I can encourage them not to stay with abusive people. I can encourage them to avoid diseases—things that give them a healthy, safe life. But I can never say, oh, you should never live with another person. That's a value issue. I can tell them my opinion but as far as putting that out there that that should be your objective, I can't do that.

Marriage advocates would disagree with Maria Bailey. Most believe that teachers should do exactly what Maria resists—"putting it out there" that marriage *should* be the ultimate objective.

Maria's student-sensitive approach to teaching Marriage and Family Life was reflected in choices about curriculum and in her style of teaching. The FACS teachers have the flexibility to incorporate all or only part of the *Connections* curriculum in their course offerings, and Maria Bailey only incorporated selected portions that she felt would be useful to her students. She also used another state-approved textbook: *Married & Single Life*.[48] Both she and several of the students I talked to expressed how useful the *Connections* workbooks were. She felt that the curriculum helped some students become more open to thinking about marriage:

> I really appreciate the book and the curriculum that [the marriage initiative] provided for me. I think it's been very important to my kids. On the first few days that they came into the class, a very high percentage of the class put up their hands that to say no, I don't want to talk about marriage. Marriage is what got me a mean stepfather. I'm not going to do it. I don't want to hear about it. And so, they had already lived pretty much a soap

opera life at fifteen. The way I had to approach the book is that if you know everything that your parents or stepparents are doing wrong, here's your chance to take this book and decide how you would do it differently. Don't just tell me what's wrong. Start making a plan on how you are going to do it right.

Maria, however, was not necessarily promoting a nostalgic vision of the nuclear family but one that dealt more with postmodern families that were the knowledge base of her students. She did not lecture on the "spiritual, moral, and civic vocation" of marriage.[49] Instead, she focused on the students' relationships, letting them discuss the workbooks together "and talk and get acquainted and not be so frightened when they are around each other."

The workbook is divided into four sections: the first section encourages students to think about self-understanding, including a page to create a collage describing "what it's like to be me"; the second focuses on relationships and dating, including emotions and breaking up; the third teaches communication skills using the speaker-listener technique; the fourth and longest section focuses on what one initiative employee called "the marriage game"—partnering students to plan their wedding and the details of their marriage. This part Maria did not teach.

My first day attending class, I traveled to the school with Natalie, an employee of the marriage initiative. While chatting with Maria, Natalie asked about the marriage game, and Maria told her she wasn't doing it because she had too many girls in the class. Later, during our interview, she explained, "In this particular grade, there's a large number that are younger, and it's like I didn't think they would get the significance of anything, that it would just . . . it just didn't fit them." She had used the marriage game with another class that was largely seniors, but she didn't have them do a ceremony. She described her approach and reservations:

No, it was not an official big thing or whatever. It was just a class period where we did all the activities on the page [describing their ideal wedding, filling out the marriage license, and creating a family album]. It was somewhat productive. I can see where two people actually wanted to go into counseling and went through this kind of thing, it would really make more sense than in a public school, where there may or may not be any relationships in the class. Out of my other group, I only had one couple out of the group, and the rest of them were one of a kind not ready to do an activity with anybody, you know, like that.

Unlike the class in New Jersey that held a mock church wedding, Maria downplayed this aspect of the curriculum, worrying that many of the students would not make sense of or feel comfortable with participation in a mock marriage.

Maria's classroom always had a vibrant buzz as students worked together on activities. When I began attending, the semester was already well under way and Maria had covered most of the first two sections of the workbook. A few students wrote quite a bit about themselves and their relationships, but most wrote just a few words in each section. While the students worked, I chatted with them about their interests, goals, and what they had learned. During the weeks I attended, I found mixed responses to the curriculum. One day, Maria asked them to fill out a section in their workbook on the types of communication that are modeled in their families. The questions included, "How would you describe the communication 'condition' at home?" (open or closed communication); "How often do your family members get together to talk about concerns?" (daily, several times a week, only when there is a problem, never); "How would you describe the overall tone of the conversation style at home?" (talk quietly, shouting, argumentative, critical). One white senior girl told me that she really enjoyed filling out these exercises; it was like having a personal journal. At another table, several boys had put "NA" (not applicable) as answers. I asked them about this, and one white boy said that his parents only talked to him when they told him what to do or he wanted something. The others (two white and one African American) described their relationship with their parents as "nonexistent." The students at this table created quite a ruckus, making jokes and laughing throughout the class period. At another table, several sophomore and junior girls were also having a good time, all except one African American girl who later told me that she didn't like filling out the workbook because it made her feel like there is something wrong with her family. She said it was something she preferred not to discuss in this environment.

The relaxed atmosphere in Maria's class allowed the students a chance to interact with one another; it also meant that the students were often unfocused and didn't get much work done. Maria showed several films, including *The Wedding Planner*, a predictable, mediocre film starring Jennifer Lopez in a genre of romantic comedy that glamorizes a wedding as the key to romance and love. The students intermittently paid attention to the film as they chatted. With thirty in an enclosed space, the norm was noise and chaos. Maria told me that she felt this population learns best by talking and sharing their ideas with one another, but it wasn't always clear *what* they were learning. It was true that these at-risk students struggled with many emotions about the future, and perhaps this class gave some space to grapple with their anxieties. After a trip to the library to research marriage, I talked to a group of girls and asked what they learned. They said they looked up stuff on teenage marriage and found that "it's stupid." One white junior said that she's going to get married at twenty-three, and she wants to marry someone whose father is a banker. I laughed and said those were very specific criteria! A Latina junior said that she wanted to get married and have three children before she is thirty.

Many of these students viewed cohabitation as an important step before marriage. One day, I talked with a white senior who said she eventually wanted to marry but that she would probably live with her boyfriend first to make sure it was right. I asked whether Ms. Bailey ever talked about living together, and she said she had told them that marriages where the couple lived together beforehand weren't as successful. However, this student still felt it was important to know that this was the right person. She said that most of her peers felt that living together was an important step to take before getting married. Scott Gardner and his colleagues in their evaluation of the *Connections* curriculum found that there was no significant difference in attitudes regarding cohabitation between those who had taken the course and the control group who had not.[50] It is possible that teaching about the outcomes of cohabitation on marriage has little effect to change students' attitudes as it becomes increasingly more normative.

Maria's approach to teaching marriage education sought to ensure that students didn't feel uncomfortable. Even so, a few students felt upset with how the curriculum seemed a negative reflection on their home life. Others enjoyed aspects of the curriculum, but it was unclear what they took home. One white senior, who had been suspended for being drunk on campus, pointed to the exercise listing seven things you should watch out for when you marry as particularly enlightening. Most of the students, however, drew a blank about what they had learned. The class did offer a safe space and helped some students become more engaged with school activities, such as was the case for a couple of female sophomores who had been getting into trouble at school but signed up to be officers with the encouragement of Maria for the school chapter of the Family, Career and Community Leaders of America (FCCLA), the former Future Homemakers of America. Maria told me that such involvement was often a turning point in students' lives. Similar to Maria's class, Pat Weston's class at Monroe High also provided a safe space for students who were having trouble in school.

Heterosexual Dreamin' in the Classroom

Attending Monroe High School offered a very different experience than the one at Red Earth High. In visiting Red Earth, I easily walked into the school and signed a visitor's sheet at the principal's office. In contrast, entering Monroe High meant gaining clearance from the security officer at the front door and passing through a metal detector. At the principal's office, I was issued a security badge. Gangs are a problem at Monroe High, as they are in other urban schools within the Oklahoma City School District. The school has adopted zero tolerance policies, campus police officers and teachers roam school grounds, and security cameras scan hallways. Pat told me that Monroe had one of the highest teenage pregnancy rates in the state. While the racial demographics of her Marriage and Family Life class were more diverse than at Red Earth, she faced similar issues to Maria in teaching students from disadvantaged backgrounds. She explained the challenges to me:

> Lower socioeconomic base, huge minority, very transient, many of them are incarcerated families or incarcerated themselves. For some reason they're very disenfranchised from society, being raised by grandparents, living in shelters and they have very little base. It takes so long to teach the program because they have to make that point of reference for each other. They don't have a point of reference and so that's what I'm having to work on.

Like Maria, Pat spent quite a bit of time adapting the curriculum to meet the needs of her students to give them "a point of reference"—helping them to understand ideas that they have not personally experienced. Trying to explain concepts like "temperament disorder" proved difficult. Unlike Maria, Pat used the entire curriculum, including the "marriage game," extending it to last for the school year, interspersed with the state-approved textbook.

Pat's class was also chaotic, and the classroom was quite messy, with student workbooks, textbooks, and magazines covering the tables and sewing/craft items spread about. At the end of each class, Pat had the students clean up, but there was still disarray. Similar to Maria's class, I acted as an informal teaching assistant, sitting at tables with students, helping them with their assignments, and answering questions. As a white woman younger than Ms. Weston—who in her mid-fifties commanded their respect, these students seemed more mistrustful of me than those at Red Earth who instantly began chatting with me. On my first day, one student asked if I was a new student, and Pat told them I was there to help out. When I returned the second day, one of the white boys said, "Not you again." Over time, I was able to build relationships as I discussed my own experiences and listened to theirs. It proved a difficult tightrope to walk, however, positioned as I was to be an authority figure, helping the students with a curriculum and working under Pat's teaching style that at times challenged my principles. Pat was socially conservative and a self-proclaimed fan of George W. Bush.[51] One day, she asked the students a question about the worst criminal in history, and one of the students answered George Bush. She replied that she resented that answer. She said that there were two things she would die for: her family and her country, and President Bush was doing his best to keep the country on the right track. I was upset by the lack of discussion about this student's comment, even if it was sarcastic.

While socially conservative, Pat cared deeply about helping her students, and her goal seemed to be maintaining a mostly nonjudgmental stance toward them. Students with serious problems often came to her for guidance because they knew she would help without reprimanding them. Juanita, one of her Latina female juniors, had slept with a guy who was HIV-positive. She had come to class in tears, and Pat had taken her outside to talk about it. After class, Pat gave Juanita the HIV-hotline number *and* her home number in case she needed to talk. Another student who trusted Pat above other teachers was Kashawn, an African American junior who was out as a lesbian. Kashawn had been sent to a foster home after spending time in juvenile hall. She was having trouble in her classes and often was a no-show. Pat told me:

> You notice I did have her respect in class, I'm probably one teacher that did. Did you also notice when she first came in she was very defensive. You know, "I'm not talking to you. I don't want to be here." Because they are so used to being beat up and abused, I work very hard at respecting my children and I demand the same back from them. And that's always a very hard, hard connection to make is that mutual respect, very hard connection to make.

Pat understood that she needed to gain Kashawn's respect. In the first weeks, Pat had students fill out the personality section of the workbook and create a poster using magazine cutouts, drawings, or another medium to depict what was important to their sense of self. Kashawn included a picture of two women kissing and announced in her class presentation, "I'm gay." Pat thanked her for sharing, and the students were, overall, accepting. A Latina senior, Mary, who had a boyfriend, went out of her way to befriend Kashawn and help her feel included. They often chatted together about problems they had in their relationships.

However, while Pat dealt with individual students in a supportive manner, she was also willing to teach her values and to push participation even if students expressed their unwillingness. In the first few weeks of class, Pat required all to apply for membership in the FCCLA. We spent an entire class looking over the FCCLA manual and learning words such as membership, programs, public relations, and professional development. Most of the students appeared completely uninterested. When some protested that they didn't want to join, Pat said it was a class requirement. She also asked them to memorize the FCCLA creed:

> We are the Family, Career and Community Leaders of America.
> We face the future with warm courage and high hope.
> For we have the clear consciousness of seeking old and precious values.
> For we are the builders of homes, Homes for America's future,
> Homes where living will be the expression of everything that is good and fair,
> Homes where truth and love and security and faith will be realities, not dreams.
> We are the Family, Career and Community Leaders of America.
> We face the future with warm courage and high hope.

When I asked Pat about the purpose of memorizing the creed, she told me that students didn't memorize enough anymore. The deeper rationale that Pat didn't mention is present in the creed itself, which calls forth the need to instill the "old and previous values" of a time past—to encourage young people to be "builders of homes," where home means "truth and love and security and faith," values essential to "America's future." The creed ties together the constellation of marriage, home, faith, and implicit heterosexuality that is central to a particular vision of a strong America.

In teaching marriage education, Pat offered a nostalgic perspective on past values in comparison to the "reality" of today's world. During one lesson, she wrote on the board the "common pattern" for relationships: Meet > Ask > Date > Engage > Marriage, asking the students where sex went on the list. They replied under dating. Pat hesitated a minute and then asked, "Where *should* sex go?" Jennifer, a Latino junior, answered, "When you are engaged." Cassandra retorted, "No, under marriage." Pat wrote the word "sex" under "marriage." Several students protested that waiting until marriage was too long, so Pat put it under "engage." Others voted for "dating," and she moved it over. Finally, Matt, a white senior, told the class that it should go under "ask," and everyone laughed. Pat told them that this was the whole point. When she was growing up, sex unquestionably went with marriage, but during the sixties society started to change where free love meant sex whenever you wanted. This Marriage and Family Life class, she emphasized, is about teaching values and thinking through these decisions.

A week later, Pat began the section on commitment and marriage. Hector, a Latino junior, told the class that marriage is worse than going to jail; he'd rather be locked up than be married. He said, "I don't want hamburgers for dinner every night" and announced that he wanted a wife, not a "ho." Pat replied, "Okay, I can agree with you on that," which began a discussion of the difference between a wife and a "ho." Pat asked, "What qualities do you look for?" Leticia, an African American junior, pointed out that guys are attracted to "hos," and that they perceive sexy women to give and unsexy *wives* not to put out. Rather than pursue this line of argument, which might have moved into a feminist critique of the sexual double standard, Pat focused on commitment. She argued that staying with one person for the rest of your life didn't have to be like "eating hamburgers every night." It's possible to keep things fresh.

Teaching her values, Pat offered a perspective different in many cases from what students had been exposed to in their upbringing. In one class, she taught from the curriculum on hidden issues—topics that are not usually discussed openly and constructively such as power, recognition, commitment, and acceptance. Many of the students responded positively to these lessons. Similar to students in Maria's class, many held negative views on marriage that Pat sought to dispel. However, in teaching about marriage, Pat relied more than Maria had on an ideology that combined nostalgia for the past with present popular cultural images, such as valorizing conservative gender norms between the "wife" and the "ho." In the fifties, the sexual double standard involved a complex set of rules and conventions meant to check and squelch female adolescent sexuality. The sociologist Wini Breines sums up this system: "Teenage sexual etiquette, dating and going steady, channeled female sexuality into a routinized sexual system that controlled and punished female spontaneity and ensured that young women followed the prescribed steps to marriage."[52] Breines uncovers how white, middle-class female sexuality was fundamentally tied to race, class, and identity; the "deviant" expression of working-class and racial minority sexuality necessitated the segregation of white, middle-class youth subcultures in suburban America.[53] Additionally, Breines demonstrates that the appearance of female sexual conformity often served as a mask for acts of subversion in suburbia.

Similar to the desire quoted at the beginning of this chapter to revive "courtship customs," Pat Weston taught her students about a time when sex only came with marriage, referring to a past ideal that placed pressure on young women to refuse men's sexual advances (or accept them but refuse the final act). Her focus on the "bad" values of the sixties such as free love failed to explain the complexity of the transformation of marriage and family that have attended postindustrial economies and women's mass entrance into the paid workforce, not the least of which has been the delayed age of marriage. Even in Oklahoma where people marry two years younger than the national average, waiting for sex until marriage can seem, as one student expressed, "too long." In discussions, Pat tended to side with students who expressed traditional beliefs about gender and sexuality. Randy, a white junior, was a vocal presence in the class who often discussed his belief that a wife should stay home with the children. Mary, also very vocal, held less traditional views on gender and often argued with Randy in class that women can work and that the husband should be willing to pitch in with household chores and child care. She, however, stood alone in openly challenging the ideas presented about conservative gender norms, and Pat did not dispute comments from boys in the class, such as one Latino senior who said women can't expect guys to change; guys are not made to take on "women's" work.

Kashawn, who came out early on as lesbian, was often absent, but when she did attend, she tended to be very quiet during discussions that inscribed gender and sexual boundaries that marked her as an outsider. This changed one day during class when Pat had the boys and girls split into separate groups to create a poster of the ten worst and best things about dating. I offered to supervise the boys in the hall outside the classroom while the girls stayed inside with Pat. Using crayons, we wrote "Good" and "Bad" on two sheets, and Randy and his friends went to work listing all the bad things about dating: Talking about the future; being "just" friends; meeting the girlfriend's family; breaking up; sex, because it ruins relationships; marriage, because we are too young for that kind of commitment; kids, because now you are stuck with that person. They listed sex at the top of the "Good" list, and all of them were having trouble coming up with other items. Just as I tried to jolt their imaginations, Kashawn arrived late and asked what we were doing. I told her we were creating a poster about dating and that she should check with Ms. Weston inside the classroom. A few minutes later, she came out and told us that everyone at the girls' table agreed with her that she didn't belong with them. She said, "I'm with you guys because I don't do guys." Kashawn sat down and began bantering with the others. The boys continued with their discussion of sex, and Kashawn told them that she liked "fucking." When they brought up pregnancy, she said it sucked that she couldn't get a girl pregnant. She and José made "guy" jokes about sex and gave each other high-fives. When we reentered the classroom for discussion, Kashawn stayed with the guys while each group looked over the other's poster. The discussion, which assumed heterosexuality, centered on how guys want sex and girls want love. Kashawn argued along with the other guys that sex is the goal.

Within the structural constraints of the Marriage and Family Life class in which heterosexuality was always assumed, Kashawn performed a "female masculinity" that challenged, to a certain extent, heterosexuality's dominance and the association of masculine norms with male bodies.[54] Displaying a butch hip-hop style, Kashawn was a striking and courageous presence as she expressed her gender and sexual nonconformity. Many times before in the classroom, she had remained quiet during discussions of heterosexual romance, dating, and family practices. On this day, however, she embraced her otherness by openly resisting the heterosexual assumption that would have placed her with the girls. Instead, she became for the day an honorary boy, a move that Pat Weston did not resist (or openly support). However, Kashawn "did gender" with the boys in a way that reinscribed a gender hierarchy that belittled "feminine" feelings of love and emotion. Being a boy meant eschewing emotion and instead just wanting sex. Kashawn let everyone know that she didn't "date" (e.g., that she expected her girlfriend to "put out"). Mary was incensed by the focus the boys had placed on sex over love, and at one point she called out Kashawn, saying that she didn't treat her girlfriend well. Kashawn responded by looking dejectedly at her feet. Her friendship with Mary made it difficult to straddle the two sides of the gender binary.

In her ethnography of sexuality and gender identity in high school, C. J. Pascoe likewise found the doing of female masculinity in high school to be fraught with contradiction. She discovered that the racially diverse basketball girls garnered student respect by defying gender expectations, but their performance of masculinity often meant objectifying girls and engaging in aggressive practices of fighting. The basketball girls were popular athletes who experienced their bodies as "agentic and powerful, much as boys might experience their bodies."[55] Together they proved a formidable group.

Likewise, another tight group of white girls who had formed a gay-straight alliance on campus, although more socially marginalized than the basketball girls, also bucked gender expectations. Gay-straight alliances (GSAs) are an emerging phenomenon in public high schools that increasingly offer safe spaces, social support, and prospects for activism to lesbian, gay, bisexual, transgender, queer, and straight students.[56] Without such support, high school can prove an extremely hostile environment for lesbian and gay youth, who lack a politicized understanding of sexuality and gender. Monroe High had no such alliance, and Kashawn was one of a few out lesbians. Her girlfriend attended the same high school, and the two had gotten into trouble for making out in the halls. Pat Weston's class offered a moderately safe space for Kashawn, but as the weeks progressed this space became more fraught as the lessons turned to consider marriage and the students began to plan their mock weddings.

The Wedding

Kashawn's girlfriend, Sandy, was added to Pat's class late in the first term, a development over which Pat was none too happy. With Sandy attending, Kashawn paid even less attention to the curriculum and the two would sometimes sneak out together (as did others), even though students were supposed to get a pass if they had to leave. With the chaos and noise, it was difficult to keep track of who was in the classroom and who was out. The two reentered in time to watch a video that Pat showed about two boys who were killed in a car crash while intoxicated. After our discussion, Pat told the students that their next major assignment would be to provide the name of the person each would marry for a series of in-class exercises, at which point Kashawn let out a loud guffaw. Pat explained that it didn't need to be someone in the class, but it would help if the person could attend for the ceremony. Kerry, a Latina senior, asked if the girls could be single mothers. Pat replied, no, this was about marriage. She used Kerry's question as an opportunity to say that according to the law in Oklahoma marriage was heterosexual (the constitutional ban against same-sex marriage had just passed), so it had to be between a guy and a girl. Kashawn and Sandy had checked out at this point, concentrating on their own stuff. Randy asked, "What if we don't want to get married?" Pat responded, "Tough. Life is full of things you don't want to do."

Pat went on to describe the activities involved in the marriage game. Together, each couple would decide on household duties and discuss plans for a wedding. Each would draw a card that designated a wedding budget, what kind of family they would have after they married (how many children, their occupation, etc.), and a family crisis that they would have to work through. They would do a family vacation, which would happen the next semester after I was gone. Pat told me that she was planning a field trip to the Boy Scout Center to "spend the day hiking, camping and doing what families would do together and we're going to do some family activities." Finally, Pat would "unmarry" them. Kerry asked whether they were getting a divorce, and Pat said no, they were not doing divorce in this class. There would be a ceremony to unmarry them, after which each of them would evaluate the experience of being married. Throughout her explanation, Kashawn and Sandy remained quiet. At this stage, Kashawn appeared no longer comfortable speaking out about not doing guys.

The school situation for Kashawn continued to deteriorate. A few days after the marriage game announcement, Pat split the class into groups to discuss things that are easier to change in oneself than in others. Sandy was absent, and Kashawn wandered around the room while the others talked. In private, Pat told me that school officials wanted to kick her out of school and that Pat had told them not to do that, but Kashawn was even failing her class. When we all got back together, Kashawn joined the group she was assigned to and participated in the class discussion, which focused on it being easier to change your own negative patterns of fighting with your partner than trying to make the other person change. When Pat introduced a new topic on the kinds of constraints that should be in place to exit a marriage, Kashawn withdrew, shuffling through her binder. The next day was the deadline to designate a marriage partner, and both Kashawn and Sandy were absent. They attended, however, the following day when Pat had students draw from a pile to designate the budget for their wedding (in amounts from $500 to $100,000). A couple of students asked if they could pass on getting married, and again Pat said no. Kashawn and Sandy got in line to do the drawing, but suddenly they were gone. About ten minutes later, they came in breathless with an administrator on their heels. Kashawn told a story about going downstairs to another teacher to get the names of two boys they would marry. Pat told the administrator that she had no idea they were gone, and he took them away. Pat later said that she wasn't going to back them up because Kashawn had just been getting worse.

The wedding was set for December 15, a few days before I planned to drive back to California. The students worked on separate computers to search for things they would need for the big day. Most of the girls browsed for wedding dresses and rings. Pat said that this is what they predominantly begin with. She instructed them to look up details about getting a license and writing their vows. The students were to write a report detailing their wedding budget to present to the class the day before the wedding. However, when the day arrived, most weren't ready. Pat was upset but decided to conduct the weddings as planned. The students were still looking up stuff, and I helped Mary find the perfect beach resort for her wedding. Later, Pat told me that Kashawn had been suspended for kissing Sandy in the hall on the day that the administrator apprehended the two for leaving class. When Kashawn's foster mother confronted her about it, she left home and hadn't been seen since. Breaking her parole, Pat thought Kashawn would probably end up back in juvenile hall. This was discouraging news, and it was the last I heard of her.

The wedding day arrived, and I arrived early to help decorate. I was in charge of the wedding table with the large sheet cake that had colored letters saying, "Good Luck!" There was punch to drink and bubbles to blow in celebration. Two students confessed that they didn't have their vows and wrote them at the last minute. Students from other classes had arrived to participate in the wedding. Pat took out the "marriage" certificates, and I signed as a witness. She told them to take off their coats and get ready to go outside to begin the ceremony. The judge, a male teacher from another class who was running late, rushed in and Pat handed him a black robe. The students lined up outside as Pat gave each couple a gold plastic ring. They entered solemnly, embarrassed grins on their faces. There were two whose partners weren't able to attend, and they had to be married by themselves. The judge told the first couple to approach, asking in a gruff manner whether they had money for their license, had brought their health certificate, and had written their vows. This couple didn't have a health certificate or money, and he sent them away, as he did the others. At first I thought this was going to be it, but Pat gave the students a few minutes to assemble the paperwork. Then, to the sounds of the wedding march, again the couples entered. After reading their vows, the judge announced each husband and wife, and told them to shake hands. He signed their "marriage" certificates, and we all had cake and punch.

After Christmas break, students would again draw from a pile to find their profession, type of family (number of children), and the crisis they would deal with. I asked one of the female freshmen observers who was helping out what she thought. She said she wanted to take the class in the future to get to look at wedding dresses and think about her wedding. Her comment jogged one of the pressing questions I had concerning what students learn from this exercise. Is it just encouraging them to focus on an idealized heterosexual wedding? When I asked Pat about what students learn, she replied that in her experience students enjoy the marriage game but also get a good dose of reality:

> When you ask them they say, "Oh, it's great. I love it." I learn more from listening and that's how I've learned about some of those nuances when they're planning their marriage, the fighting, the arguing. They say, "This is really hard," and, "I had no idea," and, "Okay, now if we have so and so in the wedding you have to have so and so," and next thing you know they're trying to figure out they have eleven attendants. It's the reality check of what it's going to be like. And you'll see them stressed out and plus some fighting.

The idea of giving students a reality check is interesting in light of the way Pat taught marriage education to emphasize values from a time past that tended to ignore the reality of transformations in intimacy, sexuality, and marriage. I also wondered, with Oklahoma's early age of marriage, whether the exercise might actually encourage students to marry early. Pat replied that she didn't see it that way, but that it had become a debated issue "in town": "They think classes like this are going to make the kids all want to—we're going to make it seem so easy they're going to want to do it. And I don't think I make it easy as much as I make it seem real. What I'm trying to help have them do is to choose the right partner for themselves and that's my goal." The idea of teaching students how to choose the right partner seems worthwhile, but it does not provide a good justification for a mock marriage. In fact, other relationship and sex education curricula teach methods for choosing a good partner within the framework of dating, romance, and sex, and not as part of a broader agenda to promote heterosexual marriage.

An overall evaluation of marriage education in high schools has begun to answer the question of what students learn. An initial study of the impact of marriage education curricula in Oklahoma and Florida indicates that these provide positive outcomes for students such as improved communication skills and a better understanding of commitment.[57] A study by Scott Gardner followed students for four years after their classroom experience and found that those who studied the *Connections* curriculum improved on attitudes toward marriage, divorce, and marriage preparation, and they gained a perceived ability to resist sexual pressure compared to a control group. However, positive gains by the *Connections* group over the course of the curriculum either diminished, or the control group caught up in the year.[58] The researchers also found that the most positive gains in relationship skills were by students raised in two-parent homes, indicating "children who already have the strongest relationship skills, according to previous research, benefit from [marriage education] the most, while those from single-parent and divorced parents struggle more and respond less to interventions like *Connections*."[59] This finding is particularly problematic in light of Oklahoma's implementation of marriage education in Marriage and Family Life classes that cater to at-risk students who often come from single-parent and divorced homes. Although my participant observation was not meant to evaluate the program's effectiveness, Maria's skepticism concerning the benefit of exercises like the marriage game seems warranted in the broader picture of the needs of at-risk students.

More problematic is teaching values to students framed by an ideology that draws distinct boundaries to promote the superiority of heterosexual, monogamous marriage, drawing on a past that doesn't reflect transformations of intimacy in American society. With the prevalence of the abstinence model for teaching about sex and relationships, teachers seem reluctant to discuss the pressing issues of contraception and safe sex that might deter teenagers from getting pregnant and contracting STDs. Teaching ideals of marriage and dating to revive a lost "innocence" might have a negative impact on students who may not wait for marriage to initiate sexuality. The agenda of marriage promotion in high school is particularly detrimental for nonheterosexual students. Kashawn was forced to make decisions about how to negotiate class exercises that depended on a matrix framing her lesbian identity as outsider. One might argue that this class was an elective and that Kashawn was not forced to take a Marriage and Family Life class that involved a marriage game. Yet the lack of school support to create safe spaces for lesbian and gay youth, and to educate other students about nonheterosexual sexualities, provided few options for students like Kashawn who land in Pat Weston's class as a way to get an easy passing grade. Ironically, this class was one space where Kashawn could, at times, express her sexual identity without reprimand. However, the ideology that dominated the teaching eventually made that safe space dangerous and harmful.

My fieldwork at Monroe High proved to be one of the more challenging experiences I had in Oklahoma. I watched with dismay the inevitable train wreck for Kashawn as the class moved toward the marriage game. There seemed no positive outcome: either she participated in a heterosexual marriage game that would deny her identity and sexuality or she would ditch the class, which meant another move toward suspension or even expulsion.

I wondered if the outcome might have been different if Pat Weston had offered other choices for her. Although Pat seemed willing to accept and help Kashawn in a limited manner, ultimately her stance on heterosexual marriage did not consider the negative impact that such a requirement would have on nonheterosexual students. There may have been others in the classes—either "out" or not—who would also feel compelled to participate in an exercise that broadcast their outsider status. Unfortunately, I never learned what happened to Kashawn.

This chapter has examined the boundary work involved in teaching marriage education in the classroom. Students tracked into elective Marriage and Family Life courses tend to be those with little economic and cultural capital, and they are seen as in need of training on the basics of marriage and family, that is, on principles of "the Mission" that are implicit to married, middle-class families. This instruction involves negotiating a boundary that situates heterosexual marriage as the mythic family model from a past when expectations were clear—when sex outside marriage was hidden, stigmatized, and unspeakable, and when same-sex desire remained in the closet. Marriage education in the classroom, in contrast to abstinence that insists that sex outside marriage is socially undesirable, more subtly prioritizes heterosexuality through exercises like the marriage game. In this way marriage promotion reinforces a boundary to mark insiders and outsiders. Whereas heterosexual, at-risk youth might take the path to becoming a marital insider—embracing an ideology that idealizes the white, middle-class, nuclear family, for students like Kashawn this ideology mandated her outsider status as a condition of its internal logic. The silence concerning the assumption of heterosexuality allows its promotion to appear obvious and uncontestable, although troubled by homosexuality's increasing visibility. Teachers cannot pair girls together to play the marriage game in a female-dominated class without raising the specter of same-sex coupledom and its prohibition as a legitimate expression of family. Likewise, same-sex desire is policed in the classroom as integral to the boundary work that maintains heterosexual marital sex's position at the top of the sex hierarchy.[60] The next chapter examines the boundary work in relation to the construction of race of two Native American tribes that seek to promote marriage and Christian morality.

Contesting Native American Marriage

In the government's intentions to accustom native Americans to the sovereignty of the United States, or else remove them from the continent, marriage patterns could not be forgotten. For if monogamy founded the social and political order, then groups practicing other marital systems on American soil might threaten the polity's soundness. Native Americans did not share Christians' common sense about marriage. . . .

To Christian settlers, missionaries, and government officials, Indian practices amounted to promiscuity.

—Nancy Cott, *Public Vows*[1]

Two-Spirit people are well aware that at one time in the history of Native America, mostly before European contact, gender and sexual diversity was an everyday aspect of life among indigenous people. They are also aware that historically they enjoyed the same rights and privileges as other tribal members.

—Affidavit of Brian J. Gilley[2]

Marriage in the United States has been a central mechanism to confer national identity, citizenship, and rights. Three predominant levels of American society shape marriage. The first level contains the communities that offer approval or disapprobation of particular family configuration and practice. At the next level, legislators and judges set the terms and limits of marriage and divorce through state law. Finally, federal laws, policies, and values circumscribe the meaning of monogamous, heterosexual marriage.[3] For individuals whose marriages have been policed or legally excluded, access has been a site of struggle for equal status. Accordingly, marriage laws and practices in the United States have formed and shaped racial distinctions and inequalities, often through imposing "Western" standards of gender and sexual practice.

In recent years, same-sex couples have taken center stage in the fight to gain access to legal marriage as a civil right.[4] By fighting their exclusion and participating in marriage-related community practices such as public commitment rituals, they contest the assumption of a natural and universal heterosexuality. These battles follow a history in the United States (and Europe) that has justified and advocated Christian, monogamous marriage to eradicate the once predominant "belief systems of Asia, Africa, and Australia, of the Moslems around the Mediterranean, and the natives of North and South America [that] all countenanced polygamy and other complex marriage practices."[5] When European colonials landed in America, they discovered native communal and polygamous practices that conflicted with their Christian beliefs. They also documented the existence of native individuals whose comportment could not be explained within standard European gender norms and recorded their surprise that indigenous tribes tolerated and even celebrated these practices.[6] Early on, legislators turned to promoting (Christian, monogamous) marriage as a way to civilize and Christianize Indians and to end the behaviors and customs that flew in the face of colonial morality.

In contemporary "Indian territory"—now the state of Oklahoma, Native American tribes have sovereignty to decide their own marriage customs and rituals, which are today more likely to share mainstream understandings of heterosexual marriage. Reflecting national dynamics, tribes confront the debate over marriage's meaning and purpose. On the one hand, the federal government seeks to promote marriage among Native Americans, instituting a Native American Healthy Marriage Initiative and offering federal grants to tribes and Native nonprofits. In Oklahoma, only a few of the thirty-eight federally recognized tribes have been awarded federal funds for marriage promotion.[7] A Chickasaw tribal leader told me that there was a general reluctance to accept money for marriage promotion that might not be sensitive to Native customs. As a solution, the Chickasaw Nation used funds to work closely with the state marriage initiative to customize "a mainstream marriage education curriculum to the customs, traditions, and values of the Chickasaw Nation."[8] On the other hand, tribes are dealing with the question of same-sex marriage. A battle has been staged in Oklahoma over a Cherokee lesbian marriage that turned the national spotlight on who is allowed to marry and why.

In this chapter, I examine a case of Native American marriage politics to uncover the tensions and contradictions involved in a history that has sought to homogenize and "Christianize" divergent native family and kinship practices in the United States. I begin with a brief history of the importance of marriage in the push to Americanize Native peoples, and then I concentrate on the particular case of marriage promotion in the Chickasaw Nation. Finally, I address the marriage politics of the Cherokee Nation, which, in reaction to a lesbian couple's Cherokee marriage, amended its constitution to define marriage as between one man and one woman. These tales reveal the unremitting tensions that chip away at marriage's hegemonic logic. The case of Native American marriage politics serves as a microcosm for studying the broader culture that relies on marriage to confer American citizenship and belonging.

America's "Indian Problem"

The United States government calibrated its dealings with American Indians as a method to develop the frontier, relying on existing precedents from the English colonial and imperial experience. During first contact and beyond, Europeans produced detailed observations of the natives to establish conceptions that continue to haunt U.S. and Indian relations today. Similar to the Europeans who designated other natives they had colonized, American colonists viewed natives to be "savages" and developed two main images.[9] The "noble savage" was viewed as an "innocent," living in an idyllic, earthly paradise untarnished by the demands of civilization. The historian Francis Paul Prucha states of this perception: "This good Indian welcomed the European invaders and treated them courteously and generously. He was handsome in appearance, dignified in manner, and brave in combat."[10] The "ignoble savage" was seen as a beast whose raison d'être was war, cruelty, and uncivilized practices such as cannibalism and human sacrifice. Prucha states, "Not a few Englishmen saw the Indians with their superstitions and inhuman practices as literally children of the Devil." He continues, "The threads of these two conceptions intertwined in strange ways, and one or the other was drawn upon as suited the occasion. What persisted, however, were the notions of otherness, dependency, and inferiority."[11] For Europeans, and later for Americans, the push was to move savagism to civility, a goal that reached its zenith at the end of the nineteenth century.[12]

This perspective influenced Thomas Jefferson, the most prominent among the first generation of American politicians to theorize about the Native population and to set the stage for their treatment. He viewed Native Americans as equal by nature to white men (whereas he thought black men inferior), and he wrote extensively about the need for their cultural amalgamation with the white population. His Enlightenment theory of civilization, which proposed an inevitable transition from savagery to culture, complemented the tenets of religion regarding the mutual compatibility of Christianizing *and* civilizing the Indian population. Government officials vigorously supported the missionary societies that formed to instruct Indians on agricultural and household arts at the turn of the nineteenth century.

Even as many officials vindicated these policies in their view that "tribes who were 'most advanced in the pursuits of industry' were the ones who were most friendly to the United States,"[13] the Native populations in the Eastern states became a hindrance to white expansion of land ownership. This led to a policy of "Indian removal" and subsequent segregation to lands uninhabited by whites. Following Indian removal and in another wave toward assimilation, the self-identified "friends of the Indian" began to fight the idea that Indians should be treated differently than other Americans.[14] Prucha explains that these reformers "set about to solve the 'Indian problem' in terms of religious sentiments and a patriotic outlook that were peculiarly American. Convinced of the superiority of the Christian civilization they enjoyed, they saw no need to inquire about positive values in Indian culture."[15] The goal of Americanizing Indians was part of a broad ethnocentrism that was also applied to European immigrant groups in the United States (and in some cases African Americans), and it sought to do away with "Indianness."

The push for assimilation meant educating Indians to adhere to the American ideal of marriage—male headship, the conventional sexual division of labor, property ownership, and inheritance rights. The Dawes Severalty Act of 1887 (also known as the Allotment Act) facilitated this ideal, allotting freeholds in "severalty" to individual Indians as property owners. The act ended collective ownership of most tribal lands—accelerating the destruction of communal living—and led to the eventual disintegration of Indian Territory because Native land was increasingly being released for white settlement. It further undermined Native American women's ties to agricultural work in its expectation that the Indian male would be landowner and farmer. The act also laid the foundation for the United States to grant citizenship to Native Americans thirty-seven years later, in 1924.[16]

Not only were the communal patterns of Native Americans, which reformers called communistic, viewed as anti-Christian, but their family practices were considered barbarous and savage. According to Henry M. Teller, Secretary of the Interior between 1882 and 1885, the "heathenish customs" of the Indians were a great hindrance to the advancement of their civilization. In a report, he states:

The marriage state, existing only by the consent of both parties, is easily and readily dissolved, the man not recognizing any obligation on his part to care for his offspring. . . . Some system of marriage should be adopted, and the Indian compelled to conform to it. The Indian should also be instructed that he is under obligations to care for and support, not only his wife, but his children, and on his failure, without proper cause, to continue as the head of such family, he ought in some manner to be punished.[17]

The regulations for courts of Indian offenses drawn up in 1883 made plural or polygamous marriages an offense warranting a fine of not less than twenty nor more than fifty dollars, or hard labor for not less than twenty nor more than sixty days. Likewise, the courts imposed a penalty for living or cohabiting with any female who was not the man's wife and provided a provision for judges to solemnize Indian marriages, issue a certificate, and collect a fee not to exceed one dollar.[18] By means of education and adherence to private property, the goal was to create loyalty to Christian morality and patriotic Americanism, ultimately readying Native Americans for the duties and obligations of citizenship.

The specific case of Americanizing Indians sheds light on the historical tenets of heterosexual marriage ideology and how it intersects with the meaning of American identity. By proselytizing an "American" vision of marriage for the Indian population, government officials participated in boundary work that sought to "whiten" them in order to downplay their otherness and ultimately blend in to become patriotic citizens. The importance of marriage in Americanization uncovers the connections of heterosexual gender norms, capitalism, and whiteness. In the case of Native Americans, it was necessary to stamp out the polygamous, communal, and more gender-egalitarian patterns of kinship and labor that were viewed as un-American. The logic of this ideology is recurrently rooted in a sense of American identity built on the principles of republicanism—an ideal vision of voluntary union based on mutual consent, and on the history of capitalism—formed by an individualized, self-sufficient nuclear family with a male head.[19]

The goal of Americanizing Indians had substantial consequences for the treatment of individual tribes. The five southern tribes who were removed to the territories that now encompass Oklahoma, known as the Five Civilized Tribes—the Cherokee, Chickasaw, Choctaw, Creek, and Seminole—consisted of those thought to be more amenable to the "civilized" ways of white settlers and would prosper on circumscribed acreage.[20] In relation to political status, control of land, and education, the Five Tribes had a unique relationship to the federal government. Section 8 of the Dawes Act, for example, exempted the Five Civilized Tribes from the law's provision to break up reservation land, which was held in common by the members of a tribe, into small allotments to be parceled out to individuals.[21] In subsequent years, the Dawes Commission and the Curtis Act of 1898 extended the allotment policy of the act to the Five Tribes. The historian Angie Debo's landmark book *And Still the Waters Run: The Betrayal of the Five Civilized Tribes* documented how agents systematically manipulated this allotment policy to deprive Native Americans of land and resources. By 1901, an amendment to the Dawes Act conferred citizenship to all Indians on Indian Territory, and tribal governments quickly became mere shadows. Government officials cheered the end of Indian government. In discussing the demise of the Cherokee Nation, Secretary of the Interior Franklin K. Lane expressed in a 1914 report:

> The word of the white man has been made good. These native and aspiring people have been lifted as American citizens into full fellowship with their civilized conquerors. The Cherokee Nation, with its senate and house, governor and officers, laws, property, and authority exists no longer. Surely there is something fine in this slight bit of history. It takes hold upon the imagination and the memory, arouses dreams of the day when the Indian shall be wholly blended into our life, and at the same time draws the mind backward over the stumbling story of our relationship with him.[22]

The desire to assimilate Native Americans into "our life" and to contradictorily segregate them on reservations and unused land has established an inconsistency and variability in tribal-federal relations that continue today. Efforts to promote marriage among Native Americans reflect this continuing tension between the effects of colonization and the desire for self-determination.

Chickasaw Marriage Promotion?

In August 2005, the Roundtable on Religion and Social Policy interviewed Quanah Crossland Stamps, Commissioner of the Administration for Native Americans (ANA), a division of the U.S. Department of Health and Human Services. Stamps, a Republican member of the Cherokee Nation, was appointed by George W. Bush in 2002. During the interview, Stamps described the planning and organization of the ANA with its three programs—the Social and Economic Development Strategies program

(SEDS), a language-preservation program, and an environmental regulatory enhancement program—and she discussed how, under the SEDS program, funding is available for projects that "focus on strengthening family relationships, strengthening marriages."[23] Accordingly, roughly $1 million was allocated for the Strengthening Marriage and Relationships in Tribal (SMART) Native American Communities (renamed later the Native American Healthy Marriage Initiative), with a cap of $150,000 on each project. Stamps offered details in a fashion similar to other marriage advocates about the negative effects of low marriage and high divorce rates in the Native American community on child well-being, justifying the need to strengthen Native families in a similar fashion to the federal Healthy Marriage Initiative.

Her broad reasoning on how to strengthen families, however, reflects a very different ideal from that of the general marriage promotion movement. Stamps described the particular status of Native American marriage and divorce: "It is all interrelated for our communities. There are extended families and the nuclear family. We raise our children together as a community. The concept of marriage is a Western concept, not necessarily a tribal concept."[24] When asked about the differences between strategies to strengthen Native families compared to Healthy Marriage Initiatives for other populations, Stamps remarked: "We're trying to focus more on a holistic approach. We're not distinguishing between married couples, non-married couples. We do have some distinctions in our communities—we have traditional marriages, and we have very extensive extended families. We have a lot of grandparents taking care of children. So we are more focused on allowing a cultural approach."[25]

In contrast to marriage advocates who seek to prioritize the importance of marriage, Stamps made it clear that the ANA is not simply focusing on married versus nonmarried people. Given the history of colonization in the United States that has sought to civilize Native Americans to be participants in the "American" ideal of marriage and family, Stamps's emphasis on recognizing the diversity of family forms in Native communities is significant. She further explained the approach of tapping the hundreds of community-based Native American nonprofit organizations around the country to help strengthen families. Continuing to highlight the differences between Native approaches and that of the marriage initiative, Stamps answered a question about whether these organizations are faith-based by noting that the majority of Native communities do not work with faith-based programs.

Regarding the small number of tribes that have a family initiative, Stamps acknowledged the Chickasaw Nation as a leader. The Chickasaw Nation, with its tribal government located in Ada, Oklahoma, has in recent years become a successful model of a wealthy tribe. With a three-branch system of government (executive, legislative, and judicial), its modern Constitution was ratified in 1983. It counts itself among the one-third of the 561 federally recognized tribes that engage in gaming, and it is among the narrower margin that do so successfully. Until the 1980s, tribes rarely had a large block of money to attend to tribal needs, which meant a lack of long-term planning and investment. Early in the 1970s, then-President Richard M. Nixon ordered federal policy to recognize Indian self-determination, acknowledging that federal services to Indians were solemn treaty obligations. For a number of tribes including the Chickasaw Nation, the growth of gaming wealth facilitated an economic road to self-determination, as well as solidifying assimilation into a capitalist system of governance.[26]

The Chickasaws, who had migrated to what is now Mississippi, Kentucky, Alabama, and Tennessee in prehistoric times, were the last of the five tribes forced by the U.S. government to leave their lands to relocate to Indian Territory during the Great Removal. After years of struggle, the tribe under the direction of Governor Bill Anoatubby has had phenomenal economic success. A Nation official told me, "I think our tribe—it's not a secret, it's in print— gosh, most months you are looking at I don't know how many million dollars we are profiting a month. The numbers are almost astronomical due to all the revenue from our enterprising efforts." In 1987, the tribe had only 250 employees; by 2008, this had increased to 10,500 and the tribe has diversified to other ventures such as health care and banking.[27] This success has meant plenty of resources to help its citizens, including housing, food and subsistence, clothing, and so on. And after receiving a Project Strong Family grant from the federal government, the Chickasaw Nation began to focus on disseminating the Prevention and Relationship Enhancement Program (PREP).

I interviewed the director of the Office of Strong Family Development, a department that includes the Chickasaw Children's Village (a residential facility for children), the transitional living program for runaway and homeless youth sixteen to twenty-one years old, and Family Services, which is "designed to facilitate the formulation of new skills for addressing family-related issues within the tribe."[28] The director told me that in 2002 the Chickasaw Nation was the only group to receive funding under a Project Strong Family grant, which totaled $140,000. The focus had been on four things, according to the director: "Fatherhood accountability; single-parent support; blended family; youth development. We got that looking at the tribe and what the need was there, and that would cover most of the bases." However, after receiving the grant, the Administration for Children and Families asked the Nation to concentrate on promoting marriage. According to the director, the marriage initiative wasn't on the initial list of approved activities for the grant. He explained:

> It became extremely important probably due to the president at the time and the political environment, and along with research indicating that there are so many negative consequences to family instability. Yes, right after we were funded there was a huge push, and it was almost after the fact we were really told look that was really a marriage initiative, the only federally funded marriage initiative program in the United States. So, we had to change gears real quickly to make sure that we were . . . and the great thing was it all fit perfectly.

As the director described, former President Bush's strong endorsement of the Healthy Marriage Initiative was one factor in the push to promote marriage among Native Americans. However, this push appears somewhat ephemeral.

As the director described, the first marriage initiative grants in 2002 were offered to tribes as part of a push toward promoting marriage. However, by 2005, Stamps, in her interview with the Roundtable, geared the conversation away from marriage promotion, stressing instead the differences between Native family structures and "Western" conceptions of marriage. Stamps characterized the need for a cultural approach to all aspects of services in relation to marriage and family, including the administration of fatherhood accountability. At the federal Office of Child Support Enforcement, there are specific regulations for administering the tribal child-support enforcement activities—specifically fathers' support of biological children, which differs from other communities. Stamps explained:

> Rather than paying back monetarily—because our communities have a difficult time with employment and high poverty—the father can get credit in paying back child support if they go to school functions with their children. If they come over and cut the wood or do things around the house that benefit the family and the children, he's considered to be providing that child support. Rather than monetary, it's being present in a child's life. We're trying to make it culturally appropriate.[29]

These regulations focus on involvement and not on marriage. It appears that perhaps the initial impetus to promote marriage among Native Americans was not very successful, and a more nuanced and holistic approach instead surfaced.

Stamps stated that the idea of strengthening families had been stressed on program announcements for several years. However, she gave a caveat: "Native communities really examine things and talk amongst themselves before they launch any type of community-based project that will affect the entire community. There's a lot of consultation going back and forth."[30] Thus, the ANA appears to receive a very limited number of Native American Healthy Marriage Initiative applications and this program is one of the least funded. For the 2008 budget year, there were a total of 133 ANA grants funded at just over $22 million. Only twelve went to fund Native American Healthy Marriage Initiative projects at a little over $2 million. In contrast, the ANA awarded almost $13 million to sixty-seven Social Economic Development and Strategies (SEDS) grants for that year. For the 2007 budget year, the ANA approved and funded only two Healthy Marriage grants for a total amount of $346,475, and, in 2006, it approved and funded ten grants for a total of $1,789,387.[31] Low rates of funding may be attributed to the fact that the Native American Healthy Marriage Initiative is a new program. It also could be the case that the ideology of marriage promotion is not as effective among Native communities.

In 2004, the Chickasaws were among the few tribes in Oklahoma willing to work with the state marriage initiative. At the time of our interview, the director estimated that roughly 300 people had participated in the PREP workshops. The director described how he began communicating with the initiative to learn more about PREP. He detailed a mutually beneficial collaboration: "By us representing the Native Americans in Oklahoma and the marriage initiative being in Oklahoma, you couldn't have a very effective marriage initiative without that piece of the puzzle." The Chickasaw Nation also benefited from the relationship as the marriage initiative offered "all the training for all the PREP instructors, tons of our workbooks for all the groups, they advertise, they will come in and help us with couples, they help promote us even at a national level." Perhaps most exciting for the marriage initiative were the modifications that the director suggested to make the curriculum more culturally appropriate to the Chickasaw people. Regarding the speaker-listener technique, several initiative leaders told me about how the director substituted a talking stick or feather for the floor (the cardboard tile each couple passes back and forth). The director said, "Our people can relate to this historically and culturally. The tribes have been doing this for centuries." Another difference the director discussed was how the role playing and interactive conversations that take place in the training can be very difficult for Native couples. He noted that it is "really taboo for Native Americans to bring things from your household and talk it over in public."

Even as the director described a willingness to work with the marriage initiative, he also felt it important for the tribe to administer the program in a culturally sensitive manner that would not be viewed as part of a broader non-Native initiative. He explained:

> Native Americans, obviously and for good reason I think historically, are a little apprehensive about just jumping on a national bandwagon in which the federal government is promoting PREP or even the University of Denver or Markman and Stanley [the creators of PREP]. I think it is important for it to be promoted more from the perspective of Native Americans. Each tribe promotes it within their boundaries.

Here again, the idea of resistance to the dominant white culture plays a significant role in how the services are disseminated. Similar to Commissioner Stamps, the director described how it is important to recognize the diverse families that populate the Native American population. He detailed the difference: "Within Native American families we don't really realize cousins and distant cousins. Everyone is like brother and sister, so it's a very tightly knit group with a lot of support. I think to tweak the curriculum to build on those supports can be a good thing." His words speak to a variance in the conception of Native family life that differs from the goal of promoting marriage as consisting of two-married parents and their biological children.

Resistance to being part of a broader federal marriage initiative is also evident in how the Chickasaw governor dealt with his family initiative after signing it into proclamation. The initiative was advertised as expanding family services into a comprehensive set of assistance programs, including an Employee Relationship Enhancement program, family and marriage counseling and therapies, family crisis resolution, PREP courses, fatherhood accountability classes, youth development groups, abstinence classes for youth, and single-parent support groups. In his 2004 State of the Nation address, however, Governor Anoatubby mentioned the family initiative only briefly toward the middle of his hour-long address. He stated: "The word 'family' has a strong meaning with the Chickasaw people. Family is something to be cherished, to be preserved. Many programs have been implemented to strengthen our families. The PREP program and our new family initiative are designed to increase the skills we need to keep our family units intact."[32]

This very short reference to the family initiative gives no details about PREP, the Chickasaw family initiative, or the statewide marriage initiative from which the governor's initiative received the PREP curriculum. This is surprising given the fact that the initiative—a major undertaking—had received government funding that year. The main focus of the speech was on education, health care, and culture, and the brief statement about the family initiative appeared under a much longer segment, "Education, Youth and Family, Arts and Humanities," which detailed programs for youth and the sustenance of Chickasaw families through home ownership programs, among others. Nowhere in his speech did Anoatubby mention the word "marriage."

In order to initiate a specifically Native program, the director created and oversaw the Governor's Family Initiative Employee Relationship Enhancement (ERE) training, a four-hour course to teach relationship skills. He described the process of creating the curriculum:

> We knew that everybody wouldn't buy into the marriage initiative. There are a lot of people who like to be single. There are a lot of people who are homosexual, who do not want to buy into the traditional marriage initiative. So, what we did was, we took those things that were very strong, relationship skills for marriage but that also would work very well in rearing children and then also would be extremely effective in building working relationships with co-workers, and we condensed them and combined them and spit out that four-hour curriculum called the Employee Relationship Enhancement.

The director drew on principles from PREP but also incorporated theories and ideas he'd learned from his past experience working as a licensed behavioral practitioner and professional counselor. The curriculum uses the "Coffee Can Theory," for example, to elucidate the amount of anger and stress one can tolerate. It asks the reader to imagine a two-pound coffee can that fits inside his or her torso. As each stressor or angering stimulus is added like a scoop of coffee—some as bigger scoops than others, it is easy to see that the can will fill and run over. The curriculum discusses how to ventilate to let off pressure, using the speaker-listener technique as one of those mechanisms. The director also included his own conceptualization of the "Iceberg Theory," to offer a visual of how anger is the tip of the iceberg that one can see. However, two-thirds of the iceberg is hidden under water that encompasses emotions such as rejection, fear, hurt, and loneliness. The lesson states: "The iceberg theory is especially important in the work environment. Many times family members or spouses will have insight into dynamics contributing to emotional states. Co-workers, however, may have limited knowledge of these dynamics." The curriculum offers advice for relationships in general but often stresses the importance of communication in work relationships.

While the curriculum focuses more on work relationships, I was surprised to find that it includes Bible verses to highlight relationship principles. It refers to Ephesians 4:26—"Do not let the sun go down while you are still angry"—to illustrate the negative consequences of holding grudges when dealing with coworkers. Further on, it states: "Respect is one way to validate a human being's worth. We must recognize that a person has value as a human being. We are instructed by the Bible, in I Peter 2:17, to show proper respect to everyone." When I asked about the reason for including Bible verses in training Nation employees, the director said:

> The fact is that the year 2004 is based on Christ's death, so if he is not a deity, if he was nothing more than a great philosopher that walked the face of the earth, for that reason alone we gain so much wisdom from the things he said. The more that I've studied psychology and the more that I read the Bible, it's amazing to me when God says things like don't let the sun set on your anger, and psychology is teaching you not to ball that up and let it build into resentment. They just go hand in hand. So, we wanted to quote it for several reasons. One, there's so much wisdom in it, and it's so right on target. Two, people take it to heart. When you look at a people that seventy something percent of the tribe says that they are Christian, then obviously that is going to impact three-fourths of your people.

The director explained in detail how the god of the Christian religion and the god—or the Great Spirit—of Native American religion really refer to the same phenomenon: "I think the Bible talks a lot about God making himself manifest to people, even to animals. . . . I mean God is God. He made himself manifest to Chickasaws for centuries before the news of Christ came." He described how difficult it had been to accept "the good news" of Christianity because of the messenger who also "wiped out ninety percent of all living Native Americans on the North American continent." He detailed how Native Americans have finally "seen past the messenger and understand the [Christian] message" as one not in conflict with Native American religion. When I asked whether the predominantly Baptist churches draw on both native and Christian religions, the director admitted that they are "tradi-

tional Baptist." Evidently, the history of colonialism and Christian proselytizing has greatly influenced current religiosity and practices of spirituality
among the Chickasaw.

ERE workshops became one of the employees' annual incentives, adding
an extra two-week paycheck in December for Chickasaw employees who
met a designated number of goals ranked by a percentage for their level of
importance to the tribe and the effort it took to achieve them. All of these
activities are meant to go above and beyond the scope of the job. The director
explained:

> We talked to the governor and he initially approved that 25 percent of
> everybody's incentive could be contingent on attending this four-hour
> course. Well, he thought about it a little bit more, and said that if we really
> want people to get involved and recruit a lot of people for that, let's make it
> 50 percent. So, he actually approved as part of his governor's family initia-
> tive proclamation that every employee that attends that four-hour course
> will get 50 percent of their annual incentive based on their attendance.
> That's just phenomenal because it's four hours. You'd be crazy not to do it.
> By far, it's been the most successful recruiting tool that we've used.

When I interviewed the director, the ERE program had just started. He said
that they were hoping to train six thousand employees over the course of
the year. Ultimately, he described the goal of aiding families by providing
"wraparound services"—housing, food, and social services—in addition
to marriage education. The director described how it is important to meet
the material needs to "take care of a lot of the dynamics that usually push
people apart." Thus, the family initiative prioritizes helping families remain
viable through economic and social support services, a component missing
from the state initiative with its focus on providing marriage education to as
many people as possible and targeting a predominantly middle-class clientele. With its smaller population and plush sources of revenue, the Chickasaw Nation has the resources to provide a broad spectrum of services to
Chickasaw individuals and families. However, even as the family initiative
has sought to promote family diversity and support, it nevertheless engages
the ideological persuasion of marriage promotion.

Attending one of the four-hour ERE training sessions, I noted that the
majority of the four hours of training with workers from a social services
division of the Nation (seven women and one man) focused on workplace
relations. However, the workshop leader, Marissa, did introduce a message

about marriage, which appeared to fall flat. The group was very lively and interactive. Most were willing to share about their personal lives; several said they were divorced, and one said she was raising her grandson. A long discussion of the iceberg theory brought up an example of a coworker not in attendance who refused to offer a greeting in the morning. This led to a conversation about the best way to deal with those who "wear their emotions on their sleeves." Marissa discussed dealing with these behaviors in terms of a technique in the ERE curriculum (drawn from PREP): When you do "X" (a behavior—not a character trait) in situation "Y," I *feel* "Z." Turning to the topic of trust in relationships, she discussed the issue of fidelity and workplace affairs. At this, the women who had been bantering throughout the workshop began to tease the only man present about scratch marks on his arms from being attacked at work by libidinous female coworkers.

The audience grew quiet and the energy in the room dropped precipitously, however, when Marissa brought up the subject of commitment in marriage. When she discussed couple relationships, she introduced the idea of dedication and constraint commitment and asked, "How much commitment is necessary to make marriage work?" She then read Ephesians 5:22–24, a verse not included in the workbook: "Wives, submit to your husbands as to the Lord. For the husband is the head of the wife as Christ is the head of the church, his body, of which he is the Savior." After explaining how important it is to hold one's spouse in high esteem, Marissa asked why be committed? One of the participants wanted clarification on whether she was referring to marriage or to the workplace. She answered either or both. Another employee looked doubtful as she asked, "What was the question?" It wasn't clear whether the participants were dodging the question or whether their attention had wandered at the end of the long workshop. One finally replied that at work one needs to keep one's commitments, and added that marriage was a whole different story. She didn't elaborate, and Marissa didn't follow up, perhaps sensing resistance to a discussion of marriage.

I wasn't able to interview Marissa to find out why she presented the Ephesians verse about male headship in marriage. Neither did I uncover a specific reason for why the training for Native employees addressed marriage. Perhaps the more pressing question, given the fact that the training was funded with a grant from the federal Healthy Marriage Initiative, was why there had not been *more* of a focus on marriage? The reason appeared to be similar to the one provided by social workers who taught PREP Relationship to Temporary Assistance to Needy Families (TANF) clients: the response was more positive when the workshop focus was on communication skills that applied to diverse relationships, in this case relationships in the workplace. As the director explained, many Native Americans, for reasons of their history, will not buy into the idea of marriage promotion.

While most of the ERE curriculum left out the word "marriage," Marissa did teach about Christian commitment and an ideology of male headship. As the one trained to provide workshops to employees, Marissa might have focused more on marriage, but overall she downplayed this aspect of the curriculum. The tightrope she walked between presenting information on marriage versus workplace relationships highlights the tensions in government efforts to promote Chickasaw marriages. On the one hand, marriage promotion principles are muted and contextualized within a wider discourse of the history of European colonialism, American hegemony, and the overall genocide of Native Americans. On the other hand, the basic assumption that motivated the marriage discourse in the ERE workshops is based on the ideal of the patriarchal, nuclear family. These tensions are also apparent in the case of a Cherokee same-sex couple who married in Oklahoma.

Cherokee Marriage Panic

The Cherokees in Oklahoma have not followed the lead of the Chickasaw Nation to initiate a family initiative, secure government funding to promote marriage, or collaborate with the statewide marriage initiative. They did receive government funding for other projects, including an ACF Compassion Capital Fund Demonstration Program grant in 2004 to expand and strengthen the role of Cherokee organizations in their ability to provide social services to low-income individuals. This grant was divided into subawards to twenty organizations with strong service history in "alcohol and drug abuse, diabetes prevention, prisoner re-entry, marriage and family counseling, and elderly services."[33] Other funding included a Social and Economic Development Strategies grant in 2008 for a three-year project to integrate the Cherokee language and culture into the regular school curriculum. In 2002, the Cherokee Nation became an honoree of the Harvard Project of American Indian Economic Development for its implementation of a Cherokee Nation History Course for employees of the Nation, which includes instruction on "matrilineal kinship, family relationships and what's appropriate" to support these.[34] Similar to the Chickasaw, the Cherokees focus on their own traditions of family networks and kinship.

As the second largest Indian tribe in the United States, almost seventy thousand Cherokees currently reside in the Cherokee Nation, a tribal jurisdiction area that includes fourteen counties in northeastern Oklahoma. Before they were forced by the United States westward in 1839 to what would later become Oklahoma, the Cherokees occupied territory primarily in Georgia, Alabama, North Carolina, and Tennessee, maintaining a distinct culture in part due to their Iroquoian language, and in part due to their unique kinship system and religious worldview. Cherokee family structure was historically a matrilineal system, which relied on Cherokee women to create and maintain the tribe. The historian Theda Perdue documents that marriage and kinship were flexible systems among the Cherokees and that polygamy and divorce were common options.[35] The matrilineal organization of the Cherokee Nation flew in the face of dominant Euro-American norms that attributed property rights solely to white men. For Cherokee women who married non-Cherokee men, their children had an indisputable claim to membership in the Nation, and, for much of Cherokee history, Cherokee kinship was tied to being born of a Cherokee woman.

U.S. expansion into Native territory in the Southeast facilitated the emergence of a national identity that relied on cultural heritage and a distinct, identifiable "homeland."[36] In the early 1800s, Cherokee officials ratified a number of laws to regulate sex and marriage as a method to govern the marital behavior of Cherokee women who had the potential to give birth to new members of Cherokee society.[37] Race was important. The American binary racial model in the United States offered little space for American Indians. To negotiate this fraught terrain, Cherokees sought to distance themselves from people of African descent. The historian Fay Yarbrough uncovers how "Cherokee law invoked a common identity for Indians and whites socially as free and racially as not black."[38] The emergence of a national identity enabled the U.S. government to manipulate a relatively small group of wealthy, slaveholding Cherokees to sign a treaty of removal, which ultimately led to the deadly "trail of tears" and annihilated a quarter of the Cherokee population.[39]

As U.S.-Indian policy has vacillated between periods of supporting tribal self-government and of forced Indian socioeconomic assimilation, marriage policy has been key to policing boundaries.[40] Since the 1980s, American Indian tribes legislate marriage according to their own principles of self-determination under the Doctrine of Tribal Sovereignty, and a number of the thirty-eight federally recognized tribes in Oklahoma issue their own marriage licenses for "tribal custom marriage."[41] The practice, however, is rare, and most Native Americans seek a license through the state.[42] In 2004, Leslie Penrose, a white minister at a lesbian/gay-accepting church, worked with a Cherokee activist, Samuel Crittenden, to obtain a license to perform marriages certified by the Cherokee Nation.[43] Crittenden had studied tribal sovereignty statutes and found a mandate for states to recognize Native marriages. He believed that, because the Cherokee legal code defined marriage in gender-neutral terms, a same-sex couple could conceivably establish a marriage not approved by the state.

Kathy Reynolds and Dawn McKinley, both citizens of the Cherokee Nation, went to Tahlequah, Oklahoma—the capital of the Nation—on May 13, 2004, to obtain a marriage license. The clerk gave it to them, explaining that she had no problem handing it to them, but they were unlikely to find a certified Cherokee minister to perform the ceremony. This simple act initiated a chain of events that has been remarkable in juxtaposing tensions between "Indian" identity and the ideology of marriage in American society. The first occurred the very next day when the Chief Justice of the Cherokee Judicial Appeals Tribunal placed a thirty-day moratorium on issuing marriage licenses to prevent other same-sex couples from obtaining a license. Henceforth, proponents and opponents of same-sex marriage in the Nation would both engage the discursive terrain of tradition to back their arguments in favor or against. Each side would claim to be the established authority on Cherokee custom regarding the practice of marriage, and each would portray its case as the best resistance to the legacy of imperial intrusion.[44]

Five days after receiving their license, Dawn McKinley and Kathy Reynolds were married on Cherokee land in Tulsa. The ceremony included native traditions for blessing the couple, witnessed by family and friends, as well as reporters and activists. Leslie Penrose, who officiated, led the couple in a prayer that incorporated earth, fire, wind, and water: "Creator God, We honor all you created as we pledge our hearts and lives together. We honor earth and ask for our marriage to be abundant and grow stronger through the seasons." Taking some red earth that had been gathered from Cherokee land at Mohawk Park, Penrose threw it in the wind. "We honor fire and ask that our union be warm and full of passion." The couple swept their hands over a candle. "We honor wind and ask for wisdom as we struggle and grow this marriage together." Another attendee blew soap bubbles to signify wind. "We honor water and ask that our marriage may never thirst for commitment or care." The water was from a sacred spring that had been flown in from the Cherokee homeland. Leslie Penrose finished, "Creator God, We honor all you created as we pledge our hearts and lives together. Amen."

By honoring Cherokee tradition, the ceremony disrupted the Christian-faith bias that is central to marriage ideology in American society. Following the vows, Leslie Penrose announced the couple "cooker and companion," in line with the Cherokee word for husband, which means "companion that I live with," and for wife, "cooker." After the ceremony, I drove with the wedding party to Tahlequah to file the license. There were a series of exchanges with Justice Stacy Leeds, who told the couple that the Chief Justice of the Cherokee Nation had "issued a moratorium on all marriages. Heterosexual, same-sex, all marriages." Finally, in protest, Dawn McKinley gave an eloquent speech:

> We're good enough to be on your roll, but not good enough to be married in the eyes of the tribe, and where does that leave us? That's saying that we are not as equal, and that's not right, because the laws of the tribe are set out to serve everyone. It doesn't say anywhere in that because you are homosexual you don't deserve the same rights as the heterosexual people in our tribe. You know, it's bad enough our state won't recognize us, but for our own tribe—for our own people to turn against us. I've always been very proud to be a part of the Cherokee people. I am very proud of my heritage. Today, I am very ashamed of it.

She identified her membership in the tribe as a powerful reason for recognition, even if the state is unwilling to authorize her marriage to Kathy. Her message mirrors the equal rights frame that mainstream lesbian and gay interest groups have used to define their position and get their message out to the public.[45] At the same time, her statement draws on an argument about heritage and the importance of cultural identity. Her words reflect a pervasive tension in the discursive terrain regarding same-sex marriage between mainstream LGBT rhetoric that draws on individual rights and a language of cultural heritage that speaks to a shared "Indian" past.

The intra-tribal legal battle over same-sex marriage reveals how a legacy of colonialism is implicated in the boundary work that engages questions of traditional custom. On June 11, 2004, Todd Hembree, the Cherokee Tribal Council attorney, filed a complaint as a private citizen to claim that individuals of the same gender do not qualify for a marriage license under the Cherokee Nation Code. Three days later, on June 14, the Cherokee Tribal Council voted fifteen to zero to amend the Cherokee Code by Legislative Act 26–04 in favor of defining marriage as between one man and one woman, drawing a strict boundary around a practice of kinship that has been much more fluid and less defined. While the language they used reflected federal and state legislation set forth in the Defense of Marriage Act, which defines marriage as explicitly heterosexual, the Cherokee Nation justified the amendment *not* as a way to bring tribal law in alignment with U.S. legal norms, but as important to preserve tribal customs.[46] Under Cherokee law, the amendment was not retroactive and did not impact the issued marriage license.

In the next months, McKinley and Reynolds were unable to find a Cherokee lawyer to represent their case, and the ACLU and other national lesbian and gay organizations did not step forward. Thus, for the first year, they were forced to represent themselves. They finally garnered representation from the San Francisco–based National Center for Lesbian Rights, and they eventually won their case. In September 2005, the Judicial Appeals Tribunal of the Cherokee Nation ruled that Todd Hembree had no standing to sue. Their victory didn't last long, however. A group of elected tribal councilors filed a new court challenge that was also found in January 2006 to have no standing. In its decision, the court found that the council members could not prove that they were individually harmed or affected by the marriage. In the same month, the Court Administrator, who is responsible for recording marriage licenses, filed a third lawsuit challenging the validity of the couple's marriage, which is still awaiting a ruling from the Cherokee Nation District Court as of September 2011.

In making his case, Hembree argued for a reading of the Cherokee Code to assess the legislative intent of its creators in 1892. In his Petition for Declaratory Judgment, for example, he stated, "Same sex marriages were not part of Cherokee history or tradition. Cherokee society in 1892 did not allow nor contemplate same sex marriage. This Court should determine that same sex marriage is not allowed under today's laws." The document further spells out: "Respondents' actions are an attempt to have the Courts redefine the traditional concept of marriage within the Cherokee Nation. Simply put Respondents are seeking to take advantage of a perceived 'loop hole' in our statute that if successful would fly in the face of the traditional definition and understanding of marriage of the Cherokee people."[47]

The judgment does not specify what constitutes a "traditional" Cherokee understanding of marriage. Instead, its language draws on the frame used by the religious right to suggest that proponents for same-sex marriage are attempting to redefine "traditional" morality.[48] The argument itself assumes a universal meaning of marriage. The conservative Heritage Foundation website, for example, states: "Regardless of religion, culture or constitutional tradition, societies have always agreed on the nature of marriage." It further contends: "Marriage is being threatened in the courts through a series of decisions that seek to overthrow the customs, laws, and social norms of human experience."[49] Thus, while arguing that the definition of marriage is grounded in "nature"—a position suggesting a universal meaning based on the "natural," two-parent, heterosexual family—the conservative position paradoxically stresses the socially constructed character of marriage in custom, social norms, and law.

In the case of Cherokee marriage, Todd Hembree's language does similar rhetorical work suggesting a universal form of marriage among the Cherokee. However, before the Cherokee Code was amended, the only specifications given were those that barred individuals from marriage based on kinship and insanity—"individuals nearer of kin than first cousins, the currently married, the insane, and the 'idiotic.'"[50] Thus, Hembree was compelled to argue for an understanding based on intent. During my interview with him, he stated:

Actually Title 43 is based on the Constitutional Law of the Cherokee Nation of 1892, which also bolsters, I believe, my argument that in 1892 the context in which this law was written and adopted definitely does not contemplate marriage between a woman and a woman or a man and a man. It was traditionally defined as a man and a woman. See, Section 8 has "husband and wife," Section 9 has "husband and wife." I'm taking the attack, you know, the stance that you read Title 43 in its entirety. You consider the time in which Title 43 was originally generated, and you can come up with the conclusion that marriage is a definition between a man and a woman. You know I might be right and I might be wrong.

His deliberation on whether he is right reflected a general disavowal of being a "social conservative," even while he employed the language of the religious right. He said, "I don't care what people do in their lives, in their bedrooms. I really don't, but I do have respect for the law, and I do have a respect for the institution of marriage."

Todd Hembree, as did other leaders in the Cherokee Nation, embraced an understanding of marriage as a central component of Cherokee heritage that "promotes stability" through biology and nature:

There are certain things that are what they are because of nature. A man and a woman joined in union together from the earliest times for procreation, to carry on the species or the village or the city, state, whatever it was. That's the way it's always worked before, because that's the way biology works. A man/man relationship and a woman/woman relationship is against that, you know. It's not what, I'll say, we're hard wired to do, so in the general sense that's not going to promote a stable society.

Whereas promoting marriage within the Chickasaw Nation meant acknowledging a nuanced, matrilineal heritage differing from dominant conceptions of marriage in the United States, the debate over same-sex marriage in the Cherokee Nation facilitated boundary work to embrace a presumptive heterosexuality. Todd Hembree, in discussing family formation in "villages and clans," relied on biological explanations to assert a universal heterosexuality. The legal case itself failed to offer any evidence of differences between hegemonic understandings of marriage and the Cherokee matrifocal clan system, which once authorized women's power over their homeland and community agriculture. Embracing this ideology meant ignoring the history under which U.S. intervention historically "educated" American Indians to emulate the dominant Euro-American family system of property ownership and male headship.

I asked Todd Hembree about anthropological studies of the "berdache," the historical name given by European invaders for American Indians who did not act according to expectations of their gender.[51] Anthropologists who study the malleability of gender among Native Americans have largely abandoned the word "berdache," which is now seen as derogatory, and have replaced it with the word "two-spirit." Recently, the two-spirit idea has also inspired a movement among lesbian, gay, bisexual, and transgender Native Americans to see it "as integral to Indigenous struggles for decolonization, self-determination, and cultural continuance."[52] Hembree told me that he was not familiar with this phenomenon in the Cherokee culture. He asserted, "I've had this conversation with [Samuel Crittenden] about whether this is part of our culture [two-spirit]. I'll say I don't believe it is. You know, it might be some other Native American tribes but it sure ain't ours. Now, I know the heck it wasn't our culture in 1892." Hembree's skepticism seems partially justified. The Two-Spirit/Queer scholar and activist Qwo-Li Driskill states, "I've encountered very little reference to Cherokee Two-Spirit people in historical accounts, though such references do exist."[53] S/he asserts that much of the knowledge is held by traditional people and not recorded.

Uncovering the knowledge of traditions that are now called two-spirit raises particular challenges in how to assess accounts that were written from the colonizers' perspectives. The anthropologist Will Roscoe begins his book on the third and fourth genders among Native Americans with a quote from Edwin T. Deng, a fur trader in Montana, who described the Crow in 1833: "Most civilized communities have but two genders, the masculine and feminine. But strange to say, these people have a neuter. Strange county this, where males assume the dress and perform the duties of females, while women turn men and mate with their own sex."[54] By all accounts, there is little doubt that these practices became a target of colonial violence, from the Spanish invasion onward. According to Driskill:

> When European invaders and missionaries began toppling Cherokee gender roles, all of *duyuktv* [a Cherokee word meaning "the right way"] was disrupted. . . . Through violent enforcement of patriarchy, gender relationships made a dramatic shift. Rather than seeing the roles of men and women as always in *duyuktv*, Christian European patriarchy enforced ideas of male supremacy, rigid gender categories, and sexuality as something to be suppressed and controlled.[55]

From this reading, traditional gender and sexual practices among American Indians cannot be understood apart from U.S. intervention and regulation of political identity. The two are intermeshed in arguments surrounding what counts as traditional Cherokee practice concerning marriage, gender, and sexuality.

Just as Todd Hembree mixes together tradition and contemporary understandings of Cherokee culture to defend his stance on marriage, Kathy and Dawn's legal case also refers a combination of these in favor of their marriage. One pleading said of the opposing party: "Petitioner's claims are rooted in cultural and historic ignorance and an ethic [*sic*] bias that seeks to erode an already fragile remnant of a once brilliant culture that embraced freedom of choice for the individual in all aspects of his or her personal life."[56] Referring to the "freedom of choice for the individual" suggests the philosophical ideal of freedom and democracy dominant among Western thinkers such as John Stuart Mill and Alexis de Tocqueville. Such phrasing suggests the fraught relationship between ideas of Cherokee tradition and contemporary political discourse.

During our interview, Kathy explained how the case shaped her perspective on being Cherokee. First, she expressed the couple's surprise at the turn of events:

> Our life has been so disrupted. I don't know; we were so naïve. We had no idea it would be like this. With the marriage certificate, we just thought, "We've bought some marriage certificate, get married and it would be done." In our heads, it wasn't going to be a big deal. It was, "Okay. Well if they accept it, then we'll do it, get married." I don't think we realized exactly what we just did.

Kathy and Dawn hadn't seen themselves as activists, and Kathy described being angered by accounts that described them as seeking political gain to challenge the Cherokee constitution. She mentioned a quote from Todd Hembree in a newspaper article:

> Todd Hembree said that we did it for going against Chad Smith in the Cherokee Nation. Honest to God, I didn't know the man's name until all of this. I didn't know anything about the politics. And I think I've taken a lot of the political knowledge that I've gotten from the Cherokee Nation and I've learned a lot and I've been very thankful for that. If nothing else comes out of it, I know a bit more about what goes on.

Kathy remarked that one of the things she learned was how the Cherokee officials "buddied up" to the Oklahoma government. She called attention to the tension between sovereignty and the laws of the state: "The whole point of being a sovereign Nation is to have your traditional ways and to carry out your historical culture and ceremony that the state will overlook." As is clear from the discursive language involved in the case, however, the influence of U.S. imperial power on the Nation has had a long and complex history that accentuates the difficulty in establishing what constitutes tradition. Dawn and Kathy's marriage brought this tension to the foreground in a way that also illuminates the colonizing power of marriage ideology.

Marriage promotion among American Indians made visible the boundaries of race in normative understandings of marriage. For Native American leaders who supported marriage promotion, including the Commissioner of the Administration for Native Americans, Quanah Crossland Stamps, who was a member of the Cherokee Nation, race was prominent in their arguments about the history of European colonialism, white American hegemony, and the overall genocide of Native Americans. They recognized that Native American families differ from the "traditional" Euro-American nuclear family that was once dominant among Euro-American societies. However, when same-sex marriage became the issue for the Cherokee Nation, officials used language that relegated race to the background. Instead, they stressed the universality of marriage and its roots in biology and nature, eschewing more nuanced understandings of its matrifocal roots. Thus, the debate over the meaning and place of marriage in Native societies cannot be understood outside of the social conditions of imperialism that have shaped tradition and memory. These dynamics point to the inherent colonizing power of marriage ideology, which organizes knowledge about American society based on its foundation in the nuclear family and its ability to subjugate any alternative.

Conclusion

The Power of the "M-Word"

Same-sex marriage would enshrine in law a public judgment that the desire of adults for families of choice outweighs the need of children for mothers and fathers. It would give sanction and approval to the creation of a motherless or fatherless family as a deliberately chosen "good." It would mean the law was neutral as to whether children had mothers and fathers. Motherless and fatherless families would be deemed just fine.

—Maggie Gallagher, "What Is Marriage For?"[1]

Yessiree, family values are hot! Capitalism is cool! Seven-grain bread is so yesterday, and red meat is back! . . .

Today Americans are consciously, deliberately embracing ideas about sex, marriage, children, and the American dream that are coalescing into a viable—though admittedly much altered—sort of bourgeois normality. What is emerging is a vital, optimistic, family-centered, entrepreneurial, and yes, morally thoughtful citizenry.

—Kay Hymowitz, *Marriage and Caste in America*[2]

For over a decade, same-sex marriage has been a contentious issue in the United States, marked by contending ballot initiatives, legislation, and lawsuits to legalize or ban it. California exemplifies this factiousness. The Supreme Court of California ruled in 2008 that its law banning same-sex marriage was unconstitutional, but a referendum in November—Proposition 8—passed and restored it. After withstanding a challenge in the state Supreme Court, a federal judge found the ban unconstitutional in a ruling that will likely move its way up to the United States Supreme Court. In the federal lawsuit, *Kristin M. Perry v. Arnold Schwarzenegger*, the marriage advocate David Blankenhorn served as one of two key witnesses for proponents of Proposition 8 to argue that redefining marriage to encompass same-sex relationships would be harmful to society.

For Blankenhorn, legalizing same-sex marriage would weaken the institution. In an op-ed article for the *Los Angeles Times*, he explains:

> Every child being raised by gay or lesbian couples will be denied his [*sic*] birthright to both parents who made him. Every single one. Moreover, losing that right will not be a consequence of something that at least most of us view as tragic, such as a marriage that didn't last, or an unexpected pregnancy where the father-to-be has no intention of sticking around. On the contrary, in the case of same-sex marriage and the children of those unions, it will be explained to everyone, including the children, that something wonderful has happened![3]

In arguing for the importance of biological parents in the court case, Blankenhorn relied on studies that compare children raised by married, biological parents with those raised by unmarried mothers, stepfamilies and cohabiting parents (in Blankenhorn's view, the latter constitute a tragedy). Judge Vaughn R. Walker ultimately determined Blankenhorn's testimony to be inadmissible, because Blankenhorn's investigation into marriage was not grounded in the "intellectual rigor" expected of social scientists.[4] Moreover, the judge determined Blankenhorn's conclusion that married biological parents offer a superior family form over married nonbiological parents to be invalid as the evidence he presented did not compare biological to nonbiological parents. According to Judge Walker, it may be true that "parents' marital status may affect child outcomes," but it does not follow that the correlation is grounded in biology.[5]

Even as Blankenhorn's testimony was discredited in the California federal trial, his reasoning exemplifies a dominant cultural repertoire of marriage promotion: marriage is the best institution for heterosexual parents to raise children and thus needs to be strengthened and prioritized in law and public policy. Some marriage advocates would likely disagree with Blankenhorn's argument in favor of biological parenting; however, most would agree with its basic ideology that prioritizes heterosexual parenting (while a few might support marriage as the best institution for same-sex parenting) and decries the tragedy of unwed childbearing and divorce in weakening the institution and creating havoc on American society. In his decision, Judge Walker also confirmed the importance of marriage in public policy and to stabilize American society: "The state regulates marriage because marriage creates stable households, which in turn form the basis of a *stable, governable populace*."[6]

The federal court decision is an important step in combating discrimination against lesbians and gay men, and it appropriately points to the prejudice of efforts to ban same-sex marriage that enable stigma. Judge Walker draws on evidence of how these bans perpetuate the inferiority of same-sex relationships. However, the decision also suggests the inferiority of intimate relationships among the nonmarried, and no mention is made of the stigma or stereotypes that the unmarried face. In fact, marriage is addressed as the highest form of relationship, "the definitive expression of love and commitment in the United States."[7] Claims about the normative superiority of marriage defend a symbolic boundary against the "harms" of illegitimacy and family pathology often attributed to single-mother and African American families. In the field of poverty research, there has been general avoidance of cultural analyses that rely on a culture-of-poverty model to "blame the victims" for their problems.[8] Marriage advocates, however, revisit this theoretical orientation. Research and policy recommendations draw on the culture-of-poverty thesis in their interpretation of survey-research findings to "prove" that high out-of-wedlock birth and divorce rates are causing social problems such as poverty. Anxiety over heterosexual marriage and its "problems" (unwed childbearing, cohabitation, and divorce) has heightened even as divorce rates stabilized in the early 1980s and have since declined. More important, perhaps, are the changing attitudes that are driving shifts in family life.[9] It is no surprise then that this renewed focus occurs during a period that has witnessed the expansive growth in mobilizations seeking to legalize or to ban same-sex marriage.

In this book, I have shed light on the practices, ideologies, and social consequences of boundary work that promotes "lifelong, internally stratified marriage" (LISM) as a standard by which to judge all heterosexual and nonheterosexual relationships.[10] Putting critical heterosexual studies and cultural sociology in conversation, this book forges a path to uncover the relationships among sexuality, culture, and poverty in creating sexual and social inequalities, and to consider how relying on an assumption of universal heterosexuality impacts policies and practices to create nonheterosexual *and* heterosexual outsiders. Rather than rely on social-psychological explanations of distinctions between "us" and "them," this study offers an examination of the structural deployment of practices and ideologies that connect to broader angst over a shared American identity. It further examines the ways culture shapes decision making and its effects on the poor and on nonheterosexuals. Mario Luis Small, David J. Harding, and Michèle Lamont clarify the need for sociologists to study culture and poverty to inform public policy: "Both the discourse and the policy reflect deeply held (if often inconsistent) assumptions about the goals of policy and especially about work, responsibility, service, agency, 'deservingness,' and the structure of opportunity."[11] A cultural analysis is important to explaining the anxiety driving policy decisions such as pro-marriage efforts to transform cultural attitudes. In the following, I offer concluding remarks on the boundary work animating marriage promotion politics to reinforce the outsider status of nonheterosexuals and to assimilate heterosexual "others" into American society.

Marital Citizenship in America
Same-Sex Marriage, Doing Gender, and (In)visibility

For marriage advocates, heterosexual marriage is foundational to American identity and society. On the one hand, my research in Oklahoma uncovered the mechanisms that maintain the invisibility of sexual and gender outlaws through an assumption of universal heterosexuality. On the other, I found that sexual and gender transformations of the past few decades produce "paradoxes of visibility." In *Freaks Talk Back*, Joshua Gamson describes the paradoxes of visibility in the talk shows of the 1990s when queers and their relationships were made public in a simultaneously "scandalizing and normalizing" manner.[12] Such tensions also occur in arenas other than pop culture, as is the case of state and local efforts to strengthen marriage that rely on an assumption of marital heterosexuality. The workshops teach about the importance of hierarchical gender differences for "normal" relationships, a philosophy haunted by the specter of same-sex relations.[13] The focus on gender hierarchy heightened the sexual outsider status of lesbians and gay men, and this was especially uncomfortable when workshops included a lesbian couple. With the increasing visibility of lesbians and gay men, and the spotlight this visibility has illuminated on their lack of citizen rights, the project of marriage promotion has been forced to grapple with the question of offering services to sexual (and marital) outsiders.

Conservative Christians populate one end of the marriage promotion spectrum in their efforts to protect their values against a globalizing world where national borders are porous and sexual boundaries are breaking down. They believe that America was founded on the Judeo-Christian principle of a one-man, one-woman marriage. In Oklahoma, the campaign against same-sex marriage relied on a moral boundary to mark marriage as essential to citizenship. Politicians and religious leaders portrayed lesbians and gay men to be "other" to the principles of American democracy; they are "radical activists" or even "family terrorists" who seek to break down the secure boundaries of marriage. Similar to the way that Mormons were represented as "metaphorically nonwhite" in American society due to the "barbarism" of polygamy, depictions of homosexual "radical activists" draw on racialized images of Muslim terrorists who are viewed as seeking to destroy America.[14] Conservative Christians also draw on a culture-of-poverty model to include same-sex marriage as part of a broader cultural and global phenomenon of family "pathology" that relates to racial images of African American and African societies.

Political conservatives and the religious right dedicate great effort to ensure that lesbians and gay men, and more importantly their relationships, remain unrecognized in law and public policy. They rally for legislation that defines marriage as between one man and one woman and prohibits offering legal benefits to partners within nonmarital relationships. In Oklahoma, these efforts were very successful; 76 percent of voters were in favor of a constitutional amendment to ban same-sex marriage. Conservative Christians rely on commonsense understandings of marriage and American identity to make a case for the "outrage" of same-sex marriage.[15] Marital heterosexuality proves to be an important dividing line, such as in the case of the Cherokee marriage panic. When a Cherokee lesbian couple received a marriage license from the Nation, the Cherokee Tribal Council followed the path of antilesbian and gay initiatives by amending their code to define marriage as between one man and one woman. Similar to the religious right, tribal leaders argued that there is a traditional concept of marriage within the Cherokee Nation that is universal and based on the concept of procreation. Such renderings ignore complex understandings of clan and kinship systems in "traditional" Cherokee culture that are matriarchal and include a history of polygamy and divorce.

Campaigns against same-sex marriage include a defensive element that speaks to the symbolic power of the language of tolerance. In the campaign against same-sex marriage, local and national news coverage provided images that often humanized the plight of gay and lesbian couples. Several moderate evangelical pastors and religious leaders I talked to were swayed by the debate to rethink their ideas about legal benefits in favor of civil unions. A year before, they had not considered it. In the video discussed in chapter 1 that was produced by the Oklahoma Family Policy Council, state senator James A. Williamson asks whether same-sex marriage can be thought of as "a civil rights issue." His answer: "There is no civil right to deny children a mother or a father." One might wonder, in a state where the majority of the population is against legalizing same-sex marriage, why engage the idea of civil rights at all, even if the goal is to cast doubt on it? Williamson later explains: "Although most Christians agree that same-sex marriage is in conflict with the word of God, some Christians claim that we have no business pushing our views of morality on everyone else. The fact is Judeo-Christian values have always been the basis for American law and culture." While the statement about pushing morality does not directly reference rights, it indirectly speaks to dominant American ideals of freedom and equality. This video, directed specifically to Christians, offers a glimpse into the increasing need to defend what many see as intolerant attitudes and policies toward lesbians and gay men. Attitudes are slowly shifting even in the heartland.

Survey data on public opinion concerning lesbian and gay issues since the 1970s point to significant increases in tolerance toward—and even approval of—lesbian and gay rights.[16] A recent study by Robert Andersen and Tina Fetner found that, unlike other shifts in attitudes that are generally based on generational differences, attitudes toward homosexuality have become increasingly more tolerant among all age groups in the past two decades. In her insightful book *How the Religious Right Shaped Lesbian and Gay Activism*, Fetner exposes the ineffectiveness of the religious right in shifting public opinion, even in a period of increased activism against lesbian and gay rights during the 1990s.[17] It was in this decade that attitudes began to shift toward more tolerance. One major takeaway point is that, despite the greater size and superior resources of the religious right, its focus on fighting against lesbian and gay rights has ironically strengthened the lesbian and gay movement and *enabled* more national visibility to foster shifting attitudes in favor of equal rights.

Paradoxes of visibility are also prevalent in the marriage initiative. In 2004, the debate over same-sex marriage dominated public attention, and the initiative did its best to steer clear of the issue. As Mary Myrick expressed, it is the state's job, and not the initiative's, to define marriage. However, the definition of marriage is disputed not only due to the issue of same-sex relations but also to its transformed place in the life script of heterosexuals. The decline of marriage and women's increased workforce participation during the past forty years has challenged traditional norms that once created social cohesion through gender hierarchy and implicit heterosexuality. Participants in these workshops represent a variety of family formations, including cohabiting couples, second and third marriages, singles, and so on. However, instructors teach as if all participants are married or will marry, rendering other possibilities invisible. Instructors rehearse dominant scripts on gender polarity concerning expectations of men's and women's "nature" in marriage. Both the training and workshops I attended revisited ideas on hierarchical relationships between men and women that are based on cultural conceptions of men as rational (strong) and women as emotional (weak). These performances provide simple answers to complex negotiations that women and men face as they juggle tight work schedules along with raising children and try to manage households that often bring children from previous marriages or relationships. The gendered performances teach that wives need to allow "men to be men" and that husbands need to cater to their wives' emotional needs.

The American marriage movement presents a public image of favoring gender equality. For example, its Statement of Principles asserts: "Support for marriage, we emphasize, does not require turning back the clock on desirable social change, promoting male tyranny, or tolerating domestic violence." In a more specific declaration, the Institute for American Values and the Institute for Marriage and Public Policy, two key organizations of the marriage movement, issued a position statement in 2006 that declares, "We are deeply committed to the moral principle of equal regard between men and women, and of marriage reforms that are consistent with the equal dignity of both genders."[18] In contrast to this public image, the sociologist Kathleen Hull found a pattern similar to my findings of emphasizing polarity and hierarchy. She employed a critical discourse analysis of presentations, reports, and position statements of the movement between 2001 and 2006, and found that the movement presents women to be more "nurturant, vulnerable, dependent, needy, feelings-focused, passive, and marriage-minded. Men are active, protective, achievement-oriented, sexual, and in need of the civilizing influences of wives and marriage."[19] As Hull explains, the leadership's claim of embracing gender equality cannot be taken at face value because so much of the movement literature and the language of its leaders expresses the importance of gender hierarchy and male privilege in marriage. At the same time, she asserts, the claims of equality should not be seen just as lip service. Movement leaders may believe their assertions of support for gender equality. The same, I believe, can be said of the marriage initiative in Oklahoma, where trainers and workshop leaders may not specifically advocate gender hierarchy (though some may), but the instruction espouses male privilege.

The boundary work in marriage workshops also reveals a paradox of visibility for lesbians and gay men. By teaching about the "opposite" sexes, marriage workshops seek to implement self-monitoring practices and carry the assumption that "good" citizens will act according to dominant gender norms, strengthening the border of heterosexual marriage against those who stand outside the one-man, one-woman box. However, this boundary is permeable, such as the case of the two lesbian couples who challenged the ideology of marital heterosexuality. The performance of gendered binaries intrinsic to institutionalized heterosexuality, a generally seamless aspect of the marriage workshops I attended, was rendered more palpable and transparent. Even while the relationships of the lesbians were disregarded, their presence created an unforeseen disruption. From the framework of heterosexual marriage ideology, the lesbians were "other" than heterosexual women (not-women) in the context of a marriage class, and the gendered prescriptions made them sexual *and* gender outsiders. Simultaneously, their presence offered a rare opportunity to bring together heterosexuals and nonheterosexuals in an equalizing environment to learn better skills of communication. All of the couples I interviewed, even those who had the strongest beliefs against homosexuality, recognized that the lesbian couples "had needs too." This was probably one of the few environments in the state, and anywhere else for that matter, with the potential to mix together heterosexual and nonheterosexual couples in an intimate and prolonged setting of relationship enrichment, albeit in a very limited manner. For heterosexuals, such exposure might challenge stereotypes and even change minds.

Lastly, marriage education in secondary schools reveals paradoxes of visibility for nonheterosexual students. Kashawn, an African American, lesbian student who was enrolled in a high school family and consumer science course, challenged the gendered and heterosexual assumptions of heterosexual marriage ideology that animated the curriculum by coming out early in the class. Her vocal presence often troubled the easy relationship of heterosexuality, home, and nation that the teacher wove into her instruction as her peers struggled to include her in the class. However, her attendance as a student with little power to change the terms of the classroom also meant an uneasy invisibility where Kashawn was forced to choose between being a "guy" or a "girl" for the purpose of class exercises. As students began to plan the marriage game, Kashawn was compelled to participate as a heterosexual. Ultimately, the boundary work that allowed Kashawn to negotiate her sexual identity in the classroom led to a reinstatement of the divide that situated her as an outsider.

The dominant frame of marital heterosexuality in the workshops and in other arenas like high school classrooms compels assimilation and accommodation by participants, a dynamic that expressly excludes nonheterosexual outsiders. In terms of sexual citizenship, heterosexual marriage ideology is a powerful tool to mark exclusion, and even as the paradoxes of visibility offer openings for inclusion, marital heterosexuality ultimately reinforces a boundary that becomes a form of social closure. A similar dynamic is at play in the case of the boundary work prevalent in marriage promotion that seeks not to exclude but to incorporate marginalized heterosexual women and men into the norm of middle-class marriage and family.

Race and Class Boundary Work

Activism to secure marriage's borders is akin to activism to defend the nation's borders as a way to safeguard America's future. Nancy Cott has theorized the relationship between nation-building and marriage: "Where citizenship comes along with being born on the nation's soil as it does here, marriage policy underlies national belonging and the cohesion of the whole."[20] The symbol of marriage has become a foothold to resist the gale of diverse perspectives and values that threaten a particular configuration of American identity. As Arlene Stein found in her study of a small town's battle over sex, faith, and civil rights, many seek to fend off the enormous economic and cultural changes that are creating a multicultural society.[21] One place Americans look to find traction is by embracing an idealized, nostalgic family to create distance from the messiness of the families "we live with."[22] Representations and ideals of family life seek to reinvent a mythical American identity that relies on conceptions of the nuclear family as timeless and universal. Marriage advocates draw on this marriage ideology as a way to assimilate poor single mothers and other outsiders into middle-class, American values.

Significant shifts in family transformation where the majority of white, middle-class women delay marriage and childbearing, marry in smaller numbers, and work outside the home have created an economic and racial divide, a "marriage gap" between the rich and the poor. Increasing numbers of white, Latino/a, and African American children are born outside marriage. For the marriage movement, the professed goal is to reduce this gap. As Kay Hymowitz puts it, "It is hard to see how our two Americas can become one without more low-income men and women making their way to the altar."[23] For marriage advocates, marriage is essentially about instilling American, middle-class, and heterosexual values. Hymowitz continues:

Traditional marriage gives young people a map of life that takes them step by step from childhood to adolescence to college or other work training—which might well include postgraduate education—to the workplace, to marriage, and only then to childbearing. A marriage orientation also requires a young woman to consider the question of what man will become her husband and the father of her children as a major, if not *the* major, decision in her life.[24]

She suggests that poor young women should follow the life script of their middle-class counterparts, which would lead to greater economic success. Such reasoning reflects the "new politics of poverty" of the past decades that concentrates on individual behavior and tends to ignore the numerous structural barriers that poor women face, even if they do marry.[25] This form of antipoverty thinking is part of a broader market fundamentalist ideology that has ended the entitlement of cash assistance provided by welfare to focus on individual responsibility. Implicit to this ideology is the idea of teaching low-income women to be accountable, to bear children after marriage, and to improve their children's lives by marrying.

American identity adheres to the core belief that economic success or misfortune is the sole responsibility of the individual. This philosophy of individualism is central to free-market capitalist ideology. Whereas scholars have often turned to communitarian ideals of marital commitment to counter free-market ideology, I argue that, rather than a haven from the messiness of public life, marriage ideology itself promotes radical individualism.[26] Drawing on nostalgia for families of the past, marriage advocates justify policies to promote marriage as the best way to stay out of poverty, placing the responsibility on the individual to marry as a poverty cure. This punitive individualism, and the lack of an alternative narrative in the American ethos, enables coalitions of various stripes (conservative Christians, economic conservatives, and centrist liberals) to join together in promoting marriage. In this way, marriage ideology connects America's market fundamentalist corporate culture with moral/religious traditions.

Thus, promoting integration into the heterosexual, married family creates and reinforces a divide that can and will perpetuate social inequality. In Oklahoma, a focus on behavior and culture facilitates the diversion of funds from needy families to focus more on middle-class marriages. Given the stated desire to reduce the marriage gap, it appears ironic that the majority of services offered by the marriage initiative go to the middle-class. This outcome results from the leadership's focus on involving churches and combating the divorce rate. One might argue that reducing divorce can ameliorate its negative economic impact on women as they are on average more impoverished after divorce than are men. However, such reasoning fails in the face of the material consequences of a strategy that sustains or even widens the marriage gap. Those who live in very poor neighborhoods are the least likely to have access to the free marriage-initiative activities. In contrast, white, middle-class couples predominantly populate the large Sweethearts Weekends (now called "Forever, For Real"), and most have the financial resources to pay. The same pattern is present in the smaller classes for the general population. Undoubtedly, the marriage initiative has made efforts to get services to low-income individuals, such as in the case of the class taught by George Young to the women from the Oklahoma housing project, and through social service programs. The "Family Expectations" program for unmarried couples on Medicaid with a new baby, which began after I left Oklahoma, means more of the services going in this direction. However, this program is funded by a separate federal grant and thus is not part of the roughly $3 million of state funds spent on the marriage initiative per year (see the below section—"Policy Implications"—for more discussion).

Why hasn't the marriage initiative prioritized the Temporary Assistance to Needy Families (TANF) population, especially because TANF money is being used to fund it? I never received a good answer to this question in my interviews with marriage initiative leaders. Some reasoned that funds for the marriage initiative only represent a small fraction of the overall TANF budget. Yet, as the director of the Oklahoma Department of Human Services (OKDHS) told me, the benefits going to women on public assistance in Oklahoma will not raise them out of poverty. In this light, it seems especially punitive to divert funds away from poor women to offer free marriage classes to the general population. Others argued that Oklahoma's high divorce rate necessitated this strategy. Again, this doesn't answer the question of why TANF funds? The logic of redistributing resources from the poor to the middle class follows a general shift that occurred with the passage of welfare reform to "expand the former entitlement program to serve non-needy families."[27] Thus, diverting scarce resources to provide services to the general population was sanctioned in the 1996 Welfare Reform Law and in the 2005 Deficit Reduction Act.

Offering benefits to the middle class over the less privileged is true of many entitlements in the United States such as housing subsidies through mortgage-interest deductions. In contrast, very little funding is bestowed on affordable housing to low-income individuals. The poor, and especially poor single mothers, are often characterized as being personally responsible for their poverty. Herein is the problem with endeavoring to assimilate low-income single mothers into middle-class marriages. The structural constraints on poor women are made invisible when poverty is seen as a personal choice attributed to marrying. Even the idea of "marriage-plus"—focusing on marriage promotion *and* socioeconomic supports—does not fend off the erasure that marriage as an antipoverty strategy has on the numerous barriers poor single mothers face. The history of racism in this country, for one, is made invisible. Kay Hymowitz offers a middle-class life script that she believes poor women could take if they didn't have children outside marriage. While it is true that nonmarital childbearing makes such a trajectory more difficult, most poor women do not have the economic, cultural, or educational resources that offer a simple route to college and a highly paid job.

Race also plays an important factor in who receives services. Even though the poverty rates are higher in Oklahoma among African Americans, Latinos, and Native Americans (as in the rest of the nation), these groups are not prioritized to receive free marriage education classes. National leaders have focused on race as an important dividing line in perpetuating poverty and what Daniel Patrick Moynihan called the "tangle of pathology" of single-mother black families that perpetuates "delinquency, joblessness, school failure, crime, and fatherlessness."[28] Leaders of marriage promotion like to say that Moynihan was right. Ron Haskins, a senior fellow at the Brookings Institution, sums up this perspective: "Today, in part because of the continuing demise of married-couple families, the average black is far behind the average white in educational achievement, employment rates, and earnings; blacks also have much higher crime and incarceration rates."[29] While most social scientists view such causal statements as suspect, it is again surprising, given the angst expressed by many marriage promotion leaders concerning the state of racial minority families, that these have not been more of a priority for on-the-ground services and activities. While the marriage initiative in Oklahoma claims on its website to develop "relationships with organizations that provide educational opportunities to Hispanic [*sic*] families" and "tribal groups to provide workshops to Native American families through appropriate social service programs," these efforts are limited to the willingness of organizations to take the lead in disseminating services.[30]

The widening marriage gap acts additionally as a symbolic boundary. For example, funding a statewide initiative that incorporates mostly white, middle-class couples reinforces the idea that marriage is more important to this population. Ideologically, the marriage cure seeks to assimilate poor women into the middle class through marriage; however, in Oklahoma, energy and resources spent on getting services to the general population sustain the marriage gap, which is further upheld by blurring the symbolic boundary between church and state. Getting religious leaders involved in disseminating a marriage message has been a top priority, and other statewide and community marriage initiatives are seeking to disseminate services through churches, religious organizations, and nonreligious environments with a Christian moral or faith message. A 2008 report discusses the "one percent solution" in which Ohio, Texas, and Utah have dedicated 1 percent of TANF funds to marriage-related initiatives. In addition, ten states— Alabama, Arizona, Colorado, Georgia, Louisiana, Michigan, New Mexico, New York, Oklahoma, and Virginia—have dedicated significant TANF funds to marriage-related activities, offer marriage services to the general population, and have targeted religious groups to help disseminate the services.[31] Again, this often means a focus on those affiliated to Protestant and Catholic churches with predominantly white, middle-class congregations, contradicting the purported goal of marriage promotion to increase the marital citizenship of poor individuals.

Examining such boundary work sheds light on how inequality is produced through symbolic language—in this case, the cultural need to strengthen marriage—that solidifies ideas of marriage along the lines of race and class. Boundary work reinforces the idea that marriage is essential to American identity and justifies the practice of promoting it in the population that is least likely to marry. Thus, while marriage education classes are offered as a free service to the public, they are *required* of welfare clients in their weeklong orientation that is a prerequisite to receiving TANF benefits or as part of their GED instruction. Targeting marriage education to the specific population of TANF clients is not widespread in Oklahoma, but in the cases where it occurs TANF clients expressed their cognizance of the motivating philosophy. Several told of frustration with the idea that their impoverished circumstances are read as a failure to marry or to remain married. As has been the case in the history of the American welfare system where discriminatory eligibility requirements demanded "moral fitness," there is a punitive element in mandating participation in relationship classes. Moreover, it offers a model to praise poor single mothers who may have fewer barriers and are able to marry, while it further demonizes those women who are the most disadvantaged. Again, boundary work is at play in defining the "bad behavior" of single mothers who need instruction on the fundamentals of relationships. The same dynamic is at play in secondary schools where racial minority and marginalized students tend to be tracked into family and consumer science courses that incorporate marriage education. Students on a college-prep track do not often take these classes and do not receive this instruction, although they might also benefit from learning communication skills.

Similar to the paradoxes of visibility, this research has shown that efforts to strengthen a marriage border are fraught with contradictions that, in small ways, unravel the efforts being made, as witnessed by the resistance to marriage promotion that instructors and recipients employ. Social workers and instructors who teach TANF clients recognize that a message about marriage is not of benefit to poor women who are seeking to better their own and their children's lives by moving forward with education, gaining skills, and seeking work. Instead of focusing on relationship skills in marriage, these instructors teach about building better communication with children, with bosses, and in other personal relationships. While this resistance doesn't challenge the symbolic boundary work of the national project that promotes a marriage-cure ideology, it does empower women in their everyday lives to strengthen relationships. On-the-ground practices of these instructors also resist the overall premise of marriage promotion as a form of marital citizenship by placing importance on the extant relationships in poor women's lives instead of on marriage as the key to the American dream. In cases where instructors did teach about marital citizenship, a number of TANF clients vociferously protested.

Attempts to promote marriage among Native Americans offers another window into the conflict between resistance and acceptance of normative understandings of marital citizenship. In the history of the United States, U.S. officials embraced an "American" vision of marriage for the Indian population that sought to whiten them as patriotic citizens. In contemporary attempts of marriage promotion, there is general resistance to efforts to impose this ideology of marriage. Native American leaders, including the U.S. Commissioner of the Administration for Native Americans, point to the relationship of an American understanding of marriage and the history of European colonialism, white American hegemony, and the overall genocide of Native Americans. They advance the idea that Native American families differ from the ideal of the "traditional" Euro-American nuclear family. Resistance to such assimilation highlights tensions in the production of marital citizenship and its relationship to inequality.

In sum, this ethnography shines light on the relationship between the boundary work of marriage promotion and conditions of social inequality in the United States. I have sought to unravel the complex ideological components of marriage promotion that include religiously based family values, the culture-of-poverty thesis, neoliberal Horatio-Alger heroism, and national identity. Linked together into an ideology of marriage, this way of knowing produces contradictory and unexpected social consequences that are at times at odds with the goals of marriage promotion. What do these findings mean to policies that use federal and state funds to promote marriage with a goal of strengthening society? I argue that the very premise of such marriage policies—the ideal of promoting one form of marriage—produces a symbolic boundary that is fundamentally discriminatory. Thus, the project of marriage promotion conflicts with the ideals of economic and social justice that are important movements in the United States. In this next section, I turn to the implications of these findings for social policy.

Policy Implications: Marriage Promotion and Family Formation

In 2010, Mathematica Policy Research issued a report on its evaluation project of eight Building Strong Families (BSF) programs around the country. The Administration for Children and Families contracted Mathematica as part of its federal Healthy Marriage Initiative to develop and test the effectiveness of marriage education to improve the relationship quality and increase the likelihood of marriage for unwed couples who are expecting a child or who have just had a baby. A little over five thousand couples were randomly assigned to either a BSF group that participated in the program or a control group that did not. Measuring the overall impact on couples fifteen months after they applied for the program (in terms of the stability and quality of the relationship), the evaluation did *not* find any significant difference in BSF programs to help couples stay together or get married, nor did these programs improve relationship quality.[32] Cheryl Wetzstein, a *Washington Times* journalist and a strong advocate of marriage promotion, wrote in her column that "a cloud has been forming on the horizon for the marriage-ed movement." She quotes Benjamin Karney and Thomas Bradbury, psychology professors at the University of California at Los Angeles, who assess the report: "Asking couples who are already spread thin to take on new tasks, even to improve their relationships and parenting, may be unreasonable." They conclude: "Emerging evidence suggests that the quality of couples' intimate relationships is powerfully constrained by the environments in which couples live."[33]

Wetzstein declares that, even with this "crushing blow" to marriage education, there is one bright spot: Oklahoma! Its BSF project—Family Expectations—was the only program to have a positive impact on whether couples were still romantically involved and the only one to improve relationship quality. Even this good news, however, was countered by another program out of the eight that actually had negative effects on couples' relationships. Couples in the Baltimore BSF program were less likely than the control group couples to remain romantically involved. More significantly, in Oklahoma the BSF program did not affect marriage rates, ultimately one of the main goals of such programs. At the fifteen-month follow-up, 25 percent of both research groups were married. Perhaps these results are not surprising given my ethnographic research on what happens on the ground in implementing pro-marriage programs. Clearly, the most successful classes target predominantly middle-class couples, and workshops for poor single mothers are better received when they don't emphasize marriage.

The words of Benjamin Karney and Thomas Bradbury ring true. Structural constraints directly impact the effectiveness of relationship classes to improve relationships, and promoting marriage in a context where poor single mothers or impoverished couples are struggling to make ends meet is a questionable strategy. In a blog on eHarmonyLabs, Bradbury suggests:

> Alternative approaches to building strong families might devote the same resources toward improving living conditions in lower-income communities. Whatever enables low-income families to manage their lives better should make it easier for them to manage their relationships as well. With greater support, couples who are motivated to be together may find ways to do so, even in the absence of programs that target their relationships directly.[34]

Karney and Bradbury codirect the Relationship Institute at UCLA, which offers "educational programs that are designed and delivered by leading scholars in the study of intimacy, marriage, and the family."[35] Bradbury has also published with Howard Markman and Scott Stanley, both key figures in the marriage movement. Thus, it is particularly significant that Karney and Bradbury offer an analysis of marriage promotion programs for poor couples that sounds similar to the words written back in 2002 by two scholars critical of marriage promotion—Stephanie Coontz and Nancy Folbre—in which they argue that nonmarriage often results from poverty and not the other way around.

There was very little discussion of the findings on the Smart Marriages listserv, but Scott Stanley addressed the BSF evaluation in depth at the 2010 Smart Marriages plenary titled "Research, Innovation, Delivery."[36] Stanley's assessment put a positive spin on the bleak findings in pointing to the history of large federal multimillion-dollar studies that evaluate different kinds of policy initiatives, such as jobs training and fatherhood programs (which he claimed lack great evidence). According to Stanley, the initial story is generally dismal. Thus, Oklahoma stands out as exceptional, because positive outcomes don't usually happen in the initial stages. He went on to focus on what Oklahoma did right—mainly getting people into the seats to get the training—and he said that Oklahoma's strategy is replicable, listing the soundness of its detailed procedures, effective management control, clear incentives and support, and highly structured curriculum. His conclusion seemed directed at Bradbury, stating, "It is *not* tenable to say that we can't help couples who already have a lot of stuff on their backs." What he doesn't mention is the finding that even in Oklahoma couples were no more likely to marry than the control group.

What does this evaluation study mean for policymakers? In some respects, Scott Stanley is correct. While it represents one of the most comprehensive to date on evaluating the effectiveness of marriage programs for low-income, at-risk couples, it is still too early to definitely conclude that teaching about relationships skills is ineffective for helping them stay together. However, and perhaps more importantly, there appears no evidence to suggest that a focus on marriage (i.e., the marriage cure) is beneficial to low-income couples. Arguments in favor of marriage promotion that treat it as a simple social fact—"Getting married and staying married is associated with economic advantages for unwed mothers"—are misleading and potentially harmful for impoverished women who are targeted by these programs (suggesting that economic mobility lies in marriage). Studying workshops on the ground, I found that TANF clients did not respond well to classes that upheld marriage as the golden standard and especially resented being stigmatized for being unmarried. At the macro level, Daniel Lichter and associates who studied whether marriage can be a "panacea" to poverty found little evidence to support the marriage cure. They state, "We have virtually no information about whether marriage *per se* lifts disadvantaged single mothers out of poverty or reduces reliance on welfare income."[37] The demographers Wendy Sigle-Rushton and Sara McLanahan found that single women, even if they were to marry, would continue to have much higher rates of poverty than currently married women due to characteristics—education, health status, and employment—that makes it difficult to attract economically stable marriage partners.[38]

Under the administration of Barack Obama, it at first appeared likely that funding for marriage promotion was on the wane. Congress did not include marriage programs in its funding for TANF from October through December 2010. However, marriage advocates lobbied hard and the programs were partially reinstated in the new extension of the federal budget through September 2011 (at only three-quarters of their previous dollar level—$75 million instead of $100 million). The administration's FY 2011 budget includes $500 million for a new Fatherhood, Marriage, and Families Innovation Fund to provide two equal streams of competitive three-year grants for:

1. State-initiated comprehensive responsible fatherhood initiatives, including those with a marriage component, that rely on strong partnerships with community-based organizations; and
2. State-initiated comprehensive family self-sufficiency demonstrations that seek to improve child and family outcomes by addressing the employment and self-sufficiency needs of parents with serious barriers to self sufficiency, and which may also address the needs of children in families that are "child-only" TANF cases.[39]

As the Obama administration's plans for the new innovation fund became evident, Diane Sollee sent out an emergency post to the Smart Marriage listserv: "TRYING to stay Calm. PLEASE VOTE. Administration's proposed plan for TANF—3/27/10."[40] In her post, she laments, "It's like the M word has been officially tabled and we're back to the old F words—can't talk about or fund Marriage or Marriage Education, only Fatherhood and Family." Marriage advocates seem to have made their voices heard as the ACF website on "Questions and Answers on the Fatherhood, Marriage, and Families Innovation Fund" states clearly that marriage education programs will continue to be funded but it would be only those programs that integrate marriage and fatherhood activities. Rather than funding community-based programs, the new fund will go to states or multistate consortia that network with experienced community-based organizations.

While the attention of the policy debates over marriage promotion focuses on marriage and fatherhood programs for low-income individuals, no one is discussing the issue of states using TANF dollars to fund marriage workshops for those who can afford to pay or how these TANF funds are being spent in general. The marriage initiative in Oklahoma demonstrates the discriminatory implementation of marriage programs that offer services to the middle class using TANF funds meant for "needy families." The language of the new Fatherhood, Marriage, and Families Innovation Fund does prioritize an integrative strategy to encourage fatherhood and marriage programs to "work together, along with other community resources, in efforts to develop more comprehensive approaches that may include assisting parents with employment, child support payment, housing stability, and parenting and relationship skills," which might be implemented at the state level.[41] However, no one in the ACF is discussing this aspect. Moreover, the inclusion of marriage programs in the blueprint for the new fund promises to extend the continued focus on marriage in public policy that draws a line between acceptable and unacceptable families and seeks to cure poverty through an ideal of "one marriage," giving further justification to state programs that do the same. Oklahoma's marriage initiative continues to grow, and Mary Myrick's company, Public Strategies, now has a national presence as it leads in offering technical assistance to the Administration for Children and Families' grantees, the Texas Healthy and Human Services Commission, and several policy research organizations.[42] Thus, the structure of the marriage initiative in Oklahoma is likely to continue to be replicated.

If policies to promote marriage are fundamentally discriminatory, what can be said of programs that focus on teaching *relationship* education (and do not focus on marriage)? I did find limited evidence that a focus on strengthening relationships might positively impact the lives of single, impoverished mothers, because many were receptive to learning communication skills and found them helpful in their personal lives. There is a nascent literature that speaks to the benefits of relationship classes for low-income participants. The Fragile Families and Child Well-being Study examined building relationship skills and found that by increasing male employment, hourly wages, *and* relationship quality, the result would be an increase in the proportion who married from 10 to 15 percent.[43] A study conducted by the Minnesota Family Investment Program found that increased family incomes for TANF clients increased marriage rates among single parents and reduced instability among two-parent families without even introducing relationship skills.[44] Philip and Carolyn Cowan and associates conducted a clinical trial of an intensive program that successfully enhances fathers' engagement with children and defends against declines in relationship satisfaction for married and cohabiting couples. This study, which involved only heterosexual couples, found that longer interventions of sixteen weeks and improved emotional support between the couples were most successful in decreasing parental stress and increasing relationship happiness.[45] There is no reason to think that such interventions would not also benefit lesbian and gay parents.

While relationship-skills instruction may be valuable, I argue against shifting TANF funds to offer relationship skills that might go to other services—

child care, education, job training, health care—as a way to lift women out of poverty. Regarding the public policy goal that seeks to lift impoverished women out of poverty, I concur with Sigle-Rushton and McLanahan (and more recently with Benjamin Karney and Thomas Bradbury) in their assessment that policymakers would do better "to focus on the structural causes of economic disadvantage—low wages and unemployment—than to divert resources to the promotion of marriage."[46] I would add that concentrating resources on the nuts and bolts of poor women's needs certainly is a more effective strategy to impact conditions of inequality. Research that informs marriage promotion policies needs to be more historical and comparative to uncover how marriage ideology informs claims making. The demographers Pamela Smock and Wendy Manning, for example, situate debates over the marriage cure by looking at historic poverty rates that were substantially higher in 1959 than 2000 for both families as a whole and for single parents. They point out that, in a time of rapidly shifting family patterns, there has also been a significant *decrease* in poverty. More expansive analyses can inform how to think about marriage as a social problem. They conclude, "It is important to take a long and broad perspective, rather than focus on narrow slices of time, when evaluating family phenomena, especially family phenomena that are being interpreted and constructed as social problems."[47] Research that compares U.S. policy with other countries is also useful to gain a long and broad perspective and to uncover how other countries deal more equitably with issues of single parenting, cohabitation, and same-sex relationships.[48]

There are limitations to my findings here that are important considerations for policy discussions. I approached this research using the "extended case method," with the goal of constructing theory to discover how the micro-processes of local marriage promotion practices impact on macro-levels of change and inequality.[49] This study, however, takes place in a state renowned for its religious and social conservatism as part of the "Bible Belt." Specifics of the marriage ideology I outline are thus tied to its location in middle America. I have included analyses of marriage movement literature as well as religious right literature to connect these local interpretations to the broader patterns. Another limitation is the focus on a marriage initiative in just one state. A plethora of programs have emerged in the last few years that offer a range of philosophies and activities, many of which are localized as "community marriage initiatives" and are not as expansive as the statewide initiative I studied. Many of these smaller programs concentrate services on low-income populations. Programs across the country utilize a number of curricula, some faith-based and some not, for reaching out to low-income residents and other populations.

Even so, as I have argued throughout this book, the marriage initiative in Oklahoma has been a leader in building the philosophy and implementation of marriage promotion, and many programs and coalitions have used its model in building their own programs. Certainly, statewide initiatives in Ohio, Texas, and other states have. While the California Healthy Marriages Coalition brings together community-based programs, I did some preliminary research in 2003 examining the emergence of the Orange County Marriage Resource Center and found that its initial trajectory was very similar to Oklahoma, with a focus on disseminating services through faith-based organizations and churches. The sociologist Jennifer Randles conducted ethnographic research in a Northern California community-based marriage education program for poor parents funded through an HHS/ACF grant. Her findings substantiate several of my discoveries in Oklahoma. Similar to some of the Oklahoma workshops for TANF clients, these workshops did not prioritize marriage as a poverty cure. In contrast to my findings where instructors focused on relationship skills, however, the classes she attended promoted marriage as an individual good, enhanced by successful coparenting and communication skills. She claims, "What isn't addressed in these classes for poor families or by marriage promotion policy advocates in general, is the fact that poverty tends to undermine poor couple's efforts to marry, not support them."[50] More research of this kind is needed to study the ideological components of these programs on the ground.

While the leaders of the marriage initiative were incredibly enthusiastic about helping people better their relationships to get and stay married, I have shown how these efforts can contribute to perpetuating social inequalities. By studying the ideological components of marriage promotion and its implementation on the ground, I demonstrate that cultural repertoires matter for inequality. In other words, the ideologies and cultural repertoires that motivate marriage promotion have social and economic consequences that cannot be ignored in discussions of policy. From a social justice perspective, the ideological project to uphold the heterosexually married family will do more harm than good. It will no doubt create more unequal families in its attempts to create a hierarchy with marriage at the top. It carries deleterious economic consequences, like using money that could be spent on needy families to offer services to more privileged ones or by offering financial incentives to poor people who marry. As Blankenhorn suggests, marriage advocates are helping to sprout marriage initiatives across the nation, and the "m-word" is increasingly on the public radar screen. The result will likely be more inequality for families across the nation—for gay and lesbian families and for poor women trying to make ends meet. A project to strengthen *families* might offer a more democratic use of government funds. In the end, a *marriage* movement disseminates a message that stigmatizes the nonmarital families "we live *with*" by idealizing an imagined marriage "we live *by*."[51] Americans must find a different way to think about families in the twenty-first century.

Appendix A

Methods

My methodology for studying the politics of marriage in Oklahoma incorporated an "extended case method," in which I first sought to dialogue with participants, and I then worked to embed this dialogue "within a second dialogue between local processes and extralocal forces that in turn can only be comprehended through a third, expanding dialogue of theory with itself."[1] During the first four months, I concentrated on participation in marriage initiative workshops for the general population that I located on the marriage initiative website. I traveled across the state to attend a total of thirty workshops for the general public that were advertised on the marriage initiative's website, including three Sweethearts Weekends (six classes), three six-week workshops (fifteen classes), and twenty-four weekend workshops (twenty-four classes). I also conducted participant observation of a state-sponsored Prevention and Relationship Enhancement Program (PREP) training weekend to discover the method for training volunteers.

In attending workshops for the general population, I approached the workshop leader before the class to tell her or him about my research and to gain permission to participate. During introductions, I would then announce to the participants who I was, the nature of my research, and let them know I could answer questions during the break or after class. Because these workshops were open to the public, I did not seek consent from individuals, and as a participant I shared my views and my background, and I then blended in as part of the class. While couples were the dominant presence in the workshops, sometimes single women and men attended because either they wanted to learn the skills or were there to coach the exercises. I blended in best when the workshops included other single participants.

The first workshop I attended accentuated the challenging dynamics I at times encountered as a researcher. Each workshop leader has her or his own style for presenting the curriculum, and Natalie used a conversational style, such as discussing negative images of marriage on television. I was startled when she abruptly changed the subject to say that she did not even want to talk about what was happening in San Francisco. She then surmised, "That doesn't have anything to do with us." It was the last week of February 2004, not too long after Mayor Gavin Newsom had authorized the city to issue marriage licenses to same-sex couples, a story that splashed across news headlines and had stirred a national debate. Later in the day, she told us that one of the things that really made her laugh was a choir singing the wedding song on television as two gay men were getting married in San Francisco, and she performed it for us in a rather sardonic tone: "We're going to the church, and we're going to get married." At this point, one of the women grimaced in disgust. I felt the blood rush to my face while I quietly looked down at my workbook, feeling conflict in my role as a researcher to not address the homophobia I perceived in this performance.

There were many such moments during my ethnographic research when I felt the need to suppress my opinions that conflicted with the conservative values I encountered. As I attended workshops and expanded my research to other marriage initiative activities, I became a regular presence and was treated as an insider. Most of the time, this worked in my favor as people assumed that I shared their perspectives, providing me the opportunity to understand their motivations and worldview. The leaders of the marriage initiative were very welcoming and were excited to share their efforts to offer an important service to the public. I appreciated their quest to better people's relationships and reduce the pain that comes from divorce. Many of the participants I interviewed attested to the power of the workshops to help couples better their relationship skills. At the same time, I sought to maintain a critical distance from the world I was immersed in to think more broadly about the implications of the politics of marriage. Thus, in this book, I have engaged a reflexive analysis that is inspired by a critical approach to ethnography, a challenge to conventional forms of realist interpretations offered by a purportedly omniscient narrator.[2] My goal, as the political theorist Nancy Fraser has proposed in her conceptualization of critical theory, is to throw light on social processes that obscure power relations, and especially those that generally remain unquestioned as the norm.[3] I question, for example, how representations from the past can organize knowledges today that draw lines between "us" and "them."

After learning that a lesbian couple attended one of the six-week workshops, I made the decision to focus in-depth interviews on participants of this workshop to understand not only motivations for attending but also how they negotiated ideas about gender and sexuality that I found were of central importance to the general instruction. I conducted ten in-depth, semi-structured interviews with participants from this first six-week workshop and eight more with participants from a second workshop that also included a lesbian couple, and two in-depth interviews with workshop leaders (see Appendix B for sample characteristics). I asked questions about individual relationship history, how the respondent had found out about the marriage workshop, what he or she learned, his or her views on the political project of the marriage initiative, and his or her feelings about attending a workshop that included heterosexual and nonheterosexual couples.

My next step in the ethnographic process was to attend more specialized classes. Over a three-month period, I attended workshops that were required of Temporary Assistance to Needy Families (TANF) recipients in one Oklahoma Department of Human Services (OKDHS) office. Altogether, I participated in twenty classes that each comprised five to twenty-five participants. My participation in these workshops was more difficult to negotiate because there was a more mandatory nature to them. Clients had to complete the weeklong orientation to be eligible for benefits. I worried that I would be seen as being connected to the marriage initiative, which might affect the willingness of clients to talk with me. I was able to sidestep these issues to some extent by introducing myself to highlight my outsider status—that I was a graduate student who was visiting from California to do research on the workshops. I also made sure to remain in the "audience" as a participant, and I would often follow the clients outside to chat during breaks while they smoked. Before returning to graduate school, I had worked for a couple years as an adult education teacher for out-of-school youth in Salinas, California, and I was able to share with the clients my past experiences. They generally viewed me as a sympathetic figure and shared with me details of their life histories and struggles. They also spoke to me about their frustrations with the constraints placed on them by welfare reform restrictions. Some had positive and others negative reactions to the PREP Relationship class included in their orientation. At the end of August 2004, I conducted two focus groups with participants during the lunch break. Each focus group lasted an hour. The first included five participants, and the second six. Additionally, I attended a six-week marriage workshop that was held during a class for TANF participants to get their high school equivalency diploma (GED), and at the end of this workshop, I held a focus group that included fifteen participants.

In addition to the TANF classes, I also began attending the Marriage and Family Life classes for high school students that incorporated the *Connections* curriculum. These classes met every day for one hour. I attended fifteen classes at Red Earth High School and thirty-five classes at Monroe High School.[4] I was only able to attend classes at Red Earth High the last month of the spring semester, whereas I began attending classes at Monroe High earlier in the fall semester. I conducted in-depth interviews with teachers from both classes. Finally, toward the end of my time in Oklahoma, I participated in a workshop for employees of the Chickasaw Nation and interviewed the director.

The services to the prison population proved more difficult to access, because observation would require special clearance and the program was fairly new. I was able to interview one married couple who had participated in the workshops in prison and also the chaplain who taught the class. The prisoner's wife visited her husband on a weekly basis for the six-week workshop. This interview focused on the particular issues that arose for a relationship constrained by imprisonment. The obstacles to doing participant observation of services for youth offenders were also insurmountable. I furthermore chose not to do fieldwork on classes for the military. Military marriage preparation classes predated the marriage initiative in Oklahoma and the initiative's choice of curriculum became another option among the ones already being used on military bases. Because the military is a closed institution with its own organizational structure and norms, I decided that trying to add this aspect to my fieldwork would overburden my analysis, so I am leaving this venue of marriage promotion for future research.

Throughout my stay in Oklahoma, I studied the campaign to pass a constitutional amendment to ban same-sex marriage and the activism to prevent the amendment's passage. Activities both in favor of and against the ban increased two months before the November election, and I spent more hours these final months studying these campaigns. I attended the church of one of the leaders of the antigay/lesbian campaign. I also attended a gay/lesbian affirmative church in Oklahoma City and conducted semistructured, in-depth interviews with fifteen gay and lesbian couples who were married outside Oklahoma, who had holy unions, or who considered themselves married. Studying anti-gay-marriage politics included attending rallies and church services that spoke out against gay marriage. I conducted semistructured, in-depth interviews with five leaders of antigay organizations in Oklahoma and with seven pro-gay/lesbian rights activists, and I did informal interviews at events to ask about members' reactions to the debate over homosexuality and the need to amend the state constitution.

The experience of doing participant observation in workshops for the general public and among targeted populations guided my theoretical focus as I coded my field notes by using a qualitative software program, Atlas.ti. I began to analyze the boundary work that I saw in play at the workshops and built on this analysis to structure questions for the fifteen in-depth, semi-structured interviews I conducted with the Oklahoma Marriage Initiative leadership and OKDHS staff, which each lasted between one and two hours.

In this book, I have provided pseudonyms for all the participants in my study with the exception of high-profile leaders of the marriage initiative who gave me permission to use their real names and those who requested that I use their real names for the purpose of activism. Mary Myrick, the president of Public Strategies, the for-profit company that manages the marriage initiative; Howard Hendrick, Cabinet Secretary for Human Services; and George E. Young, Sr., the pastor at Holy Temple Baptist Church, all gave permission to use quotes from my interviews with them. These leaders have a high profile presence in the media and have written about the marriage initiative in various capacities. All of them expressed to me that the information they provided in their interviews was consistent with statements they had made in other public venues.

Appendix B

Sample Characteristics: In-depth Interviews of Participants in Workshops for the General Population

Gender

Male	44% (13)
Female	56% (17)

Race/Ethnicity

White, European ancestry	87% (26)
African American	3% (1)
Native American	10% (3)

Current Socioeconomic Status

Upper middle class	7% (2)
Middle class	83% (25)
Lower middle class/working class	10% (3)

Education

High school graduate	7% (2)
Associate's degree or some college	17% (5)
Bachelor's degree	67% (20)
Graduate or professional degree	10% (3)

Religious Affiliation

Protestant/Evangelical	83% (25)
Other	17% (5)

Political Views

Republican	56% (17)
Democrat	27% (8)
Independent	10% (3)
Apolitical	7% (2)

Sexual Orientation

Heterosexual	83% (25)
Lesbian	14% (4)
Bisexual	3% (1)

Relationship Status

Married, in first marriage	33% (10)
Remarried	27% (8)
Cohabitating	24% (7)
Single	3% (1)
Not legally married	13% (4)

Notes

PREFACE

1. Griffith 1997; quoted in Lindsay 2007:xiii.
2. Fineman 2004.

INTRODUCTION

1. Popenoe 1999:30.
2. Blankenhorn 2007:8.
3. Blankenhorn 2007:8; Browning 2003:189.
4. Institute for American Values 2004.
5. Dion 2006; Ooms, Bouchet, and Parke 2004.
6. Coalition for Marriage, Family, and Couples Education et al. 2000:7.
7. Olson 2005.
8. Ooms, Bouchet, and Parke 2004.
9. Roberts 2006.
10. Commission on Marriage and Family Support Initiatives 2008.
11. Fetner 2008:110. The term "religious right" has been debated, especially because the organizations this term is meant to describe would not embrace it. Similar to Fetner, I employ this term to capture the connections between the activist organizations of the Christian right and the broad "pro-family" movement, which includes other conservative religious traditions. Thus, the term points to the fact that, in addition to Christians, there are conservative Jews and other religions active in a broad coalition. In Oklahoma, the religious right is predominantly Christian.
12. Coontz (2005) shows that ancient Greeks worried about deteriorating morals of wives, Romans fretted about divorce rates, and European settlers to America decried the decline of family. Likewise, marital and sexual arrangements, which for many seem unprecedented, can be found in other societies. For example, few Americans are aware of ritualized same-sex relations sanctioned in other cultures that were prototypes to and precursors of same-sex marriage.
13. Coontz 2005:5.
14. Browning 2003:188.
15. Fine and Sandstrom 1993; Hays 1996; Ghaziani and Fine 2008. Michèle Lamont (2000) uses the idea of cultural repertoires in her comparative research on working-class values and identities between the United States and France to challenge the standard framework for studying national cultural differences. Instead of viewing cultural dif-

ferences as "essentialized individual or nationalized characteristics," she views them "as cultural structures, that is, institutionalized cultural repertoires or publicly available categorization systems" (2000:243). Although this research is not comparative, it demonstrates the contingent and nonessential ways that Americans construct their identities based on marriage ideology.

16. Gillis 1996:xv.

17. Burawoy (1998:xv) theorizes the importance of ethnographic approaches as constituting four types of extensions: "the extension of the observer into the lives of the participants under study; the extension of observations over time and space; the extension from microprocesses to macroforces; and, finally and most importantly, the extension of theory." I view this research as an extended case study and as a technique to understand the responses of individuals and organizations to massive processes of change.

18. Stacey 1996:3.

19. Cherlin 1992; DaVanzo and Rahman 1993; Hull 2006a.

20. U.S. National Center for Health Statistics 1982.

21. U.S. National Center for Health Statistics 2003.

22. Cherlin 2004; Kiernan 2002.

23. Smock 2000.

24. Hull 2006a:4; U.S. Census Bureau 2001.

25. Freedman 2002.

26. Reese 2005.

27. Moynihan 1965. The "culture of poverty" model of Oscar Lewis (1959) argued that entrenched poverty created cultural values, attitudes, and practices that perpetuated themselves over time, even in the face of social changes in structural conditions. Moynihan (1965) viewed the black family as caught in a tangle of pathology as a result of the cumulative effects of slavery and the subsequent structural conditions of poverty for many African Americans. Scholars who theorized a culture of poverty were charged with "blaming the victims" for their problems, especially as conservatives used these theories to imply that people might cease to be poor if they just changed their culture. See O'Connor (2002) on how concepts like the "culture of poverty" and the "underclass" emerged from trends within the social sciences and from the central preoccupations of twentieth-century American liberalism as part of American identity. In addition, see Small, Harding, and Lamont (2010) for a good discussion of the reemergence of scholarship in cultural sociology that seeks to move beyond theorizing a model of a culture of poverty.

28. Fetner 2008.

29. Stacey 1996:54.

30. Blankenhorn 1995.

31. Stacey 1996. See also Cherlin (2009) for a discussion of how most researchers draw on their personal values for the categories to use and the questions to ask. He argues that this does not mean that all data are suspect or that all interpretations of data are equally valid.

32. Heath 2011. According to Knorr Cetina (2005:67), "Epistemic cultures are cultures of creating and warranting knowledge." Within science studies, Knorr Cetina examines how new orders of knowledge occur as a result of relational practices that gain power through reconfigurations based on everyday conventions and norms. Rather than result-

ing in a partitioning of scientific subcultures from social influences, she uncovers the broader cultural practices that manifest differently in diverse scientific domains. My article extends the concept of epistemic cultures to the areas of policymaking to shed light on collective, situated knowledge as performative practice and to acknowledge the shifting and nondeterminative processes of knowledge production. In particular, it aligns with theories of new social movements—a term applied to movements that have emerged since the 1960s that place greater emphasis on group or collective identity, values, and lifestyles—in their quest to expose unmarked categories as a way to shift power relations (Taylor and Whittier 1992).

33. Knorr Cetina 1999:8–10.

34. Wilcox, et al. 2005:1–2.

35. See Coontz 2005.

36. See Manning and Lichter 1996; Lichter, Graefe, and Brown 2003.

37. IAV 2006:1.

38. CMFCE et al. 2000:4.

39. Waite and Gallagher 2000; IAV 2006.

40. Coltrane 2001; see also Hardisty 2008. The marriage movement's growth paralleled and interacted with the "fatherhood movement," a coalition of religious and secular organizations that stresses the importance of marriage as a necessary condition of men's parenting (Blankenhorn 1995, 2003, 2007; Nock 1998; Popenoe 1996). The anthropologist Anna Gavanas (2004) in her research on this movement identified two "wings": fragile-families and pro-marriage. The fragile-families viewpoint concentrates on the specific needs of low-income, poor, and minority men, whereas the pro-marriage side promotes the cultural value of marriage as the key to responsible fatherhood. Her research uncovers commonalities among these players based on an ideology that equates "father absence" with "social ills," and lines of controversy that pit prioritizing work within the fragile-families wing against marriage in the pro-marriage wing. Similar to the fatherhood movement, a top priority for many marriage advocates is ending fatherlessness, which is viewed to be at the root of society's problems and cultural decline. In *Life Without Father,* David Popenoe advocates the social purpose of fatherhood. First, fathers have a unique role to play in child development. Popenoe says, "The two sexes are different to the core, and each is necessary—culturally as well as biologically—for the optimal development of a human being." Shifting the culture requires reducing nonmarital births and discouraging movements such as "Single Mothers by Choice." Second, children need a "*committed male and female* couple." This means promoting parenthood by a man and a woman in a nuclear family. Third, men need the cultural pressure of marriage to stay engaged with their children. Fourth, children need to feel recognition and acceptance by their fathers. Fathers need to be taught that fathering is about more than providing food and shelter. Fifth, biological fathers are more likely to be committed to the upbringing of their children. So society must reduce the necessity of father substitutes (Popenoe 1996:197, emphasis in original).

41. Coontz and Folbre 2002; U.S. Census Bureau 2000.

42. Alan Guttmacher Institute 1999; Coontz and Folbre 2002; Halpern 1999.

43. Hymowitz 2006:5.

44. For the CLASP history, see http://www.clasp.org/history.php. Theodora Ooms, a former policy analyst at CLASP, and the demographer David Fein (2006:1) describe "how

the poverty research community 'discovered' marriage, and the marriage field 'discovered' poverty." Poverty researchers have increasingly become involved in marriage promotion among low-income individuals. For example, the sociologist Kathryn Edin testified for the Human Resources Subcommittee, Committee on Ways and Means hearings on Welfare and Marriage in 2000.

45. Rector, Johnson, and Fagan 2002:8.

46. Sawhill and Thomas 2002.

47. Lichter, Graefe, and Brown 2003.

48. Coontz and Folbre 2002.

49. Tolman and Raphael 2000.

50. Meckler 2006. Still, critiques have had a strong impact on the packaging of marriage promotion policies. Wade F. Horn, the former Assistant Secretary for the Administration for Children and Families, argued that marriage promotion is not about forcing or coercing people to marry, nor should it encourage anyone to stay in an abusive relationship. He expressed that government should not withdraw support from single-parent families and that promoting marriage is not the sole means of eliminating poverty but a piece of a larger strategy: "We are not trying to move marriage rates. In fact, we may want to divert some couples *away* from marriage" (Horn 2002:4). Instead, government should help individuals who are considering marriage get the skills and education they need to build a "healthy marriage" without taking support away from vulnerable households.

51. Yakush 2007. A number of scholars and advocacy organizations have expressed concern over the overlap between pro-heterosexual marriage movements and those in favor of same-sex marriage. Arguments in favor of same-sex marriage often sidestep the broader debate over governmental policies that create and sustain social and sexual inequality. A coalition of pro-lesbian, gay, bisexual, and transgender activists, scholars, educators, writers, and community organizers issued a 2006 statement supporting a campaign to recognize diverse families, kinship relationships, and partnerships. The signatories of *Beyond Same-Sex Marriage: A New Strategic Vision for All Our Families and Relationships* link the issue of same-sex marriage to other social justice issues in the United States. (The full statement is at www.beyondmarriage.org; see also Polikoff [2008] for a nuanced and insightful argument on the legal ramifications of unjust family policies.) They point out that a conservative agenda has slashed governmental funding for a wide array of family programs and social services that hurt not only some lesbian and gay families but also disproportionately impact poor, immigrant, and racial minority communities. These critics view the politics of marriage—conservative efforts to ban same-sex marriage and the marriage promotion project—as part of a broad ideology of unjust family politics that can only be addressed through a social justice agenda that rejects attaching special benefit to marriage (Cahill 2005).

52. Peterson 2000. Supporters of the marriage movement generally assume that marriage is implicitly a union of one man and one woman. However, the movement's 2004 statement, *What's Next for the Marriage Movement?*, specifically addresses the debate over same-sex unions as one of the great cultural and legal challenges to marriage in the twenty-first century:

> At issue is whether it is possible, and in what ways it could be possible, to reconcile two important social values—one value being the importance of equal dignity and treatment for all citizens, and the

other being the importance of marriage as a vital, pro-child social institution. From the perspective of marriage and the Marriage Movement, the current controversy over equal marriage rights for same-sex couples is the most important social policy debate of our generation. It is also an issue on which we in the Marriage Movement currently hold divergent views.

The report expresses a goal of sparking a national debate that "emphasizes first the well-being of children" and helps to revive a marriage culture in the United States (IAV 2004).

53. D'Emilio and Freedman 1988:xvii.

54. Ingraham 2005.

55. In the late 1960s radical lesbian feminists initiated a sustained critique of heterosexuality as a patriarchal institution. Luce Irigaray's "Women on the Market" (1997) and Gayle Rubin's "The Traffic in Women" (1975) uncovered the phallocentric order that views women as circulating commodities of male consumption. Adrienne Rich (1980) critiqued compulsory heterosexuality for its assumption that women and men are innately sexually attracted to one another and that heterosexuality comprises a universal norm. Monique Wittig's *The Straight Mind* furthered Rich's call to investigate "unexamined heterocentricity" as a "political regime" that "rests on the submission and appropriation of women" and the categories of "men" and "women" (Wittig 1992:xiii–xiv). It took until the early or mid-1990s for heterosexuality as a conceptual category to receive sustained theoretical attention as a central sociological component of inequality.

56. Ingraham 1999:4, 2005.

57. J. Katz 1996.

58. Foucault 1981; Sedgwick 1990.

59. Sedgwick 1990:1, 71.

60. Cott 2000.

61. There is an irony that transformations in intimacy have meant the possibility of relationship recognition for lesbian and gay couples, while at the same time placing renewed focus on heterosexual romance and the wedding industry in service of capitalism to shore up heterosexual dominance. See Ingraham 1999, 2005.

62. Gross 2005:288. Marriage has acted as a conduit of the state to shape the gender and sexual order, structuring the meaning and enactment of gender and sexuality in everyday life. The ideal of the nuclear family in the United States evolved by separating "productive labor" from the home, creating a new social category: the "housewife" (Pascale 2001). Domesticity attributed to wealthy white women became the standard for all women, and the "Cult of True Womanhood" elevated the submissive housewife as morally superior (G. Brown 1990; Pascale 2001). In contrast, racial ethnic women have systematically been relegated to do the "dirty work" in domestic service and industry (Duffy 2007). By the early 1800s in the United States, state-based legal codes supplanted English-based common law, which had turned husband and wife into one person—the husband—for political, legal, and social purposes; yet political and legal understandings of marriage still confirmed male headship (Okin 1979). The republic drew on Christian principles and common law to oblige the husband to provide economically as head of the household (Gillis 1996; Yalom 2001). The husband was the one *full* citizen, establishing the basis for the economic or "patriarchal bargain" of modern marriage in which women accepted subordination in exchange for economic support (Cott 2000; Kandiyoti 1988; Stacey 1998).

63. Gross 2005:296.

64. Pascale 2007:5.

65. The progressive left has been especially critical of nostalgia movements as mobilizing past traditions into a false consciousness, using a familiar Marxian term, as a way to avert conflict and promote social solidarity (see Caputi 2005; Davis 1979:109; Radstone 2007:113–14). Nostalgia movements, however, are not singularly located in conservative coffers but have also been important to the radical left, such as in idealizations of the proletariat (Davis 1979; Radstone 2007). Cultural theorists have traced the way nostalgia organizes knowledge for both progressive and regressive social change (Battaglia 1995; Boym 2001). Thus, my goal is not to narrowly define the marriage movement as nostalgic, nor is it to paint marriage advocates as charlatans promoting false representations. Instead, I consider how marriage ideology lends itself to specific manifestations of social division and inequality that derive from nostalgia.

66. Coontz 1992; see also Coontz 2002.

67. Caputi 2005.

68. Davis 1979:105–6.

69. Caputi 2005:110.

70. Fromm 1994.

71. May 1988; Caputi 2005:142.

72. Polikoff 2005:573; see also Franke 2006.

73. The "tangle of pathology" is from Moynihan (1965). Brief for American Psychological Association and New Jersey Psychological Association as Amici Curiae in Support of Plaintiffs-Appellants at 51–52, Lewis v. Harris 875 A.2d 259, quoted in Franke 2006:241.

74. Indiana Court of Appeals 2005. 821 N.E.2d 15, quoted in Franke 2006:244.

75. M. Gallagher 2003. See chapter 4 (in this book) for a discussion concerning the different stances on stigma among marriage advocates.

76. Cott 2000.

77. Heglar 2001; Nagel 2003; Stanley 1998.

78. Cott 2000:60.

79. Funderburg 1994; Kennedy and Ullman 2003; Moran 2001; Sollors 2000; Wallenstein 2002.

80. Rubin 1984:11–15.

81. Weeks 1995.

82. Hymowitz 2006:148.

83. Somers 2008:2. Similar to Somers, I find the term "market fundamentalism" preferable to that of neoliberalism. As Somers explains, American liberalism has a very different meaning than that of European (or classical) liberalism, referring to social democratic government political philosophy. In contrast, the meaning of European liberalism is closer to what many think of as neoliberalism—denoting a laissez-faire free market. See note 15 in Somers 2008:74.

84. Bellah, Madsen, Swidler, and Tipton 1985.

85. These principles are central to what has come to be known as neoconservatism, a U.S.-based intellectual project rooted in liberal Cold War anticommunism and a backlash to the social liberation movements of the 1960s and 1970s. There has been much debate over the origins, deviations, and hybrid forms of neoconservatism. As neoconservative thinking is now often simply equated with the Bush Doctrine rather than its more com-

plex roots, I refrain from using this term. For a discussion of the merging of conservative and neo-family values interests, see Stacey 1996.

86. See Bourdieu 1984; Epstein 1992; Gamson 1998; Gerson & Peiss 1985; Lamont 1992, 2000; Lamont and Fournier 1992; Lareau 2003; Ong 1996; Pachuki, Pendergrass, and Lamont 2007; Stein 1997, 2001; Waters 1999.

87. Lamont and Molnar 2002:168; Swidler 1986; 2001.

88. Lamont 1992, 2000.

89. Quoted in Lan 2006:11.

90. For a discussion of the concepts of purity and danger and their relation to meanings of dirt in different contexts, see Douglas 1966.

91. Stein 2001.

92. Horn 2000. Wade Horn was sworn in as the Assistant Secretary for Children and Families in the Administration for Children and Families, U.S. Department of Health and Human Services on July 30, 2001.

93. Recently, the marriage initiative changed the name of its workshops for the general public to "Forever. For Real." An announcement states, "The 'Forever. For Real.' program continues the Oklahoma Marriage Initiative's history of providing marriage and relationship education free and open to the public. While the message of the OMI programs is the same, with the new 'Forever. For Real.' branding, the curriculum has been updated to include new content, games, music and many more fun components." Retrieved June 2, 2009 (http://www.okmarriage.net/programhighlights/OklahomaMarriageNewsDetail.asp x?WebsiteInformationID=1565).

94. Each participant signed a consent form before the focus group. To ensure that none of them felt coerced to participate, I told them to grab a sandwich or pizza and that they could stay or take their food to one of the common rooms to eat lunch, if they were not interested in participating. None of them took this latter option, but several had other commitments during the lunch hour, so they declined to participate.

95. See Luker 1996.

CHAPTER 1

1. Keating 2000.

2. Author fieldnotes, February 17, 2004.

3. The Heritage Foundation, "About Us." Retrieved February 17, 2000 (http://www.heritage.org/about/).

4. Oklahoma Family Policy Council, "Marriage Initiative." Retrieved February 16, 2009 (http://www.okfamilypc.org/marriage_initiative.htm).

5. Keating 2000.

6. Fagan 2001; Dion 2006. The Oklahoma Director of the Department of Human Services (OKDHS) explained that the $10 million originally came from "surplus" TANF funds, which were generated from a substantial decline in welfare caseloads. The 1996 federal welfare reform law substantially changed the relationship between states and the federal government for providing welfare services. Under the old AFDC system, states and the federal government shared the cost or savings from any increase or decrease in the welfare caseload. The new system gives each state a relatively fixed TANF block grant. If caseloads decrease, the state reaps the benefits, whereas if they increase, the state

bears the fiscal responsibility. After welfare reform became law, most states experienced a substantial decline in caseloads, which created surplus funds. By the time I arrived in Oklahoma the financial situation had reversed, and Oklahoma was overspending its TANF block grant.

7. Keating 2000. The marriage initiative was receiving a budget of between $2 and $3 million per year that amounted to $10 million (for the first four years of the initiative's funding). Howard Hendrick, the director of the Oklahoma Department of Human Services, explained what was meant by "undedicated" or surplus TANF funds, which were gathered from an excess in TANF money as welfare recipients dropped off the welfare rolls. In order to receive the block grant, the state is required to spend a fixed amount of state dollars called Maintenance of Effort (MOE). The federal government gave Oklahoma a block grant of $145 million with a MOE of $45 million that must be paid by the state. So, the state has $190 million to spend, but one year it only spends $150 million—it spent the required $45 million by the state and only $95 million of the federal grant. This creates a "surplus." After using up the designated $10 million, Director Hendrick told me that the budget for the marriage initiative would remain about the same, even though the state was facing budget cuts.

8. This is also the position of leaders of the religious right, a term I use to capture the diversity of the pro-family religious movements in the United States (see the introduction). In Oklahoma, there is a strong Baptist component to the religious right that gives it a particularly conservative Christian focus. However, there is diversity, such as Frank Keating himself who is a practicing Catholic.

9. Cherlin 2003.

10. Lofton and Haider-Markel 2007:316–17.

11. Blankenhorn 2007:3, 8.

12. Dobson 2004:17; 20–21.

13. Dill and Williams 1992:100. There is more diversity among Southern religions than the appellation "Bible Belt" accounts for. In recent years globalization has increasingly brought the religious practices of Hindus, Buddhists, Muslims, and others into conversation with other Protestant religions in Southern states (Hill 2006).

14. Campbell 2002.

15. Bednar and Hertzke 1995; Morgan and Meier 1980; Satterthwaite 2005.

16. Tugend 1985.

17. Overall 1996:A19.

18. In a television interview, Graves told reporters that the legislation "is just showing that that sort of activity is repulsive. I think it is and a lot of other people do, too." Politicians, pundits, and activists equated homosexuality and sexual promiscuity in order to argue the need for moral regeneration. A radio talk show host told the crowd at a rally, "The moral compass is shifting. We are on the brink of hedonism."

19. Lesbian and gay activists in Oklahoma told me they thought politicians rallied for this legislation, even with the statement of the attorney general that declared it unnecessary, as a political maneuver to fire up conservative Christians to vote. After the election, evangelical Christian leaders contended that a desire to protect traditional marriage drew millions of evangelicals to the polls (Cooperman 2004).

20. On the day of the House vote, an invited Baptist pastor delivered a mini-sermon to discuss a battle between good and evil:

> You play tug-of-war between parties and between debates quite often,
> wanting to win the debate. But, I want you to know there's a tug-of-
> war going on for your soul and for my soul in this world and in this
> society. And it is not a tug-of-war between democrats and repub-
> licans. It is not a tug-of-war between politicians. It's a tug-of-war
> between Jesus Christ and Satan. And it is your soul that the tug-of-
> war is happening.

Although he never mentioned the bill, his sermon implied the tug-of-war was over
moral issues like same-sex marriage.

21. Wilcox, Merolla, and Bear 2007.

22. Watt 1991. The history of evangelicals in America has witnessed a series of shifts
from major influence in American society to a separatist identity to more active engagement within politics and culture (Rieder and Steinlight 2003). Despite the lack of an
established state religion, historians have pointed to the cultural hegemony of Christianity and its moral principles throughout much of America's history. The historian
George Marsden states, "In 1870 almost all American Protestants thought of America as
a Christian nation" (1980:11). The collapse of this mainstream position, spurred by social
and intellectual challenges such as Darwinism, created the conditions for the growth of
the contemporary religious right. In the face of these challenges, a group of evangelicals
formed a separatist, fundamentalist identity that held fast to the tenets of biblical literal-
ism (Oldfield 1996). Up to the 1960s, evangelicals (and especially fundamentalists) largely
withdrew from mainstream cultural and political activity, building instead a vast network
of organizations and media resources geared specifically for evangelical interests and
needs. In contrast, the past fifty years has seen increased political activism and cultural
visibility with the rise of the religious right, which brings together the interests of religious conservatives under one uneasy umbrella (Fetner 2008).

23. Caputi 2005:6.

24. Caputi 2005.

25. Oldfield 1996:57.

26. T. Smith 1996, quoted in Rieder 2003:29.

27. Green 2004:4, 45. Green divides evangelicals among the traditionalists who are
characterized by a high level of orthodox belief, high religious engagement, and also a
desire to preserve traditional beliefs. Modernists had a high level of heterodox belief, a
lower level of religious engagement, and an ability to adopt modern beliefs and practices.
Centrists were neither traditionalists nor modernists but mixed orthodox and heterodox
beliefs. Within this subdivision, traditionalists were the largest subgroup (12.6 percent),
followed by centrists (10.8 percent), and modernists were the smallest subgroup of 2.9
percent.

28. MacQuarrie 2005. Dobson blames organizations and groups ranging from "radical
feminists, liberal lawmakers, and profiteers in the entertainment industry" for weakening
the institution of marriage and seeking "the utter destruction of the family" (2004:19, 39).
While the rise of the religious right and its pro-family agenda coalesced three conservative movements based on antifeminist, prolife, and antigay activism, in the past two
decades homosexuality has become *the* mobilizing issue for many (Fetner 2008:9). Cultural battles over same-sex marriage have captured the most public attention as an issue
that speaks to the potent symbol of American identity—the "universality" of heterosexual

marriage as a foundation of democracy and national culture. In today's world, conservative evangelicals view a once solid moral order slipping into moral chaos, and the issue of homosexuality has been key to mark this decline.

29. Goldberg 2006:44.

30. See Badgett 2004.

31. Caputi 2005:10.

32. Gallagher 2004:6, 11.

33. The announcement for the First Lady and Governor's Conference on Marriage 1999 was provided on the Smart Marriages website. Retrieved July 25, 2008 (http://lists101.his.com/pipermail/smartmarriages/1999-April/002095.html).

34. Ibid.

35. Regier 1999. Regier identified a program model based on Marriage Savers, founded by Michael J. McManus, a conservative Christian writer of a syndicated column in *Ethics & Religion,* and his wife, Harriet. The two travel to churches and communities across the nation, launching "Community Marriage Policies" that require congregations to adopt the program's testing and workbook materials.

36. The Oklahoma Marriage Covenant n.d. Retrieved July 25, 2008 (http://www.okmarriage.org/downloads/images/oklahoma marriage covenant2.doc).

37. Covenant Marriage n.d. Retrieved October 21, 2008 (www.covenantmarriage.com).

38. Only small numbers of couples have opted to participate in a covenant marriage in these states, somewhere from 1 percent to 2 percent, according to studies (Sanchez, Nock, Wilson, and Wright, 2006).

39. Retrieved March 1, 2009 (http://www.smartmarriages.com/oklahoma.covenant.html).

40. Pew Forum on Religion and Public Life 2008. Over 750 of the signatories of the covenant were from Baptist churches.

41. Parrott and Parrott 1997.

42. The annual salary of the Parrotts was reported on the No Promotion of Marriage website. Retrieved December 18, 2008 (http://falcon.arts.cornell.edu/ams3/promarriagegrants2.html).

43. Strong 2008.

44. Myrick and Ooms 2002.

45. Farris, Nathan, and Wright 2004:1. This challenge to the constitutional limits of religion neutrality has created controversy and inspired a number of lawsuits. In June 2007, the Supreme Court closed the door on a lawsuit challenging the Bush administration's use of taxpayer money to support its Office of Faith-Based and Community Initiatives (Greenhouse 2007).

46. The sociologist James Davison Hunter (1999) theorized the culture war as pitting traditionalists, who view truth to be derived from a transcendent authority, usually defined by religious beliefs, against progressives, who view truth as contextual and in flux. Beliefs about truth, whether absolute or relative, shape attitudes to social issues, such as abortion, gay rights, and welfare reform. However, reflecting on the culture-war thesis, scholars have in recent times argued that media accounts tend to sensationalize polarization and have led to an overstatement of conflict. Most Americans have not become more divided on public opinion as the thesis suggests (DiMaggio 2003; Smith, Emerson, Gallagher, Kennedy, and Sikkink 1997). The sociologist Paul DiMaggio (2003) argues that

culture-war rhetoric comprises a campaign undertaken by the religious right to shape new forms of political identity and the public's understanding of the issues that divide it.

47. First Lady and Governor's Conference 1999.

48. Keating 2000.

49. Keating 2000.

50. Regier 1999.

CHAPTER 2

1. Stanley, McCain, and Trathen 1996.

2. Cott 2000:3.

3. Caputi 2005:22.

4. Parsons and Bales 1956.

5. Ibid.:79–80.

6. A. Gordon 2008; Sedgwick 1990.

7. Keating 2004. The initiative held a one-day orientation for high-level senior administrators and community leaders, which was videotaped and downloaded via satellite to DHS county offices. Every year, they have offered a two-day staff development meeting for "gatekeepers"—those who might refer couples to workshops. Finally, there are several three-day training workshops a year for state employees and private individuals to teach the curriculum.

8. Myrick and Ooms 2002:13.

9. Smart Marriages n.d. The development of PREP was funded through the National Institute of Mental Health. The roots of the curriculum date back to the 1970s when Howard Markman was completing his Ph.D. at Indiana University. Out of a longitudinal study examining the predictors of marital distress, Markman helped to found the preventive program that was eventually named PREP, and he later collaborated with Scott Stanley and Susan Bloomberg to write *Fighting for Your Marriage* (Markman, Stanley, and Bloomberg 2001). More than twenty-five years of empirical research on the PREP technique, mostly among white, middle-class couples, points to its benefits to lower premarital breakups and divorce rates (Smart Marriages n.d). Howard Markman and Scott Stanley teach the PREP training workshops offered two to three times a year in Oklahoma, and both sit on the research advisory board for the initiative.

10. Smart Marriages n.d.

11. The creator, Scott Stanley, identifies himself as a devout Christian whose goal in designing the curriculum was to integrate PREP with Christian principles.

12. Unless otherwise noted, all biblical passages quoted in this book are taken from the New International Version translation of the Bible.

13. Stanley, McCain, and Trathen 1996:8, 21.

14. John Gray's best-selling book is *Men Are from Mars, Women Are from Venus* (1992). In his talk at the Smart Marriages conference, he analogized wallets and purses as instructive of broader patterns. Soliciting examples from members of the audience, he held up a wallet to show how lightweight and compact it is. Men have an "efficiency gene," he told us. Women may perceive men as lazy, but according to Gray, this is being organized. Men will "never do something they don't have to do." He began removing the contents from a purse, which he characterized as full of "little stuff." Gray informed us that women's

purses are big enough to carry the weight of the world, and women want to be recognized for the load they are carrying. It is the man's job to listen to his wife so that she will feel connected (and her oxytocin level will rise). A wife must give the husband the space to feel like the "king" (and keep his testosterone levels high).

15. M. Gray 2000.

16. This ethos is captured in AMC's television series *Mad Men*, a stylized drama of the men and women who work for an ad agency in early 1960s New York. A junior executive, Pete Campbell, announces a revelation about the benefits of marriage to his coworkers after a telephone conversation with his new wife: "I have dinner waiting at home for me." The idea that a woman's place is to prepare the home for the king's entry after a long day's work is represented throughout the show.

17. Popenoe and Whitehead 2000.

18. Butler 1999; West and Zimmerman 1987.

19. Gallagher 2003; Heath 2003; Stacey and Gerard 1990.

20. Gallagher 2003:71–72.

21. The marriage initiative has participants fill out an informational survey but these are not recorded by the workshop, so I was unable to obtain specific demographic information.

22. Gallagher and Smith 1999; Heath 2003.

23. Kandiyoti 1988; Stacey and Gerard 1990.

24. Ingraham 2005:3.

25. Stoever and Morera 2007. In addition, the fact that the classes consisted mostly of white, middle-class couples made it easier for a white lesbian couple to integrate.

26. Calhoun 2000.

27. Herek and Capitanio 1996.

28. Brekhus 1998.

29. Connell 1995.

CHAPTER 3

1. Hymowitz 2006:3.

2. Boo 2003.

3. Popenoe 2008:1, 4.

4. Hymowitz 2006:25.

5. M. Gallagher 2007.

6. Hymowitz 2006:51.

7. J. Q. Wilson 2002:2.

8. U.S. Congress (1996, PL 104-193, Title I, Section 101), emphasis added.

9. Boo 2003. The American Society of Magazine Editors selected Katherine Boo's story "The Marriage Cure" (in *The New Yorker*) as the winner for "Best Feature Magazine Writing" in 2003.

10. Ibid.

11. Ibid.

12. Ingraham 1999:88.

13. See http://www.tomtierney.com/contents/01/01–04/page01.htm.

14. Lowe 1998:29.

15. Barna Research Group 1999.

16. Talley 2002. The National Center for Health Statistics stopped compiling divorce data in 1996.

17. Between September 2001 and January 2002, the bureau conducted telephone interviews of two samples totaling 2,323 adults age eighteen years or older. The first sample included 2,020 individuals selected through a random digit sampling frame of telephone numbers, and the second involved active DHS Medicaid clients, allowing the researchers to oversample low-income families (Johnson et al. 2002).

18. Myrick and Ooms 2002.

19. Cherlin 2003. Some social scientists, however, interpret data in the extreme to either support or reject a thesis of harm. The demographer Andrew Cherlin (1999) provides an example of this tendency in the research of the psychologist Judith Wallerstein, who argues that divorce causes harm to most children who experience it, and in the research of Judith Rich Harris, who argues the opposite extreme: that what parents do makes little difference in childhood outcomes. The family demographer Sara McLanahan also argues that language matters in how data are understood. For example, some social scientists portray negative effects as "small, noting that most children living apart from their fathers graduate from high school (80 percent, as compared with 90 percent for children in two-parent families). Others argue that the effects are large, noting that dropout rates double (from 10 percent to 20 percent) when fathers are gone" (2002:37).

20. McLanahan and Sandefur 1994.

21. Cherlin, Chase-Lansdale, and McRae 1998.

22. Institute for American Values 2006 (emphasis added).

23. Hymowitz 2006:25.

24. Fraser and Gordon 1994.

25. For data on U.S. and Oklahoma poverty rates, including how the U.S. Census measures the poverty threshold, see U.S. Census Bureau 2001. Demographic information on Oklahoma can be found at http://quickfacts.census.gov/qfd/states/40000.html (retrieved July 25, 2008).

26. OMI changed the name of these large marriage workshops from "Sweethearts Weekends" to "All About Us."

27. I didn't ask Mary Myrick about her salary or if she was profiting from the marriage initiative. I would imagine that the marriage initiative did give her company a financial boost.

28. U.S. Census Bureau 2005.

29. Institute for Women's Policy Research 2004.

30. Wuthnow 1988.

31. M. Katz 1989.

32. For a history of mothers' pensions, see L. Gordon 1994; Ladd-Taylor 1994; Mink 1995, 1998, 1999, 2002. The number of states passing mothers' pension laws is found in Neubeck and Cazenave 2001:42. The term "marriage ethic" is cited in Reese 2005 and was coined by Abramovitz 1989. For a discussion of "welfare racism" in this period, see Neubeck and Cazenave 2001:41–65. See also Quadagno 1994.

33. Reese 2005.

34. Friedan 1983; Rupp and Taylor 1987.

35. Coontz 1997:45–46.

36. Massey and Denton 1993; W. Wilson 1996.

37. Cherlin 1992; W. Wilson 1996; Reese 2005:58. Reese further argues that black men were more likely to migrate than women in the 1950s, producing the first shortage of "marriageable" men.

38. Reese 2005:59; Komisar 1977.

39. Nancy Rose 1995; Reese 2005:28, 107. Other factors for caseload growth include female-headed households, labor market inequalities, and urban decline (Durman 1973; Loewenberg 1981; Reese 2005:245n1).

40. Moynihan was quoted in Neubeck and Cazenave 2001:153; Quayle 1992.

41. Quayle 1992.

42. Hays 2003; Lawrence Mead quoted in Reese 2005:161. Neubeck and Cazenave (2001:135–43) define paternalism as a dominant group's treatment of others whose well-being is dependent on the largesse of others. They assess the idea of a New Paternalism to argue that this appellation distorts the continuity of the paternalistic treatment of welfare recipients since welfare's inception. On the values of welfare recipients, Sharon Hays, in her book *Flat Broke with Children* (2003), demonstrates that their values are "our" values, meaning that many buy into the dominant ideologies about welfare and single parenting most often to their own detriment.

43. The social Darwinist perspective has historically been utilized to defend the policies of entrepreneurial free-market capitalism. William Graham Sumner argued that capitalism rewarded men of sound character and punished the shifty and irresponsible. While largely vilified in the 1960s and 1970s, the ideas of social Darwinism resurfaced in the 1980s in the writings of conservative thinkers like Charles Murray (Hofstadter 1955; B. O'Connor 2004:31–34). Sharon Hays (2003:125–27) argues that individualistic arguments about poverty adhere to a circular logic. By asking questions about why women become single mothers, the answer necessitates an individual-level response that excludes social factors. No matter the answer provided, the respondent is made responsible for her choices, and structural factors disappear. According to Hays, cultural arguments are faulty because they (1) level the diversity of values, beliefs, and practices of welfare recipients into a homogenized explanation; (2) ignore the broader social and historical bases of poverty, single parenting, and welfare use; and (3) rely on the assumption that welfare alone impacts the behavior of poor single mothers.

44. Polikoff 2008:66–67.

45. Stacey 1996.

46. Whitehead 1993.

47. Murray 1993.

48. Reese 2005:175–76. Peter Edelman, Assistant Secretary for Planning and Evaluation in the Clinton Administration, resigned in response to the signing of PRWORA (B. O'Connor 2004).

49. The quotes from PRWORA can be found in Hays 2003:17 (emphasis added).

50. See the introduction for discussion of other statewide programs.

51. The "Family Economic Security Profile" of Oklahoma from the National Center for Children in Poverty cites Oklahoma's annual maximum TANF family benefit for a family of three at $3,504/year or $292/month. Retrieved December 30, 2009 (http://nccp.org/profiles/fes.html).

52. Dion 2006.

53. Barbara Dafoe Whitehead's article (1993) was published in the *Atlantic Monthly* and not the *New Yorker*.

54. Hymowitz 2006:78.

55. National Fatherhood Initiative et al. 2004.

56. Kiernan 2004.

CHAPTER 4

1. *Frontline* interviewed James Q. Wilson on August 22, 2002, as part of its special feature "Let's Get Married." Retrieved April 7, 2009 (http://www.pbs.org/wgbh/pages/frontline/shows/marriage/interviews/wilson.htm).

2. Ooms 2002.

3. J. Q. Wilson 2002:217.

4. Popenoe 1996:222 (emphasis in original).

5. J. Q. Wilson 2002:221; see also Blankenhorn 2007.

6. Edin and Lein 1997.

7. Lichter, Graefe, and Brown 2003. See also McLanahan, Garfinkel, and Mincy 2001; Ooms 2002; Parke 2004.

8. McLanahan, Garfinkel, and Mincy 2001; see also Jarchow 2003.

9. Edin and Kefalas 2005:202; Edin and Reed 2005.

10. Edin and Kefalas 2005.

11. See W. Wilson 1987.

12. R. Lerman 2002.

13. Ooms 2002.

14. The two stances can represent a tug-of-war among marriage advocates, such as evidenced in the response of Robert Rector, Melissa G. Pardue, and Lauren R. Noyes of the conservative Heritage Foundation (2003), who criticize the marriage-plus perspective for trying "to cripple the President's [Bush's] initiative by siphoning off limited marriage funds into traditional government activities that have little or nothing to do with marriage."

15. National Campaign for Jobs and Income Support 2002.

16. Hinton 2002.

17. The "Family Economic Security Profile" of Oklahoma from the National Center for Children in Poverty cites Oklahoma's annual maximum TANF family benefit for a family of three at $3,504/year or $292/month. Retrieved December 30, 2009 (http://nccp.org/profiles/fes.html).

18. Hays 2003.

19. Smith 2007.

20. Myrick and Ooms 2002.

21. Nikolas Rose 1999:263.

22. Cohen 1985:57.

23. Myrick and Ooms 2002.

24. Leonard 2004.

25. Diane Sollee, Smart Marriages archives, August 29, 2005. Retrieved April 21, 2009 (http://lists101.his.com/pipermail/smartmarriages/2005-August/002791.html).

26. Oklahoma Department of Mental Health and Substance Abuse Services 1999.

27. Oklahoma Coalition Against Domestic Violence and Sexual Assault n.d.

28. Smock and Coontz 2004.

29. See Van Epp 2007.

30. Dion, Silman, Strong, and Santos 2009:3.

31. Ibid.; statistics on the female prison population can be found at the Oklahoma DOC. Retrieved April 29, 2009 (http://www.doc.state.ok.us/newsroom/faag.htm).

32. Ibid.:3.

33. Ibid.:6.

34. Ibid.:7.

35. Ibid.

36. Pearson, Stanley, and Kline 2005.

37. Dion, Silman, Strong, and Santos 2009:7.

CHAPTER 5

1. Whitehead and Pearson 2006:10.

2. Mack 2001:19.

3. Smart Marriages listserv, May 28, 2009. Retrieved June 8, 2009 (http://lists101.his. com/pipermail/smartmarriages/2009-May/003984.html).

4. Shipman and Kazdin 2009.

5. Lindberg, Jones, and Santelli 2008.

6. Luker 2006:26. According to Kristin Luker, the probability that a female between fifteen and nineteen years would be sexually active and not married went from 29 percent in 1995 to 25 percent in 2002, amounting to about half a million teens. She also notes that teenage girls have doubled their likelihood of being on the pill the first time they had sex (from about 8 percent to 17 percent) between 1988 and 2001; condom use soared from half to two out of three.

7. Luker 1996:82.

8. Ibid.:86.

9. Murray 1993.

10. U.S. Census Bureau 2004.

11. Luker 2006:28.

12. Ibid.:29.

13. Whitehead and Pearson 2006:28.

14. Irvine 2002:36. See also D'Emilio and Freeman 1988.

15. Quoted in Irvine 2002:75.

16. Darroch, Landry and Singh 2000.

17. Bruckner and Bearman 2005.

18. U.S. House of Representatives Committee on Government Reform—Minority Staff, Special Investigations Division 2004.

19. Weiss 2007. According to the SIECUS website, the federal government spends about $176 million a year promoting abstinence until marriage. Retrieved June 8, 2009 (http://www.siecus.org/index.cfm?fuseaction=page.viewpage&pageid=522&grandparentID=477 &parentID=523).

20. Irvine 2002:102.

21. Wetzstein 2005.

22. Baumgardner 2005.

23. *Choosing the Best*, an abstinence-only sex education curriculum, devotes a whole lesson to "relationship education." It also includes lessons on "risks of teen sexual behavior, rewards of abstinence, and peer pressure and refusal skills." Retrieved June 9, 2009 (http://www.choosingthebest.org/about_us/index.html). The sex education program *Life Planning Education: A Youth Development Program* includes chapters on "sexuality, relationships, health, violence prevention, and community responsibility as well as chapters on skills-building, values, self-esteem, parenting, employment preparation, and reducing sexual risk." Retrieved June 9, 2009 (http://www.advocatesforyouth.org/index.php?option=com_content&task=view&id=555&Itemid=177).

24. *Love U2: Philosophy and Goals*, The Dibble Institute: Resources for Teaching Relationship Skills to Teens. Retrieved August 11, 2011 (http://www.dibbleinstitute.org/?page_id=2937).

25. Whitehead and Pearson 2006:8.

26. Pearson n.d.

27. Mack 2001:18.

28. Ibid.:19.

29. Blankenhorn 2000.

30. Glenn 1997:5.

31. Ibid.:7.

32. Cott 2000.

33. Glenn 1997:19.

34. Cott 2000:9.

35. On contentious debates of values in the public school system, see Binder 2002.

36. Coeyman 2001.

37. Quoted in T. Lewin 1998.

38. T. Lewin 1998.

39. Del Medico 2001.

40. Ibid.

41. Oklahoma Family Policy Council n.d.

42. Archer 2009.

43. Blassingame 1999.

44. Dion and Silman 2008.

45. The names of the high schools and teachers are pseudonyms.

46. The average racial makeup in Oklahoman schools is 11 percent black, 2 percent Asian, 10 percent Latino, and 19 percent Native American. Oklahoma has one of the largest Native American populations in the country (see chapter 6).

47. For a historical perspective that places union formation in the context of the culture and traditions of the Western world over the last half millennium, see Thornton, Axinn, and Xie 2007.

48. Riker and Brisbane 1997.

49. Mack 2001:19.

50. Gardner, Giese, and Parrott 2004.

51. The other FACS teacher, Maria Bailey, never discussed with me her political affiliation. From our conversations, I assumed she was most likely moderately conservative. Pat Weston, on the other hand, was more open about her political affiliation. Her views were

more tolerant than some religious conservatives, especially about the issue of homosexuality. For example, she told me that she had a number of gay friends and took a live-and-let-live response.

52. Breines 2001 [1992]:113.

53. Ibid.:96.

54. Halberstam 1998.

55. Pascoe 2007:154.

56. Fetner and Kush 2008.

57. Sarah Halpern-Meekin, a graduate student at Harvard, conducted research on marriage education in Oklahoma and Florida high schools. See her dissertation, titled "A Relationship Legacy: The Intergenerational Transmission of Marriage and Divorce." Preliminary results are reported in Frykholm 2008.

58. Gardner and Boellard 2007.

59. Halpern-Meekin, quoted in Frykholm 2008.

60. Rubin 1984.

CHAPTER 6

1. Cott 2000:25.

2. Affidavit of Brian J. Gilley, Assistant Professor of Anthropology, University of Vermont (dated 11/20/05), entitled Gender Diversity and the Cultural Crossfire, filed with Cherokee Nation Supreme Court, December 20, 2005, in Case Number 05–11, *Baker et al. v McKinley et al.* Gilley defines Two-Spirit as "a term adopted by gay, lesbian, bi-sexual, and transgender American Indians, [that] draws on a tradition that recognized that individuals could have a gender and sexuality that incorporated aspects of both male and female characteristics."

3. Cott 2000:5.

4. Chauncey (2004) offers a compelling account of the history of LGBT activism and the path to fighting for marriage as a civil right.

5. Cott 2000:9–10.

6. Jacobi 2006.

7. The Administration for Native Americans awarded three-year healthy marriage grants to the following: $900,000 to the Chickasaw Nation in 2004, $438,936 to the Choctaw Nation in 2005, $442,832 to the Citizen Potawatomi Nation in 2005, $431,781 to the National Indian Women's Health Resource Center, Inc. in 2005, and $250,000 to the Miami Tribe in 2008. See the Comprehensive List of ACF's Healthy Marriage Grantees. Retrieved July 28, 2009 (http://www.acf.hhs.gov/healthymarriage/archive/index.html#funding/).

8. Department of Health and Human Services n.d.

9. According to Francis Paul Prucha (1984:7), the term *savage* in its early meaning connoted a person who lived in the wilderness. The term did not necessarily refer to current understandings that connote cruelty and ruthlessness.

10. Prucha 1984:7.

11. Ibid.:7–8.

12. Ibid.:9.

13. Ibid.:143.

14. Prucha 1973:3.

15. Ibid.:1.

16. Cott 2000:122–23.

17. Prucha 1973:297.

18. Ibid.:302–4.

19. Nancy Cott (2000:10–12) points out that the republican theory that applied to the formation of the United States was based on utilitarian reasoning that equated marriage and the state as forms of governance: "Of the husband over the wife, the ruler over the people."

20. Debo 1970.

21. Prucha 1984:897.

22. Ibid.:899.

23. The Roundtable on Religion and Social Welfare Policy 2005.

24. Ibid.

25. Ibid.

26. Adamson 2001.

27. Choate 2008.

28. Chickasaw Nation n.d.

29. The Roundtable on Religion and Social Welfare Policy 2005.

30. Administration for Native Americans n.d.

31. Ibid.

32. Anoatubby 2004.

33. Office of Community Service n.d.

34. Dixon 2006:42.

35. Perdue 1999.

36. Sturm 2002.

37. Yarbrough 2007.

38. Yarbrough 2004:386.

39. Sturm 2002. These politics continue. In 2011, the Cherokee Nation formally expelled from its membership thousands of descendants of black slaves who were brought to Oklahoma more than 170 years ago by Native American owners. Those removed from membership rolls will no longer be eligible for free health care and other benefits such as education concessions.

40. Cott 2000.

41. *Montana v. United States*, 450 U.S. 544, 564 (1981), cited in Jacobi 2006.

42. Kannady 2004/2005:363.

43. Leslie Penrose requested to use her real name. She viewed using her real name as important to her activism to bring legal rights to lesbian and gay couples. Likewise, Kathy Reynolds and Dawn McKinley asked to have their real names used in this research. Samuel Crittenden is a pseudonym.

44. Rifkin 2008.

45. Tadlock, Gordon and Popp 2006.

46. An Act Amending Title 43 of the Cherokee Nation Marriage and Family Act, Providing for Severability and Declaring Emergency, No. 26–04 (2004). (see Kannady 2004/2005; Rifkin 2008).

47. Petition for Declaratory Judgment, McKinley & Reynolds (No. CV-04-36). Quoted in Kannady 2004/2005:370.

48. Tadlock, Gordon, and Popp 2006.

49. The Heritage Foundation n.d.

50. Kannady 2004/2005:368.

51. Jacobi 2006.

52. Driskill n.d. As a Two-Spirit/Queer activist, Driskill uses gender-neutral pronouns (e.g., s/he, hir, and so forth).

53. Ibid.:131.

54. Roscoe 1998:3.

55. Driskill n.d.:127.

56. Kannady 2004/2005:379.

CONCLUSION

1. M. Gallagher 2003.

2. Hymowitz 2006:148.

3. Blankenhorn 2008.

4. Judge Walker noted that none of Blankenhorn's publications had been submitted for peer review and that his research on marriage mainly constituted reading other research, summarizing this body of literature, and providing his own opinion. See *Perry v. Schwarzenegger*, 704 F. Supp. 2d 921 (N.D. Cal. 2010).

5. *Perry v. Schwarzenegger*, 704 F. Supp. 2d 921 (N.D. Cal. 2010):45.

6. Ibid.:111 (emphasis added).

7. Ibid.:80.

8. See Alice O'Connor (2002) for an informative study of how concepts like the "culture of poverty" and the "underclass" emerged from trends within the social sciences and from the central preoccupations of twentieth-century American liberalism as part of American identity.

9. The proportion of marriages that end through divorce has been stable over the last twenty years in the United States and began to decline in the late 1990s (Raley and Bumpass 2003). In contrast, rates of unwed childbearing and cohabitation have continued to climb. For a good review of the changing attitudes concerning marriage and family, see the Pew Research Center Social and Demographic Trends Report titled, "The Decline of Marriage and Rise of New Families." Retrieved January 1, 2011 (http://pewsocialtrends. org/2010/11/18/the-decline-of-marriage-and-rise-of-new-families/2/#ii-overview).

10. Gross 2005:288.

11. Small, Harding, and Lamont. 2010:12.

12. Gamson 1998:212.

13. Avery Gordon (2008) examines haunting as a "social phenomenon." She states that "haunting describes how that which appears to be not there is often a seething presence . . . the ghost or the apparition is one form by which something lost or barely visible . . . makes itself known or apparent to us" (8). In this sense, I use the concept to shine light on the importance of considering the impact of what is missing or ignored.

14. Nancy Cott (2000:4) traces the ways that historically Mormons have been treated as nonwhite in American law and society.

15. Sprigg 2004.

16. Loftus 2001; Persell, Green, and Gurevich 2001; Yang 1997.

17. Andersen and Fetner 2008; Fetner 2008.

18. Coalition for Marriage, Family and Couples Education, Institute for American Values, and Religion, Culture, and Family Project 2000; Institute for American Values and Institute for Marriage and Public Policy 2006.

19. Hull 2006b:36.

20. Cott 2000:5.

21. Stein 2001.

22. Gillis 1996:xv.

23. Hymowitz 2006:30.

24. Ibid.:29.

25. In his 1992 book, *The New Politics of Poverty: The Nonworking Poor in America*, Lawrence Mead blames most poverty since 1960 on the breakdown in the work ethic among the poor.

26. See Bellah, Madsen, Swidler, and Tipton 1985; Etzioni 1998.

27. National Healthy Marriage Resource Center 2007.

28. Hymowitz 2006:54.

29. Haskins 2009:281.

30. Oklahoma Marriage Initiative n.d.

31. Commission on Marriage and Family Support Initiatives 2008. See also Ooms, Bouchet, and Parke 2004.

32. Wood, Moore, and Clarkwest 2011.

33. Wetzstein 2010.

34. Thomas Bradbury, "Poverty 1, Relationship Education 0," eHarmonyLabs Blog, July 12, 2010. Retrieved January 26, 2011 (http://www.eharmony.com/labs/2010/07/relationship-education/).

35. The Relationship Institute at UCLA. Retrieved January 26, 2011 (http://www.relationshipinstitute.ucla.edu/about.php).

36. Smart Marriages, "Research, Innovation, Delivery." Retrieved January 26, 2011 (http://www.iplaybacksmartmarriages.com/product/2065/71).

37. Lichter, Graefe, and Brown 2003:79–80.

38. Sigle-Rushton and McLanahan 2002.

39. Administration for Children and Families, "Questions and Answers on the Fatherhood, Marriage, and Families Innovation Fund." Retrieved January 26, 2011 (http://www.acf.hhs.gov/programs/cse/pubs/2010/Fatherhood_Marriage_and_Families_Innovation_Fund_QA.html).

40. Smart Marriages, "TRYING to stay Calm. PLEASE VOTE. Administration's proposed plan for TANF—3/27/10." Retrieved January 26, 2011 (http://lists101.his.com/pipermail/smartmarriages/2010-March/004224.html).

41. Administration for Children and Families, "Questions and Answers."

42. Public Strategies, "Team: Mary Myrick." Retrieved January 26, 2011 (http://www.publicstrategies.com/default1.asp?ID=19).

43. Fragile Families 2003. See also England and Edin 2007.

44. Knox, Miller, and Gennetian 2000.

45. Cowan, Cowan, Pruett, and Wong 2009.

46. Sigle-Rushton and McLanahan 2002:524.

47. Smock and Manning 2004:107.

48. See, for example, Bailey 2004 and Barlow 2004.
49. Burawoy 1998.
50. Randles 2009.
51. Gillis 1996.

APPENDIX A

1. Burawoy 1998:5.
2. Clifford and Marcus 1986; Stacey 1998.
3. Fraser 1989:113.
4. The names of the two high schools are pseudonyms.

Bibliography

Abramovitz, Mimi. 1989. *Regulating the Lives of Women: Social Policy from Colonial Times to the Present*. Boston: South End Press.

Adamson, Rebecca L. 2001, July/August. "Way to Give: Smoothing Out the Road." *Foundation News & Commentary*. Retrieved August 26, 2009 (http://www.foundationnews.org/CME/article.cfm?ID=1005).

Administration for Native Americans. n.d. "ANA Grant Awards." Retrieved August 29, 2009 (http://www.acf.hhs.gov/programs/ana//grants/grant_awards.html).

Alan Guttmacher Institute. 1999. "Married Mothers Fare the Best Economically, Even If They Were Unwed at the Time They Gave Birth." *Family Planning Perspectives* 31:258–60.

Andersen, Robert, and Tina Fetner. 2008. "Cohort Differences in Tolerance of Homosexuality: Attitudinal Change in Canada and the United States, 1981–2000." *Public Opinion Quarterly* 72:311–30.

Anoatubby, Bill. 2004. "2004 State of the Nation." The Chickasaw Nation. Retrieved April 26, 2009 (http://www.chickasaw.net/governor/index_2114.htm).

Archer, Kim. 2009, January 8. "Teen Birth Rate in Oklahoma Rises to No. 6 in Nation." *Tulsa World*. Retrieved June 27, 2008 (http://www.tulsaworld.com/news/article.aspx?subjectid=11&articleid=20090108_17_A8_Oklaho762252).

Badgett, M. V. Lee. 2004. "Will Providing Marriage Rights to Same-Sex Couples Undermine Heterosexual Marriage? Evidence from Scandinavia and the Netherlands." A discussion paper prepared for the Council on Contemporary Families and the Institute for Gay and Lesbian Strategic Studies.

Bailey, Martha. 2004. "Regulation of Cohabitation and Marriage in Canada." *Law & Policy* 26:153–75.

Barlow, Anne. 2004. "Regulation of Cohabitation, Changing Family Policies and Social Attitudes: A Discussion of Britain Within Europe." *Law & Policy* 26:57–86.

Barna Research Group. 1999. "Christians Are More Likely to Experience Divorce Than Are Non-Christians." Retrieved April 30, 2009 (http://www.barna.org/cgi-bin/).

Battaglia, Debbora. 1995. "On Practical Nostalgia: Self-Prospecting among Urban Trobrianders." Pp. 77–96 in *Rhetorics of Self-Making*, edited by Debbora Battaglia. Berkeley: University of California Press.

Baumgardner, Julie. 2005, February 17. "Love U2." Posted on the Smart Marriages listserv. Retrieved June 8, 2009 (http://lists101.his.com/pipermail/smartmarriages/2005-February/002647.html).

Bednar, Nancy L., and Allen D. Hertzke. 1995. "Oklahoma: The Christian Right and Republican Realignment." Pp. 91–107 in *God at the Grassroots: The Christian Right in the 1994 Elections,* edited by Mark J. Rozell and Clyde Wilcox. Lanham, MD: Rowman and Littlefield.

Bellah, Robert N., Richard Madsen, William Sullivan, Ann Swidler, and Steven Tipton. 1985. *Habits of the Heart: Individualism and Commitment in American Life.* Berkeley: University of California Press.

Belluck, Pam. 2000, April 21. "States Declare War on Divorce Rates, Before Any 'I Dos.'" *New York Times.*

Binder, Amy. 2002. *Contentious Curricula: Afrocentrism and Creationism in American Public Schools.* Princeton, NJ: Princeton University Press.

Blankenhorn, David. 1995. *Fatherless America: Confronting Our Most Urgent Social Problems.* New York: Harper Perennial.

———. 2000, Winter. "The New Laws of Love." *Propositions.* Retrieved June 9, 2009 (http://lists101.his.com/pipermail/smartmarriages/2001-January/000483.html).

———. 2003, Spring. "The Marriage Problem." *American Experiment Quarterly:*61–71.

———. 2007. *The Future of Marriage.* New York: Encounter.

———. 2008, September 19. "Protecting Marriage to Protect Children." *Los Angeles Times.* Retrieved January 21, 2011 (http://articles.latimes.com/2008/sep/19/opinion/oe-blankenhorn19).

Blassingame, Kelly M. 1999. "Then and Now." *Techniques: Connecting Education and Careers* 74:26–29.

Boo, Katherine. 2003. "A Less Perfect Union." *The New Yorker.* Retrieved March 13, 2009 (http://lists101.his.com/pipermail/smartmarriages/2003-August/001643.html).

Bourdieu, Pierre. 1977. *Outline of a Theory of Practice.* Cambridge: Cambridge University Press.

———. 1984. *Distinction: A Social Critique of the Judgment of Taste.* Cambridge: Harvard University Press.

Boym, Svetlana. 2001. *The Future of Nostalgia.* New York: Basic Books.

Breines, Wini. 2001 [1992]. *Young, White, and Miserable: Growing Up Female in the Fifties.* Chicago: University of Chicago Press.

Brekhus, Wayne. 1998. "A Sociology of the Unmarked: Redirecting Our Focus." *Sociological Theory* 16(1):34–51.

Brown, Gillian. 1990. *Domestic Individualism: Imagining Self in Nineteenth-Century America.* Berkeley: University of California Press.

Browning, Don S. 2003. *Marriage and Modernization: How Globalization Threatens Marriage and What to Do about It.* Grand Rapids: William B. Eerdmans.

Bruckner, Hannah, and Peter S. Bearman. 2005. "After the Promise: The STD Consequences of Adolescent Virginity Pledges." *Journal of Adolescent Health* 36:271–78.

Burawoy, Michael. 1998. "The Extended Case Method." *Sociological Theory* 16:4–33.

Butler, Judith. 1993. *Bodies That Matter: On the Discursive Limits of "Sex."* New York: Routledge.

———. 1999. *Gender Trouble.* New York: Routledge.

Cahill, Sean. 2005. "Welfare Moms and the Two Grooms: The Concurrent Promotion and Restriction of Marriage in US Public Policy." *Sexualities* 8:169–87.

Calhoun, Cheshire. 2000. *Feminism, the Family, and the Politics of the Closet: Lesbian and Gay Displacement*. Oxford: Oxford University Press.

Campbell, Kim. 2002, July 18. "Can Marriage Be Taught?" *The Christian Science Monitor*. Retrieved January 3, 2010 (http://www.csmonitor.com/2002/0718/p01s02-ussc.html).

Campbell, Kim, and Marilyn Gardner. 2004, January 23. "Can a Class Encourage Couples to Marry?" *Christian Science Monitor*. Retrieved December 15, 2009 (http://www.csmonitor.com/2004/0123/p13s01-lifp.htm).

Caputi, Mary. 2005. *A Kinder, Gentler America: Melancholia and the Mythical 1950s*. Minneapolis: University of Minnesota Press.

Chauncey, George. 2004. *Why Marriage? The History Shaping Today's Debate*. New York: Basic Books.

Cherlin, Andrew. 1992. *Marriage, Divorce, Remarriage: Revised and Enlarged Edition*. Cambridge: Harvard University Press.

———. 1999. "Going to Extremes: Family Structure, Children's Well-Being, and Social Science." *Demography* 36(4):421–28.

———. 2003. "Should the Government Promote Marriage?" *Contexts* 2:22–29.

———. 2004. "The Deinstitutionalization of American Marriage." *Journal of Marriage and Family* 66:848–61.

———. 2009. "Council on Contemporary Families Briefing Paper: One Thousand and Forty-Nine Reasons Why It's Hard to Know When a Fact is a Fact." Council on Contemporary Families Briefing Paper.

Cherlin, Andrew J., P. Lindsay Chase-Lansdale, and Christine McRae. 1998. "Effects of Parental Divorce on Mental Health throughout the Life Course." *American Sociological Review* 63:239–49.

Chickasaw Nation. n.d. "Office of Family Development." Retrieved August 26, 2009 (http://www.chickasaw.net/services/index_276.htm).

Choate, Tony. 2008. "State of Chickasaw Nation Stronger, and Getting Stronger." Chickasaw Nation. Retrieved August 26, 2009 (http://www.chickasaw.net/governor/index_2849.htm).

Clifford, James, and George E. Marcus. 1986. *Writing Culture: The Poetics and Politics of Ethnography*. Berkeley: University of California Press.

Coalition for Marriage, Family, and Couples Education [CMFCE], Institute for American Values [IAV], and Religion, Culture, and Family Project [RCFP]. 2000. *The Marriage Movement: A Statement of Principles*. New York: Institute for American Values.

Coeyman, Marjorie. 2001, April 17. "Terms of Endearment: High-school Marriage Classes Look at the Poetic—and the Practical." *The Christian Science Monitor*. Retrieved February 2, 2009 (http://lists101.his.com/pipermail/smartmarriages/2001-April/000590.html).

Cohen, Stanley. 1985. *Visions of Social Control*. Cambridge: Polity.

Collins, Patricia Hill. 1986. "Learning from the Outsider Within: The Sociological Significance of Black Feminist Thought." *Social Problems* 33(6):S14–S31.

Coltrane, Scott. 2001. "'Marketing the Marriage Solution': Misplaced Simplicity in the Politics of Fatherhood." *Sociological Perspectives* 44:387–418.

Commission on Marriage and Family Support Initiatives. 2008, February. "The One-Percent Solution: Using TANF Funds to Empower Families and Promote Healthy

Marriages in Florida." Retrieved January 15, 2010 (http://floridafamilies.org/pdfs/2008TANFOnePercentBreif.pdf).

Connell, R. W. 1995. *Masculinities*. Berkeley: University of California Press.

Coontz, Stephanie. 1992. *The Way We Never Were: American Families and the Nostalgia Trap*. New York: Basic Books.

————. 1997. *The Way We Really Are: Coming to Terms with America's Changing Families*. New York: Basic Books.

————. 2002, April 7. "Nostalgia as Ideology." *The American Prospect*. Retrieved February 1, 2011 (http://www.prospect.org/cs/articles?article=nostalgia_as_ideology).

————. 2005. *Marriage, A History: From Obedience to Intimacy or How Love Conquered Marriage*. New York: Viking.

Coontz, Stephanie, and Nancy Folbre. 2002. "Marriage, Poverty, and Public Policy." Discussion paper from the Council on Contemporary Families. Retrieved January 12, 2007 (http://www.contemporaryfamilies.org).

Cooperman, Alan. 2004, November 4. "Same-Sex Bans Fuel Conservative Agenda." *Washington Post*.

Cott, Nancy F. 2000. *Public Vows: A History of Marriage and the Nation*. Cambridge: Harvard University Press.

Council on Civil Society. 1998. *A Call to Civil Society: Why Democracy Needs Moral Truths*. New York: Institute for American Values and the University of Chicago Divinity School.

Council on Families. 1995. *Marriage in America: A Report to the Nation*. Retrieved March 5, 2009 (http://www.americanvalues.org/html/r-marriage_in_america.html).

Cowan, Philip A., Carolyn Pape Cowan, Marsha Kline Pruett, Kyle Pruett, and Jessica J. Wong. 2009. "Promoting Fathers' Engagement with Children: Preventive Interventions for Low-Income Families." *Journal of Marriage and Family* 71:663–79.

Darroch, Jacqueline E., David J. Landry, and Susheela Singh. 2000, September/October. "Changing Emphases in Sexuality Education in U.S. Public Secondary Schools, 1988–1999." *Family Planning Perspectives* 32(5).

DaVanzo, Julie, and M. Omar Rahman. 1993. "American Families: Trends and Correlates." *Population Index* 59:350–86.

Davis, Fred. 1979. *Yearning for Yesterday: Nostalgia, Art and Society*. New York: Free Press.

Debo, Angie. 1970. *A History of the Indians of the United States*. Norman: University of Oklahoma Press.

Del Medico, Jennifer. 2001, March 4. "More Than a Prom, Less Than a Promise: High School Students Get an Education in Marriage." *The Star-Ledger*. Retrieved January 2, 2009 (http://lists101.his.com/pipermail/smartmarriages/2001-March/000539.html).

D'Emilio, John, and Estelle B. Freedman. 1988. *Intimate Matters: A History of Sexuality*. Chicago: University of Chicago Press.

Department of Health and Human Services. n.d. "The Healthy Marriage: Building Real Solutions for Real People." Retrieved July 28, 2009 (www.acf.hhs.gov/healthymarriage/pdf/healthmarrbk.pdf).

Diamond, Sara. 1995. *Roads to Dominion: Right-Wing Movements and Political Power in the United States*. New York: Guilford Press.

Dill, Bonnie Thornton, and Bruce B. Williams. 1992. "Race, Gender, and Poverty in the Rural South: African American Single Mothers." Pp. 97–110 in *Rural Poverty in America*, edited by Cynthia M. Duncan. Westport, CT: Greenwood.

DiMaggio, Paul. 2003. "The Myth of Culture War: The Disparity between Private Opinion and Public Politics." Pp. 79–97 in *The Fractious Nation? Unity and Division in Contemporary American Life*, edited by Jonathan Rieder and Stephen Steinlight. Berkeley: University of California Press.

Dion, M. Robin. 2006. *The Oklahoma Marriage Initiative: An Overview of the Longest-Running Statewide Marriage Initiative in the U.S.* ASPE Research Brief. Washington, DC: U.S. Department of Health and Human Services.

Dion, M. Robin, and Timothy Silman. 2008. *Starting Early: How the Oklahoma Marriage Initiative Helps Schools Prepare Young People for Healthy Marriages.* ASPE Research Brief, Office of the Assistant Secretary for Planning and Evaluation. Washington, DC: U.S. Department of Health and Human Services. Retrieved June 1, 2009 (http://aspe.hhs.gov/hsp/06/OMI/StartingEarly/rb.pdf).

Dion, M. Robin, Timothy Silman, Debra A. Strong, and Betsy Santos. 2009. *The Oklahoma Marriage Initiative: Marriage and Relationship Skills Education as a Way to Prepare Prisoners for Reintegration.* ASPE Research Brief, Office of the Assistant Secretary for Planning and Evaluation. Washington, DC: U.S. Department of Health and Human Services.

Dixon, Mim. 2006. *Strategies for Cultural Competency in Indian Healthcare.* Washington, DC: American Public Health Association.

Dobson, James. 2004. *Marriage under Fire: Why We Must Win This Battle.* Sisters, OR: Multnomah.

Douglas, Mary. 1966. *Purity and Danger: An Analysis of Concepts of Pollution and Taboo.* London: Routledge & Kegan Paul.

Driskill, Qwo-Li. n.d. "Breaking Our Shells: Cherokee Two-Spirits Rebalancing the World." Pp. 121–41 in *Beyond Masculinity*, edited by Trevor Hoppe. Retrieved December 10, 2009 (http://www.beyondmasculinity.com/articles/driskill.php).

Duffy, Mignon. 2007. "Doing the Dirty Work: Gender, Race, and Reproductive Labor in Historical Perspective." *Gender & Society* 21:313–36.

Durman, Eugene. 1973. "Have the Poor Been Regulated? Toward a Multivariate Understanding of Welfare Growth." *Social Service Review* 47(3):339–59.

Edin, Kathryn, and Maria Kefalas. 2005. *Promises I Can Keep: Why Poor Women Put Motherhood before Marriage.* Berkeley: University of California Press.

Edin, Kathryn, and Laura Lein. 1997. *Making Ends Meet: How Single Mothers Survive Welfare and Low-Wage Work.* New York: Russell Sage Foundation.

Edin, Kathryn, and Joanna Reed. 2005. "Why Don't They Just Get Married? Barriers to Marriage among the Disadvantaged." *The Future of Children* 15(2):117–30.

Elshtain, Jean Bethke. 1999. "A Call to Civil Society." *Society* 36(5):11–19.

England, Paula, and Kathryn Edin. 2007. *Understanding Low-Income Unmarried Couples with Children.* Council for Contemporary Families Briefing Paper.

Epstein, Cynthia F. 1992. "Tinker-bells and Pinups: The Construction and Reconstruction of Gender Boundaries at Work." Pp. 232–56 in *Cultivating Differences: Symbolic Boundaries and the Making of Inequality*, edited by Michèle Lamont and Marcel Fournier. Chicago: University of Chicago Press.

Etzioni, Amitai. 1998. *The New Golden Rule: Community and Morality in a Democratic Society.* New York: Basic Books.

Fagan, Patrick F. 2001, March 26. *Encouraging Marriage and Discouraging Divorce.* Washington, DC: The Heritage Foundation Backgrounder, no. 1421.

Farris, Anne, Richard P. Nathan, and David J. Wright. 2004. *The Expanding Administrative Presidency: George W. Bush and the Faith-Based Initiative*. New York: Nelson A. Rockefeller Institute of Government, State University of New York.

Feldstein, Ruth. 2000. *Motherhood in Black and White: Race and Sex in American Liberalism, 1930–1965*. Ithaca: Cornell University Press.

Fetner, Tina. 2008. *How the Religious Right Shaped Lesbian and Gay Activism*. Minneapolis: University of Minnesota Press.

Fetner, Tina, and Kristin Kush. 2008. "Gay-Straight Alliances in High Schools: Social Predictors of Early Adoption." *Youth & Society* 40(1):114–30.

Fine, Gary Alan, and Kent Sandstrom. 1993. "Ideology in Action: A Pragmatic Approach to a Contested Concept." *Sociological Theory* 11(1):21–38.

Fineman, Martha Albertson. 2004. *The Autonomy Myth: A Theory of Dependence*. New York: New Press.

Foucault, Michel. 1981. *The History of Sexuality*. Vol. 1, *An Introduction*. Harmondsworth, UK: Penguin.

Fragile Families. 2003, January. *Union Formation and Dissolution in Fragile Families*. Fragile Families Research Brief, No. 14. Princeton, NJ: Center for Research on Child Well-Being.

Franke, Katherine. 2006. "The Politics of Same-Sex Marriage Politics." *Columbia Journal of Gender and Law* 15(1):236–48.

Fraser, Nancy. 1989. *Unruly Practices: Power, Discourse, and Gender in Contemporary Social Theory*. Minneapolis: University of Minnesota Press.

Fraser, Nancy, and Linda Gordon. 1994. "A Genealogy of 'Dependency': Tracing a Keyword of the US Welfare State." *Signs: Journal of Women in Culture and Society* 19(2):309–36.

Freedman, Estelle. 2002. *No Turning Back: The History of Feminism and the Future of Women*. New York: Ballantine Books.

Friedan, Betty. 1983. *The Feminine Mystique*. New York: Dell Publishing. (Orig. pub. 1963).

Fromm, Erich. 1994. *Escape from Freedom*. New York: Owl Books.

Frykholm, Amy. 2008, September 9. "Relationship Smarts: A Curriculum on Dating and Marriage." *Christian Century*. Retrieved June 6, 2009 (http://findarticles.com/p/articles/mi_m1058/is_18_125/ai_n28569990).

Funderburg, Lise. 1994. *Black, White, Other: Biracial Americans Talk about Race and Identity*. New York: William Morrow.

Gallagher, Maggie. 2003. "What Is Marriage For?" *Weekly Standard,* 8(45). Retrieved January 1, 2010 (http://www.weeklystandard.com/content/public/articles/000/000/002/939pxiqa.asp?pg=1).

———. 2004. *Can Government Strengthen Marriage? Evidence from the Social Sciences*. New York: National Father Initiative, the Institute for Marriage and Public Policy, Institute for American Values.

———. 2007. "The Marriage Gap Threatens the Black American Dream." Retrieved March 3, 2009 (http://townhall.com/columnists/MaggieGallagher/2007/11/13/the_marriage_gap_threatens_the_black_american_dream).

Gallagher, Sally K. 2003. *Evangelical Identity and Gendered Family Life*. New Brunswick: Rutgers University Press.

Gallagher, Sally K., and Christian Smith. 1999. "Symbolic Traditionalism and Pragmatic Egalitarianism: Contemporary Evangelicals, Family, and Gender." *Gender & Society* 13:211–33.

Gamson, Joshua. 1998. *Freaks Talk Back: Tabloid Talk Shows and Sexual Nonconformity*. Chicago: University of Chicago Press.

Gardner, Scott P., and Rila Boellard. 2007. "Does Youth Relationship Education Continue to Work After a High School Class? A Longitudinal Study." *Family Relations* 56:490–500.

Gardner, Scott P., Kelly Giese, and Suzanne M. Parrott. 2004. "Evaluation of the Connections: Relationships and Marriage Curriculum." *Family Relations* 53:521–27.

Gavanas, Anna. 2004. *Fatherhood Politics in the United States: Masculinity, Sexuality, Race, and Marriage*. Urbana: University of Illinois Press.

Gerson, Judith M., and Kath Peiss. 1985. "Boundaries, Negotiation, Consciousness: Reconceptualizing Gender Relations." *Social Problems* 32:317–31.

Ghaziani, Amin, and Gary Alan Fine. 2008. "Infighting and Ideology: How Conflict Informs the Local Culture of the Chicago Dyke March." *International Journal of Politics, Culture, and Sociology* 20:51–67.

Giddens, Anthony. 1992. *The Transformation of Intimacy: Sexuality, Love and Eroticism in Modern Societies*. Stanford: Stanford University Press.

Gillis, John R. 1996. *A World of Their Own Making: Myth, Ritual, and the Quest for Family Values*. Cambridge: Harvard University Press.

Glendon, Mary Ann. 1991. *Rights Talk*. New York: Free Press.

Glendon, Mary Ann, and David Blankenhorn, eds. 1995. *Seedbeds of Virtue: Sources of Competence, Character, and Citizenship in American Society*. Lanham, MD: Madison Books.

Glenn, Norval. 1997. *Closed Minds, Closed Hearts: The Textbook Story of Marriage*. New York: Council on Families.

Glover, Mike. 2009, December 22. "GOP Sees 'Hottest' Issue as Same-Sex Marriage." *Associated Press*. Retrieved December 23, 2009 (http://m.desmoinesregister.com/BETTER/news.jsp?key=574662).

Goldberg, Michelle. 2006. *Kingdom Coming: The Rise of Christian Nationalism*. New York: Norton.

Goldstein, Amy. 2001, September 6. "Looking beyond Jobs in Welfare Reform: Conservatives Advise States to Promote Marriage, Abstinence, Stronger Families." *Washington Post*.

———. 2002, April 1. "Tying Marriage Vows to Welfare Reform: White House Push for State Strategies to Promote Family Ignites Dispute." *Washington Post*.

Gordon, Avery. 2008. *Ghostly Matters: Haunting and the Sociological Imagination*. 2nd ed. Minneapolis: University of Minnesota Press.

Gordon, Linda. 1994. *Pitied but Not Entitled: Single Mothers and the History of Welfare*. Madison: University of Wisconsin Press.

Gray, John. 1992. *Men Are from Mars, Women Are from Venus: A Practical Guide for Improving Communication and Getting What You Want in Your Relationships*. New York: HarperCollins.

Gray, Marion W. 2000. *Productive Men, Reproductive Women: The Agrarian Household and the Emergence of Separate Spheres during the German Enlightenment*. Oxford: Berghahn Books.

Green, John C. 2004. "The American Religious Landscape and Political Attitudes: A Baseline for 2004." Pew Forum on Religion & Public Life. Retrieved December 9, 2009 (pewforum.org/publications/surveys/ green-full.pdf).

Greenhouse, Linda. 2007, June 26. "Justices Reject Suit on Federal Money for Faith-Based Office." *New York Times*. Retrieved December 23 2009 (http://www.nytimes.com/2007/06/26/washington/26faith.html).

Greiner, John. 2001a. "Senator Accuses Regier over Bids." *The Oklahoman*.

———. 2001b, March 21. "Senator Calls for Suspension of Marriage Initiative." *The Oklahoman*.

Griffith, Marie R. 1997. *God's Daughters: Evangelical Women and the Power of Submission*. Berkeley: University of California Press.

Gross, Neil. 2005. "The Detraditionalization of Intimacy Reconsidered." *Sociological Theory* 23(3):286–311.

Halberstam, Judith. 1998. *Female Masculinity*. Durham: Duke University Press.

Halpern, Ariel. 1999. *Poverty among Children Born Outside of Marriage: Preliminary Findings from the National Survey of America's Families*. Washington, DC: The Urban Institute.

Hardisty, Jean. 2008. *Pushed to the Altar: The Right Wing Roots of Marriage Promotion*. Marriage Promotion Series, Part I, Political Research Associates/Women of Color Resource Center.

Haskins, Ron. 2009. "Moynihan Was Right: Now What?" *Annals of the American Academy of Political and Social Science* 621:281–314.

Hays, Sharon. 1996. *The Cultural Contradictions of Motherhood*. New Haven: Yale University Press.

———. 2003. *Flat Broke with Children: Women in the Age of Welfare Reform*. Oxford: Oxford University Press.

Heath, Melanie. 2003. "Soft-Boiled Masculinity: Renegotiating Gender and Racial Ideologies in the Promise Keepers Movement." *Gender & Society* 17:423–44.

———. 2011. "Making Marriage Promotion into Public Policy: The Epistemic Culture of a Statewide Initiative." Unpublished manuscript.

Heglar, Charles. 2001. *Rethinking the Slave Narrative: Slave Marriage and the Narratives of Henry Bibb and William and Ellen Craft*. Santa Barbara: Greenwood Press.

Herek, Gregory M., and John P. Capitanio. 1996. " 'Some of My Best Friends': Intergroup Contact, Concealable Stigma, and Heterosexuals' Attitudes toward Gay Men and Lesbians." *Personality and Social Psychology Bulletin* 22(4):412–24.

Heritage Foundation. n.d. "The Marriage Debate." Retrieved December 6, 2009 (http://www.heritage.org/Research/Family/marriagedebate/themarriagedebate.cfm).

Hill, Samuel, ed. 2006. *New Encyclopedia of Southern Culture, Volume 1: Religion*. Chapel Hill: University of North Carolina Press.

Hinton, Carla. 2002, February 22. "Oklahoma Places Third on List of 'Worst Welfare States.' " *The Oklahoman*.

Hofstadter, Richard. 1955. *The Age of Reform: From Bryan to F.D.R.* New York: Knopf.

Horn, Wade F. 2000, April 4. "Use Welfare Money to Promote Marriage." *Fatherly Advice*. Retrieved July 22, 2008 (http://www.smartmarriages.com/tanf.oklahoma.html).

———. 2002. "Statement by Wade F. Horn, Ph.D., Assistant Secretary for Children and Families, Department of Health and Human Services, Before the Committee on Finance, United States Senate."

———. 2003. "Closing the Marriage Gap." *Crisis: Politics, Culture & the Church* 21:33–37.

Hull, Kathleen E. 2006a. *Same-Sex Marriage: The Cultural Politics of Love and Law*. Cambridge: Cambridge University Press.

———. 2006b. " 'Humanity Is Male and Female': Gender Discourses in the American Marriage Movement." Unpublished manuscript.

Hunter, James Davison. 1991. *Culture Wars: The Struggle to Define America.* New York: Basic Books.

Hymowitz, Kay S. 2006. *Marriage and Caste in America: Separate and Unequal Families in a Post-Marital Age.* Chicago: Ivan R. Dee.

Ingraham, Chrys. 1999. *White Weddings: Romancing Heterosexuality in Popular Culture.* New York: Routledge.

———, ed. 2005. *Thinking Straight: The Power, the Promise, and the Paradox of Heterosexuality.* New York: Routledge.

Institute for American Values [IAV]. 2004. *What Next for the Marriage Movement?* New York: Institute for American Values.

———. 2006, February. "What Is America's Most Serious Social Problem?" Center for Marriage and Families Fact Sheet, No. 1.

Institute for American Values and Institute for Marriage and Public Policy. 2006. *Marriage and the Law: A Statement of Principles.* New York: Institute for American Values.

Institute for Women's Policy Research. 2004. "The Status of Women in Oklahoma." Retrieved January 30, 2009 (http://www.iwpr.org/States2004/PDFs/Oklahoma.pdf).

Irigaray, Luce. 1997. "Women on the Market." Pp. 174–89 in *The Logic of the Gift: Toward an Ethic of Generosity*, edited by Alan D. Schrift. Translated by Catherine Porter and Carolyn Burke. New York: Routledge.

Irvine, Janice M. 2002. *Talk about Sex: The Battles over Sex Education in the United States.* Berkeley: University of California Press.

Jacobi, Jeffrey S. 2006. "Note: Two Spirits, Two Eras, Same Sex: For a Traditionalist Perspective on Native American Tribal Same-Same Marriage Policy." *University of Michigan Journal of Law Reform* 39:823–50.

Jarchow, Courtney. 2003. *Strengthening Marriage and Two-Parent Families.* Denver: National Conference of State Legislature.

Johnson, Christine, Scott Stanley, Norval Glenn, Paul Amato, Steve Nock, Howard Markman, and M. Robin Dion. 2002. *Marriage in Oklahoma: 2001 Baseline Statewide Survey on Marriage and Divorce.* Oklahoma: Oklahoma State University Bureau for Social Research.

Johnson, Paul. 2005. *Love, Heterosexuality, and Society.* New York: Routledge.

Kandiyoti, Deniz. 1988. "Bargaining with Patriarchy." *Gender & Society* 2(3):274–90.

Kannady, Christopher L. 2004/2005. "The State, Cherokee Nation, and Same-Sex Unions: In Re: Marriage License of McKinley and Reynolds." *American Indian Law Review* 29(2):363–81.

Katz, Jonathan Ned. 1996. *The Invention of Heterosexuality.* New York: Plume.

Katz, Michael B. 1989. *The Undeserving Poor: From the War on Poverty to the War on Welfare.* New York: Pantheon.

Keating, Frank. 2000. "Making Marriage Matter." Heritage Lecture #684. Retrieved February 17, 2009 (http://www.heritage.org/Research/Family/HL684.cfm).

———. 2004. "Healthy Marriage: What Is It and Why Should We Promote It?" Testimony before the Health, Education, Labor and Pensions Committee, Subcommittee on Children and Families. U.S. Senate Hearing.

Kennedy, Kathleen, and Sharon Rena Ullman. 2003. *Sexual Borderlands: Constructing an American Sexual Past*. Columbus: Ohio State University Press.

Kiernan, Kathleen. 2002. "Cohabitation in Western Europe: Trends, Issues, and Implications." Pp. 3–31 in *Just Living Together: Implications of Cohabitation on Families, Children, and Social Policy*, edited by A. Booth and A. C. Crouter. Mahwah, NJ: Erlbaum.

———. 2004. "Redrawing the Boundaries of Marriage." *Journal of Marriage and Family* 66:980–87.

Knorr Cetina, Karin. 1999. *Epistemic Cultures: How the Sciences Make Knowledge*. Cambridge, MA: Harvard University Press.

———. 2005. "Culture in Global Knowledge Societies: Knowledge Cultures and Epistemic Cultures." Pp. 65–79 in *Blackwell Companion to the Sociology of Culture*, edited by Mark Jacobs and Nancy Weiss Hanrahan. Malden, MA: Blackwell Publishing.

Knox, Virginia, Cynthia Miller, and Lisa Gennetian. 2000. *Reforming Welfare and Rewarding Work: A Summary of the Final Report of the Minnesota Family Investment Program*. Washington, DC: Manpower Demonstration Research Corporation.

Komisar, Lucy. 1977. *Down and Out in the USA: A History of Public Welfare*. Rev. ed. New York: Franklin Watts.

Ladd-Taylor, Molly. 1994. *Mother-Work: Women, Child-Welfare and the State, 1890–1930*. Urbana: University of Illinois Press.

Lamont, Michèle. 1992. *Money, Morals, and Manners: The Culture of the French and American Upper-Middle Class*. Chicago: University of Chicago Press.

———. 2000. *The Dignity of Working Men: Morality and the Boundaries of Race, Class, and Immigration*. Cambridge: Harvard University Press and Russell Sage Foundation.

Lamont, Michèle, and Marcel Fournier, eds. 1992. *Cultivating Differences: Symbolic Boundaries and the Making of Inequality*. Chicago: University of Chicago Press.

Lamont, Michèle, and Virág Molnar. 2002. "The Study of Boundaries in the Social Sciences." *Annual Review of Sociology* 28:167–95.

Lan, Pei-Chia. 2006. *Global Cinderellas: Migrant Domestics and Newly Rich Employers in Taiwan*. Durham: Duke University Press.

Lareau, Annette. 2003. *Unequal Childhoods: Class, Race, and Family Life*. Berkeley: University of California Press.

Leonard, Mary. 2004. "Marriage Class Plays National Role." *Boston Globe*. Retrieved September 15, 2008 (http://www.religionandsocialpolicy.org/news/article.cfm?id=1310).

Lerman, Robert. 2002. *Family Structure and Childbearing before and after Welfare Reform*. Washington, DC: The Urban Institute.

Lerner, Sharon 2004, July 5. "Marriage on the Mind." *The Nation*. Retrieved September 18, 2009 (http://www.thenation.com/doc/20040705/lerner).

Lewin, Tamar. 1998, October 14. "Debate over Marriage Education for High-School Students." *New York Times*. Retrieved June 11, 2009 (http://www.smartmarriages.com/highschoolsnytimes.html).

Lewis, Oscar. 1959. *Five Families: Mexican Case Studies in the Culture of Poverty*. New York: Basic Books.

Lichter, Daniel, Deborah Roempke Graefe, and J. Brian Brown. 2003. "Is Marriage a Panacea? Union Formation among Economically-Disadvantaged Unwed Mothers." *Social Problems* 50:60–86.

Lindberg, Laura Duberstein, Rachel Jones, and John S. Santelli. 2008. "Noncoital. Sexual Activities among Adolescents." *Journal of Adolescent Health* 43(3):231–38.

Lindsay, D. Michael. 2007. *Faith in the Halls of Power: How Evangelicals Joined the American Elite*. New York: Oxford University Press.

Loewenberg, Frank M. 1981. "The Destigmatization of Public Dependency." *Social Service Review* 55(3):434–52.

Lofton, Katie, and Donald P. Haider-Markel. 2007. "The Politics of Same-Sex Marriage vs. the Politics of Gay Civil Rights: A Comparison of Public Opinion and State Voting Patterns." Pp. 316–17 in *The Politics of Same-Sex Marriage*, edited by Craig Rimmerman and Clyde Wilcox. Chicago: University of Chicago Press.

Loftus, Jeni. 2001. "America's Liberalization in Attitudes toward Homosexuality, 1973 to 1998." *American Sociological Review* 66:762–82.

Lowe, Lisa. 1998. *Immigrant Acts: On Asian American Cultural Politics*. Durham: Duke University Press.

Luker, Kristin. 1996. *Dubious Conceptions: The Politics of Teenage Pregnancy*. Cambridge: Harvard University Press.

———. 2006. *When Sex Goes to School: Warring Views on Sex—and Sex Education—Since the Sixties*. New York: Norton.

Lyman, Rick. 2005, April 16. "Marriage Programs Try to Instill Bliss and Stability Behind Bars." *New York Times*. Retrieved July 30, 2009 (http://www.nytimes.com/2005/04/16/national/16marriage.html).

Mack, Dana. 2001, March. "Educating for Marriage, Sort Of." *First Things: A Monthly Journal of Religion and Public Life*. Retrieved September 10, 2010 (http://www.firstthings.com/article/2007/01/-educating-for-marriage-sort-of-11).

MacQuarrie, Brian. 2005, October 9. "Dobson Spiritual Empire Wields Political Clout." *Boston Globe*. Retrieved October 9, 2008 (http://www.boston.com/news/nation/articles/2005/10/09/dobson_spiritual_empire_wields_political_clout/).

Manning, Wendy D., and Daniel T. Lichter. 1996. "Parental Cohabitation and Children's Economic Well-Being." *Journal of Marriage and Family* 58:998-1010.

Markman, Howard, Scott Stanley, and Susan Bloomberg. 2001. *Fighting for Your Marriage: Positive Steps for Preventing Divorce and Preserving a Lasting Love*. San Francisco: Jossey-Bass.

Marsden, George M. 1980. *Fundamentalism and American Culture: The Shaping of the Twentieth Century Evangelicalism 1870–1925*. Oxford: Oxford University Press.

Marty, Martin E. 1998. *The One and the Many: America's Struggle for the Common Good*. Cambridge: Harvard University Press.

Massey, Douglas, and Nancy Denton. 1993. *American Apartheid: Segregation and the Making of the Underclass*. Cambridge: Harvard University Press.

May, Elaine Tyler. 1988. *Homeward Bound: American Families in the Cold War Era*. New York: Basic Books.

McClain, Linda C. 2006. *The Place of Families: Fostering Capacity, Equality, and Responsibility*. Cambridge: Harvard University Press.

McLanahan, Sara. 2002. "Life without Father: What Happens to the Children?" *Contexts* 1(1):35–44.

McLanahan, Sara, Irwin Garfinkel, and Ronald Mincy. 2001. *The Fragile Families and Child Wellbeing Study Baseline Study*. Princeton, NJ: Center for Research on Child Wellbeing.

McLanahan, Sara, and Gary Sandefur. 1994. *Growing Up with a Single Parent*. Cambridge: Harvard University Press.

Mead, Lawrence M. 1992. *The New Politics of Poverty: The Nonworking Poor in America*. New York: Basic Books.

Meckler, Laura. 2006, November 16. "Matchmaker: How a U.S. Official Promotes Marriage to Fight Poverty." *Wall Street Journal*.

Mink, Gwendolyn. 1995. *The Wages of Motherhood: Inequality in the Welfare State, 1917–1942*. Ithaca: Cornell University Press.

———. 1998. *Welfare's End*. Ithaca: Cornell University Press.

———. 1999. *Whose Welfare?* Ithaca: Cornell University Press.

———. 2002. "From Welfare to Wedlock: Marriage Promotion and Poor Mothers' Inequality." *The Good Society* 11:68–73.

Moran, Rachel F. 2001. *Interracial Intimacy: The Regulation of Race and Romance*. Chicago: University of Chicago Press.

Morgan, David R., and Kenneth J. Meier. 1980. "Politics and Morality: The Effect of Religion on Referenda Voting." *Social Science Quarterly* 61:144–48.

Moynihan, Daniel P. 1965. *The Negro Family: The Case for National Action*. Washington, DC: U.S. Department of Labor. Retrieved January 19, 2010 (http://www.dol.gov/oasam/programs/history/webid-meynihan.htm).

Murray, Charles. 1984. *Losing Ground: American Social Policy, 1950–1980*. New York: Basic Books.

———. 1993, October 29. "The Coming White Underclass." *Wall Street Journal*.

Myrick, Mary, and Theodora Ooms. 2002, November 7. "What If a Governor Decides to Address the M-Word? The Use of Research in the Design and Implementation of the Oklahoma Marriage Initiative." Paper presented at the American Association of Public Policy and Management annual conference in Dallas.

Nagel, Joane. 2003. *Race, Ethnicity, and Sexuality: Intimate Intersections, Forbidden Frontiers*. New York: Oxford University Press.

National Campaign for Jobs and Income Support. 2002. *States Behaving Badly: America's Ten Worst Welfare States*. Retrieved October 15, 2009 (http://www.nationalcampaign.org/download/ngareport.pdf).

National Commission on Civic Renewal. 1998. *A Nation of Spectators: How Civic Disengagement Weakens America and What We Can Do about It*. College Park: University of Maryland.

National Fatherhood Initiative, Institute for Marriage and Public Policy, and Institute for American Values. 2004. *Can Government Strengthen Marriage? Evidence from the Social Sciences*. New York: Institute for American Values.

National Healthy Marriage Resource Center. 2007. "TANF Funds and Healthy Marriage Activities." Fact Sheet. Retrieved January 17, 2010 (http://www.healthymarriageinfo.org/docs/tanffundhmact.pdf).

Neubeck, Kenneth J., and Noel A. Cazenave. 2001. *Welfare Racism: Playing the Race Card against America's Poor*. New York: Routledge.

Nock, Steven L. 1998. *Marriage in Men's Lives*. Oxford: Oxford University Press.

O'Connor, Alice. 2002. *Poverty Knowledge: Social Science, Social Policy, and the Poor in Twentieth-Century U.S. History*. Princeton, NJ: Princeton University Press.

O'Connor, Brendon. 2004. *A Political History of the American Welfare System: When Ideas Have Consequences.* Lanham, MD: Rowman and Littlefield.

Office of Community Service. n.d. "Demonstration Grants." U.S. Department of Health and Human Services, Administration for Children and Families. Retrieved November 18, 2009 (http://www.acf.hhs.gov/programs/ocs/ccf/about_ccf/history_funding/demo_summary.html).

Okin, Susan Moller. 1979. *Women in Western Political Thought.* Princeton, NJ: Princeton University Press.

Oklahoma Coalition against Domestic Violence and Sexual Assault. n.d. "Domestic Violence Quick Facts." Retrieved April 22, 2009 (http://www.ocadvsa.org/dv_quickfacts.htm).

Oklahoma Department of Mental Health and Substance Abuse Services. 1999. "Oklahoma State Treatment Needs Assessment Project: 1999 General Household Survey Domestic Violence Component." Retrieved April 22, 2009 (www.odmhsas.org/eda/stnap/r11.pdf).

Oklahoma Family Policy Council. n.d. "Abstinence Education." Retrieved June 27, 2009 (http://www.okfamilypc.org/abstinence_education.htm).

Oklahoma Marriage Initiative. n.d. "Who Are Our Workshop Leaders." Retrieved January 19, 2010 (http://www.okmarriage.org/TrainingInstitute/WorkshopLeaders.asp).

Oldfield, Duane M. 1996. *The Right and the Righteous: The Christian Right Confronts the Republican Party.* Lanham, MD: Rowman and Littlefield.

Olson, Sarah. 2005, January/February. "Marriage Promotion, Reproductive Injustice, and the War against Poor Women of Color." *Dollars & Sense.*

Ong, Aihwa. 1996. "Cultural Citizenship as Subjectmaking. Immigrants Negotiate Racial and Cultural Boundaries in the United States." *Current Anthropology* 37(5):737–62.

Ooms, Theodora. 2002. "Marriage Plus." *The American Prospect* 13(7):24–25.

Ooms, Theodora, Stacey Bouchet, and Mary Parke. 2004. *Beyond Marriage Licenses: Efforts in States to Strengthen Marriage and Two-Parent Families.* Washington, DC: Center for Law and Social Policy.

Ooms, Theodora, and David Fein 2006. *What Do We Know about Couples and Marriages in Disadvantaged Populations? Reflections from a Research and a Policy Analyst.* Washington, DC: Center for Law and Social Policy.

Overall, Michael. 1996, September 8. "Rights Activist Addresses Senate Bills Affecting Gays." *Tulsa World.*

Pachucki, Mark A., Sabrina Pendergrass, and Michèle Lamont. 2007. "Boundary Processes: Recent Theoretical Developments and New Contributions." *Poetics* 35:331–51.

Parke, Mary. 2003, May. *Are Married Parents Really Better for Children? What Research Says about the Effects of Family Structure on Child Well-Being.* Center for Law and Social Policy, Couples and Marriage Series, Policy Brief #3.

———. 2004. "Who Are 'Fragile Families' and What Do We Know about Them?" Couples and. Marriage Policy Series Brief No. 4. Washington, DC: Center for Law and Public Policy.

Parrott III, Dr. Les, and Dr. Leslie Parrott. 1997. *Becoming Soul Mates.* Grand Rapids: Zondervan.

Parsons, Talcott, and Robert F. Bales. 1956. *Family Socialization and Interaction Process.* London: Routledge & Kegan Paul.

Pascale, Celine-Marie. 2001. "All in a Day's Work: A Feminist Analysis of Class Formation and Social Identity." *Race, Gender & Class* 8:34–59.

———. 2007. *Making Sense of Race, Class, and Gender: Commonsense, Power, and Privilege in the United States.* New York: Routledge.

Pascoe, C. J. 2007. *Dude, You're A Fag: Masculinity and Sexuality in High School.* Berkeley: University of California Press.

Pearson, Marline. n.d. *The LoveU2: Becoming Sex Smart.* Berkeley: The Dibble Fund for Marriage Education. Retrieved August 11, 2011 (http://www.dibbleinstitute. org/?page_id=514).

Pearson, Marline, Scott M. Stanley, and Galena H. Kline. 2005, November. *Within My Reach: Instructors Manual.* PREP for Individuals, Inc., Version 1.2.

Perdue, Theda. 1999. *Cherokee Women: Gender and Culture Change, 1700–1835.* Lincoln: University of Nebraska Press.

Persell, Caroline, Adam Green, and Liena Gurevich. 2001. "Civil Society, Economic Distress, and Social Tolerance." *Sociological Forum* 16:203–30.

Peterson, Karen S. 2000, March 23. "Oklahoma Weds Welfare Funds to Marriage." *USA Today.* Retrieved June 30, 2006 (http://lists101.his.com/pipermail/ smartmarriages/2000-March/000119.html).

Pew Forum on Religion and Public Life. 2008. "U.S. Religious Landscape Survey." Pew Research Center.

Polikoff, Nancy D. 2005. "For the Sake of the Children: Opponents and Supporters of Same-Sex Marriage Both Miss the Mark." *New York City Law Review* 8:573–98.

———. 2008. *Beyond (Straight and Gay) Marriage: Valuing All Families under the Law.* Boston: Beacon.

Popenoe, David. 1996. *Life without Father: Compelling New Evidence That Fatherhood and Marriage Are Indispensable for the Good of Children and Society.* Cambridge: Harvard University Press.

———. 1999. "Can the Nuclear Family Be Revived?" *Society* 36(5):28–30.

———. 2008, August. *The American Family, 1988–2028: Looking Forward and Looking Back.* Center for Marriage and Family, Institute for American Values, Research Brief No. 13.

Popenoe, David, and Barbara Dafoe Whitehead. 2000. *Should We Live Together? What Young Adults Need to Know about Cohabitation before Marriage.* The National Marriage Project: The Next Generation Series. New Brunswick: Rutgers University.

Prucha, Francis Paul. 1973. *Americanizing the American Indian: Writings by the "Friends of the Indian," 1880–1900.* Cambridge: Harvard University Press.

———. 1984. *The Great Father: The United States Government and the American Indians.* Lincoln: University of Nebraska Press.

Putnam, Robert D. 2000. *Bowling Alone: The Collapse and Revival of American Community.* New York: Simon & Schuster.

Quadagno, Jill. 1994. *The Color of Welfare: How Racism Undermined the War on Poverty.* New York: Oxford University Press.

Quayle, Dan. 1992, May 9. *Prepared Remarks by the Vice President.* Presented to the Commonwealth Club of California. Retrieved August 9, 2010 (http://www.vicepresidentdan-quayle.com/speeches_StandingFirm_CCC_1.html).

Radstone, Susannah. 2007. *The Sexual Politics of Time: Confession, Nostalgia, Memory.* New York: Routledge.

Raley, R. Kelly, and Larry L. Bumpass. 2003. "The Topography of the Plateau in Divorce: Levels and Trends in Union Stability after 1980." *Demographic Research* 8:246–58.

Randles, Jennifer. 2009. "Parenting in Poverty and the Politics of Commitment: Promoting Marriage for Poor Families through Relationship Education." *UC Berkeley: Institute for the Study of Social Change*. Retrieved December 15, 2009 (http://escholarship.org/uc/item/0tp2b2xm).

Rector, Robert, Kirk A. Johnson, and Patrick F. Fagan. 2002, April 15. "The Effect of Marriage on Child Poverty." A Report of the Heritage Center CDA02–04.

Rector, Robert, Melissa G. Pardue, and Lauren R. Noyes. 2003. *"Marriage Plus": Sabotaging the President's Efforts to Promote Healthy Marriage*. Washington, DC: The Heritage Foundation Executive Backgrounder Summary. Retrieved December 19, 2009 (http://www.heritage.org/research/family/bg1677.cfm).

Reese, Ellen. 2005. *Backlash against Welfare Mothers: Past and Present*. Berkeley: University of California Press.

Regier, Jerry. 1999. *Oklahoma Marriage Policy: A Strategic Plan*. Retrieved September 21, 2006 (http://lists101.his.com/pipermail/smartmarriages/1999-April/002095.html)

———. 2001, May 22. "Statement of the Hon. Jerry Regier, Cabinet Secretary, Oklahoma Health and Human Services, and Acting Director, Oklahoma Department of Health. Testimony before the Subcommittee on Human Resources of the House Committee on Ways and Means." Hearing on Welfare and Marriage Issues. Retrieved July 25, 2008 (http://waysandmeans.house.gov/legacy/humres/107cong/5-22-01/5-22regi.htm).

Rich, Adrienne. 1980. "Compulsory Heterosexuality and Lesbian Existence." *Signs* 5:631-60.

Rieder, Jonathan, and Stephen Steinlight, eds. 2003. *The Fractious Nation? Unity and Division in Contemporary American Life*. Berkeley: University of California Press.

Rifkin, Mark. 2008. "Native Nationality and the Contemporary Queer: Tradition, History, and Sexuality in *Drowning in Fire.*" *American Indian Quarterly* 32/4:443-70.

Riker, Audrey Palm, and Holly E. Brisbane. 1997. *Married & Single Life*. 6th ed. New York: McGraw-Hill.

Roberts, Paula. 2006, February 10. *Update on the Marriage and Fatherhood Provisions of the 2006 Federal Budget and the 2007 Budget Proposal*. Center for Law and Social Policy. Retrieved March 30, 2007 (http://www.clasp.org/publications/marriage_fatherhood_budget2006.pdf).

Roscoe, Will. 1998. *Changing Ones: Third and Fourth Genders in Native North America*. New York: St. Martin's Press.

Rose, Nancy. 1995. *Workfare or Fair Work: Women, Welfare, and Government Work Programs*. New Brunswick: Rutgers University Press.

Rose, Nikolas. 1999. *Powers of Freedom: Reframing Political Thought*. Cambridge: Cambridge University Press.

Roundtable on Religion and Social Welfare Policy. 2005, August 15. *An Interview with Quanah Crossland Stamps of the Administration for Native Americans*. Retrieved August 1, 2009 (http://www.religionandsocialpolicy.org/interviews/interview_upd.cfm?id=96&pageMode=general).

Rubin, Gayle S. 1975. "The Traffic in Women: Notes on the 'Political Economy' of Sex." Pp. 157-210 in *Toward an Anthropology of Woman*, edited by Rayna R. Reiter. New York: Monthly Review.

————. 1984. "Thinking Sex: Notes for a Radical Theory of the Politics of Sexuality." Pp. 267–319 in *Pleasure and Danger: Exploring Female Sexuality*, edited by Carole S. Vance. Boston: Routledge & Kegan Paul.

Rupp, Leila, and Verta Taylor. 1987. *Survival in the Doldrums: The American Women's Rights Movement, 1945 to the 1960s*. New York: Oxford University Press.

Sanchez, Laura, Steven L. Nock, Julia L. Wilson, and James D. Wright. 2006. "Is Covenant Marriage a Policy That Preaches to the Choir? A Comparison of Covenant and Standard Married Newlywed Couples in Louisiana." Bowling Green State University, Working Paper Series 02–06.

Satterthwaite, Shad. 2005. "Faster Horses, Older Whiskey, and More Money: An Analysis of Religious Influence on Referenda Voting." *Journal for the Scientific Study of Religion* 44:105–12.

Sawhill, Isabel V., and Adam Thomas. 2002, October 8. *For Richer or for Poorer: Marriage as an Antipoverty Strategy*. Wiley Interscience. Retrieved April 15, 2006 (http://www.brook.edu/views/papers/sawhill/20021016.htm).

Schaffer, Michael. 2002, March 3. "Marriage Proposal: Should the Government Spend Your Tax Dollars to Encourage Holy Vows?" *U.S. News*. Retrieved April 30, 2009 (http://www.usnews.com/usnews/news/articles/020311/archive_020308.htm).

Sedgwick, Eve Kosofsky. 1990. *Epistemology of the Closet*. Berkeley: University of California Press.

Shipman, Claire, and Cole Kazdin. 2009, May 28. "Oral Sex and Casual Prostitution No Biggie." *ABC News*. Retrieved June 6, 2009 (http://abcnews.go.com/GMA/Parenting/Story?id=7693121).

Sigle-Rushton, Wendy, and Sarah McLanahan. 2002. "For Richer or Poorer? Marriage as an Anti-poverty Strategy in the United States." *Population* 57:509–26.

Small, Mario Luis, David J. Harding, and Michèle Lamont. 2010. "Reconsidering Culture and Poverty." *Annals of the American Academy of Political and Social Science* 629:6–27.

Smart Marriages n.d. *PREP®: The Prevention & Relationship Enhancement Program*. Retrieved October 25, 2008 (http://www.smartmarriages.com/prep.overview.html).

Smith, Anna Marie. 2007. *Welfare Reform and Sexual Regulation*. Cambridge: Cambridge University Press.

Smith, Christian, Michael Emerson, Sally Gallagher, Paul Kennedy, and David Sikkink. 1997. "The Myth of Culture Wars: The Case of American Protestantism." Pp. 175–95 in *Cultural Wars in American Politics: Critical Reviews of a Popular Myth*, edited by Rhys H. Williams. New York: Aldine de Gruyter.

Smith, Tom W. 1996. *A Survey of the Religious Right: Views on Politics, Society, Jews, and Other Minorities*. New York: American Jewish Committee.

Smock, Pamela. 2000. "Cohabitation in the United States: An Appraisal of Research Themes, Findings, and Implications." *Annual Review of Sociology* 26:1–20.

Smock, Pamela J., and Stephanie Coontz. 2004. *"Marriage Preparation" Prescriptions for Welfare Reform and Poverty Reduction: Take with a Couple of Grains of Salt*. Retrieved June 28, 2009 (www.contemporaryfamilies.org/marriagetext.htm).

Smock, Pamela J., and Wendy D. Manning. 2004. "Living Together Unmarried in the United States: Demographic Perspectives and Implications for Family Policy." *Law & Policy* 26(1):87–117.

Sollors, Werner. 2000. *Interracialism: Black-White Intermarriage in American History, Literature, and Law*. Oxford: Oxford University Press.

Somers, Margaret R. 2008. *Genealogies of Citizenship: Markets, Statelessness, and the Right to Have Rights*. Cambridge: Cambridge University Press.

Sprigg, Peter. 2004. *Outrage: How Gay Activists and Liberal Judges Are Trashing Democracy to Redefine Marriage*. Washington, DC: Regnery.

Stacey, Judith. 1996. *In the Name of the Family: Rethinking Family Values in the Postmodern Age*. Boston: Beacon.

———. 1998. *Brave New Families: Stories of Domestic Upheaval in Late-Twentieth Century America*. Berkeley: University of California Press.

———. 2001, July 9. "Family Values Forever." *Nation*.

Stacey, Judith, and Susan E. Gerard. 1990. "'We Are Not Doormats': The Influence of Feminism on Contemporary Evangelicals in the United States." Pp. 98–117 in *Uncertain Terms: Negotiating Gender in American Culture*, edited by F. Ginsburg and A. L. Tsing. Boston: Beacon.

Stanley, Amy Dru. 1998. *From Bondage to Contract: Wage Labor, Marriage and the Market in the Age of Slave Emancipation*. Cambridge: Cambridge University Press.

Stanley, Scott M., Savanna C. McCain, and Daniel W. Trathen. 1996. *The Christian PREP Couple's Manual*. Greenwood Village: PREP Educational Products.

Stanton, Glenn T. 1997. *Why Marriage Matters: Reasons to Believe in Marriage in Postmodern Society*: Colorado Springs: NavPress.

Stein, Arlene. 1997. *Sex and Sensibility: Stories of a Lesbian Generation*. Berkeley: University of California Press.

———. 2001. *The Stranger Next Door: The Story of a Small Community's Battle over Sex, Faith, and Civil Rights*. Boston: Beacon.

Stoever, Colby J., and Morera, Osvaldo F. 2007. "A Confirmatory Factor Analysis of the Attitudes toward Lesbians and Gay Men (ATLG) Measure." *Journal of Homosexuality* 52(3):189–209.

Strong, Deborah A. 2008. *Putting Marriage on the Agenda: How Oklahoma Laid the Foundation for Its Marriage Initiative*. Office of Assistant Secretary for Planning and Evaluation Research Brief. Washington, D.C.: U.S. Department of Health and Human Services.

Sturm, Circe. 2002. *Blood Politics: Race, Culture, and Identity in the Cherokee Nation of Oklahoma*. Berkeley: University of California Press.

Swidler, Ann. 1986. "Culture in Action: Symbol and Strategies." *American Sociological Review* 51:273–86.

———. 2001. *Talk of Love: How Culture Matters*. Chicago: University of Chicago Press.

Tadlock, Barry L., Ann C. Gordon, and Elizabeth Popp. 2006. "Frame the Issue of Same-Sex Marriage: Traditional Values versus Equality Rights." Pp. 193–214 in *The Politics of Same-Sex Marriage*, edited by Craig A. Rimmerman and Clyde Wilcox. Chicago: University of Chicago Press.

Talley, Tim. 2002, September 27. "Researchers Say One-third Cut in Divorce Rate Unlikely." *Associated Press Newswire*.

Taylor, Verta, and Nancy E. Whittier. 1992. "Collective Identity in Social Movement Communities: Lesbian Feminist Mobilization." Pp. 104–29 in *Frontiers in Social Movement Theory*, edited by A. D. Morris and C. M. Mueller. New Haven: Yale University Press.

Thornton, Arland, William G. Axinn, and Yu Xie. 2007. *Marriage and Cohabitation*. Chicago: University of Chicago Press.

Thornton, Arland, and Linda Young-DeMarco. 2001. "Four Decades of Trends in Attitudes towards Family Issues in the United States: The 1960s through the 1990s." *Journal of Marriage and Family* 63:1009–37.

Tolman, Richard M., and Jody Raphael. 2000. "A Review of Research on Welfare and Domestic Violence." *Journal of Social Issues* 56:655–81.

Tugend, Alina. 1985, January 23. "Homosexuality Law Weighed by Court." *Education Week*. Retrieved February 19, 2009 (http://www.edweek.org/).

Tyre, Peg. 2002, February 18. "Giving Lessons in Love: Oklahoma Is Fighting Its Sky-High Divorce Rate with Controversial, State-funded 'Marriage Ambassadors.'" *Newsweek*.

U.S. Census Bureau. 2000. *Historical Poverty Statistics—Table 4. Poverty Status of Families, by Type of Family, Presence of Related Children, Race, and Hispanic Origin: 1959–2000*. Washington, DC: U.S. Government Printing Office.

———. 2001. *Poverty in the United States*. Current Population Reports, Series P60–214. Washington DC: U.S. Government Printing Office.

———. 2004. Table MS-2, *Estimated Median Age at First Marriage, by Sex: 1890 to Present*. Washington, DC. Retrieved June 6, 2009 (http://www.census.gov/population/socdemo/hh-fam/tabMS-2.pdf).

———. 2005. *Current Population Survey: Annual Social and Economic Supplements*. Washington, DC: U.S. Government Printing Office.

U.S. Congress. 1996. *Personal Responsibility and Work Opportunity Reconciliation Act of 1996*. Public Law 104–93, H.R. 3734.

U.S. House of Representatives Committee on Government Reform—Minority Staff, Special Investigations Division. 2004. *The Content of Federally-funded Abstinence-only Education Programs*. Retrieved June 8, 2009 (oversight.house.gov/documents/20041201102153–50247.pdf).

U.S. National Center for Health Statistics. 1982. *Vital Statistics of the United States, 1978 (Volume I—Natality)*. Washington, DC: U.S. Government Printing Office.

———. 2003. *Births: Preliminary Data for 2002*. Retrieved March 30, 2006 (http://www.cdc.gov/nchs/data/nvsr/nvsr51/nvsr51_11.pdf).

Van Epp, John. 2007. *How to Avoid Marrying a Jerk: The Foolproof Way to Follow Your Heart without Losing Your Mind*. New York: McGraw-Hill.

Waite, Linda, and Maggie Gallagher. 2000. *The Case for Marriage: Why Married People Are Happier, Healthier, and Better Off Financially*. New York: Doubleday.

Wallenstein, Peter. 2002. *Tell the Court I Love My Wife: Race, Marriage, and Law—An American History*. New York: Palgrave Macmillan.

Waters, Mary C. 1999. *Black Identities. West Indian Immigrant Dreams and American Realities*. New York: Russell Sage Foundation.

Watt, David Herrington. 1991. *A Transforming Faith: An Exploration of Twentieth-Century American Evangelicalism*. News Brunswick: Rutgers University Press.

Weeks, Jeffrey. 1995. *Invented Moralities: Sexual Values in an Age of Uncertainty*. Oxford: Polity Press.

Weiss, Mike. 2007, February 11. "Abstinence-only Sex Ed Finds Few Scientific Fans." *San Francisco Chronicle*. Retrieved June 27, 2009 (http://sfgate.com/cgi-bin/article.cgi?f=/c/a/2007/02/11/MNG7VO2LUV1.DTL).

West, Candace, and Don Zimmerman. 1987. "Doing Gender." *Gender & Society* 1:125–51.

Wetzstein, Cheryl. 2002a, July 12. "Pro-Marriage Initiatives Win Enthusiastic Survey Support." *Washington Times.*

———. 2002b, September 16. "Welfare Promotes Marriage: Education Courses Up for Renewal Aim to Stabilize Families." *Washington Times.*

———. 2005, February 10. "Middle Ground on Sex Ed." *Washington Times.* Retrieved June 8, 2009 (http://www.washingtontimes.com/news/2005/feb/10/20050210–125526–4111r/).

———. 2010, July 5. "Let's Not Give Up on Idea of Marriage Ed." *Washington Times.* Retrieved January 26, 2011 (http://www.washingtontimes.com/news/2010/jul/5/wetzstein-lets-not-give-up-on-idea-of-marriage-ed/)

Whitehead, Barbara Dafoe. 1993, April. "Dan Quayle Was Right." *Atlantic Monthly*:47–84.

Whitehead, Barbara Dafoe, and Marlene Pearson. 2006. *Making a Love Connection: Teen Relationships, Pregnancy, and Marriage.* Washington, DC: National Campaign to Prevent Teen Pregnancy.

Wilcox, Clyde, Linda M. Merolla, and David Beer. 2007. "Save Marriage by Banning Marriage: The Christian Right Finds a New Issue in 2004." Pp. 56–75 in *The Values Campaign? The Christian Right and the 2004 Elections,* edited by John C. Green, Mark J. Rozell, and Clyde Wilcox. Washington, DC: Georgetown University Press.

Wilcox, W. Bradford. 2002. *Sacred Vows, Public Purposes: Religion, the Marriage Movement, and Marriage Policy.* Washington, DC: Pew Forum on Religion and Public Life.

Wilcox, W. Bradford, William Doherty, Norval Glenn, and Linda Waite. 2005. *Why Marriage Matters, Second Edition: Twenty-Six Conclusions from the Social Sciences.* New York: Institute for American Values.

Wilson, James Q. 2002. *The Marriage Problem: How Our Culture Has Weakened Families.* New York: Harper Paperbacks.

Wilson, William Julius. 1987. *The Truly Disadvantaged.* Chicago: University of Chicago Press.

———. 1996. *When Work Disappears: The World of the New Urban Poor.* New York: Knopf.

Wittig, Monique. 1992. *The Straight Mind and Other Essays.* Boston: Beacon.

Wood, Robert G., Quinn Moore, and Andrew Clarkwest, 2011. *BSF's Effects on Couples Who Attended Group Relationship Skills Sessions: A Special Analysis of 15-Month Data,* OPRE Report # 2011-17. Washington, DC: Office of Planning, Research and Evaluation, Administration for Children and Families, U.S. Department of Health and Human Services.

Wuthnow, Robert. 1983. "The Political Rebirth of American Evangelism." Pp. 168–85 in *The New Christian Right: Mobilization and Legitimation,* edited by R. C. Lieberman and R. Wuthnow. New York: Aldine.

———. 1987. *Meaning and Moral Order: Explorations in Cultural Analysis.* Berkeley: University of California Press.

———. 1988. *The Restructuring of American Religion: Society and Faith Since World War II.* Princeton, NJ: Princeton University Press.

Yakush, Jen Heitel. 2007. *Legalized Discrimination: The Rise of the Marriage-Promotion Industry and How Federally Funded Programs Discriminate against Lesbian, Gay, Bisexual, and Transgender Youth and Families.* Special Report. SEICUS Public Policy Office.

Yalom, Marilyn. 2001. *A History of the Wife.* New York: HarperCollins.

Yang, Alan S. 1997. "The Polls—Trends: Attitudes toward Homosexuality." *Public Opinion Quarterly* 61:477–507.

Yarbrough, Fay. 2004. "Legislating Women's Sexuality: Cherokee Marriage Laws in the Nineteenth Century." *Journal of Social History* 38(2):385–406.

———. 2007. *Race and the Cherokee Nation: Sovereignty in the Nineteenth Century.* Philadelphia: University of Pennsylvania Press.

Index

Clinton, Bill, 2, 6, 26, 90
Coalition for Marriage, Family, and Couples Education (CMFCE), 2
Cohabitation, 6, 20, 24, 48, 125, 128, 134, 137, 155, 176, 177, 194, 204, 224n9
Cohen, Stanley, 98
Colonialism, 152, 153, 156, 157, 164, 166, 169, 174, 188
Coltrane, Scott, 8
Commitment, 11, 28, 45, 48, 50, 113, 165, 184; students learning, 141, 142, 147
Communication: at home, 136; patterns, 115; skills, xii, 45, 46, 55, 57–59, 64, 75, 103, 110, 114, 122, 131, 135, 147, 163, 165, 182, 188, 193, 195; skills for prisoners, 117, 119, 120–21; students learning, 129, 131, 135, 136, 147
Compromise, 46, 52, 53, 115
Connections+PREP, 199–200; curriculum, 130–31, 133, 137, 147; in high schools, 131; workbooks, 134–35
Conservative Christians, xi–xii, 24, 25, 51, 81, 89, 178, 184, 212n19; American identity and, 29–31, 33–34; culture-of-poverty model of, 179; homosexuality and, 26–27, 32–33; marriage politics and, 8, 22, 35; values, 28. *See also* Religious right
Consumerism, 86–87
Contraception, 124, 126, 148
Coontz, Stephanie, 4, 9, 12, 190, 205n12
Cott, Nancy, 14, 43, 128, 129, 151, 183, 223n19, 224n14
Court cases, 4, 13, 26, 176
Covenant Marriage Movement, 35, 214n38
Cowan, Carolyn, 193
Cowan, Philip, 193
CPREP. *See* Christian Prevention and Relationship Enhancement Program
Crime, 5, 32, 72, 186
Critical heterosexual studies, 11, 177; institutionalized heterosexuality, 11, 15, 61, 182; marital heterosexuality, 49, 60, 61, 69, 73, 178–79, 182; queer theory and, 11, 14; thinking straight, 61. *See also* American identity; Heterosexuality; Lifelong internally stratified marriage (LISM); Nostalgia

Cultural repertoires, 5, 14, 16, 176, 195, 205n15
Culture, 22; change in sexual, 124–25, 178; decision making and, 32, 50, 177–78; diversified, 40, 183; identity and, xiii, 13, 169; marriage education adapted to Native American, 160–64; Native American, 152, 157, 170, 172; war, 40, 214n46
Culture of poverty, 6, 177, 179, 189, 206n27, 224n8

"Dan Quayle Was Right" (Whitehead), 89
Darwinism, 88, 213n22, 218n43
Dating, 123, 131, 135, 140–41, 142–43, 147
Davis, Fred, 12
Debo, Angie, 156
Defense of Marriage Act (DOMA) (1996), 3–4, 15, 26, 27, 169
Deficit Reduction Act (2005), 3, 185
D'Emilio, John, 10
Department of Corrections (DOC), 117, 118
Department of Health and Human Services, Administration for Children and Families, U.S. (HHS/ACF), 3, 19, 99, 195
Deservingness, 86, 178, 196
Discrimination, 10, 21, 73, 86, 87, 93, 95, 177, 187, 189, 192, 193; gender, 6; against homosexuals, 13, 26, 29, 35, 38–39, 64
Divorce, 9, 23–24, 41, 71, 167, 217n19; decreased, rate, 76, 77; effect of, 48, 76, 89, 176, 184–85; fear of, 94; poverty and, 75, 77; rate, 5–6, 8, 12, 34, 57, 73, 75, 77, 83, 84, 103, 157, 177, 184, 185, 215n9; rate for prisoners, 118; risk of, 133; stigma, 93
Dobson, James, 24, 29, 213n28
DOC. *See* Department of Corrections
Doctrine of Tribal Sovereignty, 167
Doherty, William, 2
DOMA. *See* Defense of Marriage Act (1996)
Domesticity, 209n62
Domestic violence, 9, 93, 94, 96, 99, 100–102, 181; marriage education workshops and, 108–10
Driskill, Qwo-Li, 172, 173

Military bases, marriage education workshops on, 78, 200
Monogamy, 1, 11, 14, 15, 32, 151, 152
Monroe High School, 131; marriage education at, 138–49, 200
Morality, xiii, 4, 6, 14, 25, 29; boundaries of, 50, 51, 54, 91–92, 122; Christian, 10, 15, 17, 24, 25, 33, 129, 149, 155, 170, 180, 187; colonial, 152; in public school system, 129
Moral Majority, 6
Mothers: stay-at-home, 86; working, 86, 87. *See also* Single mothers/motherhood
Mothers' pensions, 86, 217n32
Moynihan, Daniel Patrick, 6, 72, 87, 186, 206n27
Murray, Charles, 88, 89, 124
Myrick, Mary, 37, 38, 39, 75–76, 77, 81, 97, 102, 180, 193, 201, 217n27

National Association of Marriage Enhancement (NAME), 17
National Campaign for Jobs and Income Support, 95
National Fatherhood Initiative, 8, 18, 34
National identity, xiii, 151, 167, 189
National Marriage Project, 7
Nation building, marriage politics and, 91, 183
Native American(s), 3, 20, 22, 38, 131; Christianity and, 163–64; citizenship for, 152–56; civilizing, 152, 154, 157; customs and culture, 152, 154, 157, 170, 172; family, 152, 154, 155, 157, 159, 161, 166; Five Civilized Tribes, 155–56; gender roles, 167, 172–73; identity, 168, 169; marriage, 167–68; marriage education adapted to, culture, 160–64; marriage politics, 152–53; marriage promotion, 156–66, 174, 188; marriage promotion funding, 160; poverty rates, 82; self-determination, 156, 158, 167, 172; support services, 164; "two spirit," 151, 172, 222n2. *See also* Administration for Native Americans; Cherokee Nation; Chickasaw Nation

Native American Healthy Marriage Initiative, 152, 157, 159, 160
Neoconservatism, 210n85
New Paternalism, 88, 218n42
New Yorker, 82
Nippert-Eng, Christena, 16
Nixon, Richard M., 158
Nock, Steven L., 2
Nostalgia, 10, 12, 13, 15, 33, 47, 140, 141, 142, 184, 210n65

Obama, Barack, 3, 126, 191
OKDHS. *See* Oklahoma Department of Human Services
Oklahoma: constitution, 27; demographics, 35, 75–76; divorce rate, 23, 24, 34, 75, 77, 83–84, 184, 185; legislation, 26; marriage initiative, 18–21, 22, 34, 35–36; religious institutions and politics, 25–26, 34–35; worst welfare state, 2–3, 95
Oklahoma Department of Human Services (OKDHS), 38–39, 44, 77, 95, 97, 98, 100, 185, 199
Oklahoma Department of Mental Health and Substance Abuse Services, 100
Oklahoma Family Policy Council, 26, 31, 35, 39, 179
Oklahoma Marriage Covenant, 35
Oneness, 46, 51, 54
Ooms, Theodora, 34, 75–76, 93, 94, 97
Original sin, 47, 55
Out-of-wedlock birth, 6, 8, 12, 13, 14, 23, 24, 34, 41, 71, 183; African American, 86, 87; poverty and, 72, 79, 89, 177; rates, 71, 73, 75, 224n9; stigma, 86, 88, 93, 176, 191
Outsider status, 16–17, 22, 32, 41, 69, 71, 142, 148–49, 153, 177–78, 199; marriage ideology and, 182, 183

Parrott, Les, 36
Parrott, Leslie, 36
Parsons, Talcott, 44
Partner, choosing right, 115–16, 121, 147, 191
Pascoe, C. J., 143
Pathology, tangle of, 6, 13, 73, 87, 88, 179, 186, 206n27, 210n73

Patriarchy, 166, 173, 209n55, 209n62
Patriotism, 13, 24, 29, 154, 155, 188
Pearson, Marline, 123, 127
Penrose, Leslie, 167, 168, 223n43
Personal Responsibility and Work Opportunity Reconciliation Act (PRWORA), 2, 218n48; goals, 90
Pew Research Center, 35
Policy, 1, 3, 7, 17, 183; antipoverty, 72; implications, 189–96; inequality and, 16, 17; social, 8–9, 34, 37–38, 76, 88, 94; welfare, 86, 97
Polygamy, 14, 32, 152, 155, 167, 179
Popenoe, David, 1, 2, 7, 48, 207n40
Pornography, 123, 126
Postindustrialism, 4, 13, 142
Poverty, xii–xiii, 5, 18; of African Americans, 85–86, 88; causes and conditions of, 76–77; children and, 7, 8, 9, 76; culture of, 6, 177, 179, 189, 206n27, 224n8; diminished, rates, 9; divorce and, 75, 77; intergenerational, 72, 89; marriage politics and, 7, 8, 9; marriage promotion and, 184, 185, 191, 193–94, 207n44; out-of-wedlock birth and, 72, 79, 89, 177; rates, 194; rates for African Americans, 82, 186; rates for Latinos, 82; rates for Native Americans, 82; research, 94, 177; of single mothers, 8, 9, 10, 20, 22, 71–73, 77, 86, 87, 94, 96, 183, 184, 185–86; threshold, 78; of women, 85–86, 87, 194
PREP. See Prevention and Relationship Enhancement Program
PREP Relationship, 98–99, 106, 108, 121, 165, 199
Prevention and Relationship Enhancement Program (PREP), 197; for Chickasaw Nation, 160–61; curriculum, 45–46, 48, 50, 52, 55, 58, 100, 102–4, 111, 119, 120, 121, 215n9; curriculum modified, 113–15, 121, 130–31, 162–63; effectiveness of, 103–17; instructors, 103–17; for men, 116–17; TANF recipients and, 97–99, 103–17, 121, 122. See also PREP Relationship; Prison PREP

Prison, marriage education workshops in, 20, 22, 37, 38, 94, 95, 117–21, 200
Prisoners: communication skills for, 117, 119; divorce rate for, 118; marriage promotion for, 117–19, 121; same-sex relationships of, 119–20
Prison PREP, 117–20; at female correction facility, 121–22
Privacy, 11, 16
Privilege, 93
Pro-family movement, 34, 126, 205n11, 213n28
Promise Keepers, xii, 8
Property ownership, 154, 172
Proposition 8 (2008), 4, 175–76
Prostitution, 96, 123–24
Protect Marriage, 1, 28, 40
"Protect the boundaries of marriage" (Institute for American Values), 91
Prucha, Francis Paul, 153
PRWORA. See Personal Responsibility and Work Opportunity Reconciliation Act
Public Strategies, 24, 37, 75, 77, 193, 201
Public Vows (Cott), 43, 151

Quayle, Dan, 87, 89, 91
Queer theory, critical heterosexual studies and, 11

Race, 5, 14, 17, 22, 76, 141–42; barriers, 73; boundary work, 17, 82, 86, 186–87; exclusion and, 87; welfare and, 88
Racism, 31–32, 186
Rape, 14, 119
Reagan, Ronald, 6, 12, 88
Reagan Revolution, 12
Rector, Robert, 9
Red Earth High School, 131; marriage education at, 132–37, 200
Refugee Resettlement Program, 3
Regier, Jerry, 34, 41, 214n35
Relationship, 135, 188, 189–93, 198; education, 193; environment and, 189, 190; high school, workshops, 125; quality, 9; safe, 121, 122, 127, 134; same-sex, of prisoners, 119–20; skills, 75, 78, 110,

115, 127, 129, 148, 162, 188, 193, 195, 198;
workplace, 161–66. *See also* Christian
Prevention and Relationship Enhancement Program; PREP Relationship;
Prevention and Relationship Enhancement Program
Religion, xii, 15, 25, 30, 40, 74, 127, 163,
205n11; diversity of, 212n13; in Oklahoma politics, 25–26, 34–35
Religious neutrality, 38, 214n38
Religious right, xii, 3, 6, 8, 81, 170, 171, 180,
194, 205n11, 213n22, 213n28; boundary
work of, 24, 25; family values in, 28–29;
groups, 28; Judeo-Christian principles,
30, 31–32, 33, 40, 46, 178, 179, 180
Research, 7–8, 34, 35, 94, 189, 193–94; poverty, 94, 177, 193; on same-sex couples,
38. *See also* Social scientific research
Research method: Atlas.ti software
program, 201; extended case method,
197, 206n17; interviews, 199, 200, 201;
reflexive analysis, 198
Responsibility, 10, 15; family, xii, 104; individual, 2, 15, 16, 23, 184, 185–86
Reynolds, Kathy, 168–70, 223n23
Rockwell, Norman, 28
Roscoe, Will, 172
Rubin, Gayle, 14, 209n55

Same-sex couples, 10, 125, 182; gender
hierarchy and, 60–61, 62–63; invisibility of, 60–61, 178; marriage education
workshops and, 38–39, 44, 56–57, 58–60,
61–69, 111–12, 198–99; marriage movement and, 208n52; research on, 38; states
granting marriage license to, 4. *See also*
Outsider status
Same-sex marriage, xii, xiii, 1, 10, 198,
205n12, 213n28; campaign against, 2,
20–21, 24–25, 26–28, 32–33, 39–40, 177,
178–79, 200, 208n51; Cherokee Nation,
152, 168–71, 173–74, 179; constitutional
amendment against, xii, 4, 15, 21, 27–28,
38, 144, 171, 179, 200; illegitimacy and,
13–14; legalizing, 4, 24, 32, 68, 152,
175–76, 177, 180; recognition of, 3–4

Same-sex relationships, of prisoners, 119–20
Sandefur, Gary, 76
Sawhill, Isabel, 9
Scarborough, Rick, 30
Sedgwick, Eve Kosofsky, 11
Segregation, 142, 154
SEICUS. *See* Sexuality Information and
Education Council
Self-determination, native American, 156,
158, 167, 172
Self-sufficiency, 91, 96, 155, 192
Sex: commercialization of, 123, 125; before
marriage, 124–25, 126, 130, 140; for trade,
123
Sex education, 124–25, 126–28, 133, 147,
221n23
Sexual behavior: hierarchy of, 14–15;
sequence of, 123, 127, 140–41; standard
for, 11, 151
Sexual culture, transformation in, 124–25,
178
Sexuality, xii, 5, 125–26, 177; female, 141–42;
gender hierarchy and, 53, 54, 60; impos-
ing standards of, 151; privacy of, 16;
social science research on teenage, 127;
teenage, 123–24, 133, 141, 220n6
Sexuality Information and Education
Council (SEICUS), 10
Sexually transmitted disease (STD), 127,
130, 133, 148
Sexual regulation, 10–11, 14–15, 96
Shame, 93
Sigle-Rushton, Wendy, 191, 194
Sin, 29–30, 68
Single mothers/motherhood, 19, 38;
African American, 5, 6, 72, 82, 177; basic
needs of, 103–8; childhood outcome and
low-income, 71, 72; marriage education
workshops and, 38, 72–73, 82, 94, 97–99,
101–17; marriage promotion for, 95;
poor, 6, 8, 9, 10, 17, 22, 38, 71–73, 77, 80,
86, 94, 96, 101, 111, 121, 183, 184, 185–86,
187, 190; stereotype of African American, 88; welfare and, 88
Single parent, 6, 9, 76, 97; low-income, 94,
193–94; white families, 89

Slavery, 14, 206n27
Small, Mario Luis, 178
Smart Marriage, 2, 18, 19, 47, 99, 115, 123, 190
Smith, Anna Marie, 96
Smock, Pamela, 194
Social and Economic Development Strategies Program, 3
Social justice, 128, 189, 195, 208n51
Social scientific research, 16, 34, 36, 54, 76, 81, 89; marriage politics and, 7, 24; teenage sexuality and, 127
Social services, xii–xiii, 37, 101, 105; family, 9, 161; funding, 185, 208n51; Native American, 161, 164, 166, 186. *See also* *specific social services*
Society: family and, 40; heterosexuality and, 178; marriage and, 72, 170–71, 176–77; multicultural, 33, 183; transformations in, xiii, 16–17, 33, 124, 125, 142, 148
Sollee, Diane, 2, 99, 123, 129, 192
Somers, Margaret, 15
Speaker-listener technique, 105, 106, 113–14, 135, 160, 162
Stacey, Judith, 7
Stamps, Quanah Crossland, 156–57, 159, 160, 161, 174
Stanley, Scott, 48, 49, 50, 51, 54, 80, 100, 161, 190, 191
STD. *See* Sexually transmitted disease
Stein, Arlene, 16–17, 183
Stereotype: of gender, 63, 65–66; of lesbians and gay men, 112, 182; of single African American mother, 88; "welfare queen," 88
Stigmatization, 14, 86, 88, 93, 121, 176, 191, 196
Students: at-risk, 132–34, 137, 148; commitment taught to, 141, 147; homosexual, 125, 126, 139, 142–46, 148, 149; marriage education adapted to needs of, 138; sex among, 123–24, 133, 141; values taught to, 132–37, 140, 148; white middle class, 142
Suitable home regulations, 86, 87

Sullivan, John, 23
Sullivan, William, 16
Swidler, Ann, 16
Symbolism, xiii, 5, 22, 179, 183, 187

Talk about Sex (Irvine), 125–26
TANF. *See* Temporary Assistance to Needy Families
Teenage: pregnancy, 5, 20, 76, 78; pregnancy rate, 124, 130, 138; sexuality, 123–24, 133, 141, 220n6; sexuality and social scientific research, 127
Teller, Henry M., 154–55
Temporary Assistance to Needy Families (TANF), 2, 18; cash assistance stipend, 2, 90, 95–96, 184; distribution of funds, 17–18, 84, 90, 91, 184, 185, 192, 193–94; eligibility, 79, 96, 99, 110, 199; funding, 2, 3, 18, 23, 24, 69, 211n6, 212n7; mandates, 95; marriage initiative and, funding, 2, 73, 75, 77–79, 80–81, 84, 86, 90–91, 97, 101, 185, 187, 211n6; orientation, 97, 98–99, 103, 105–7, 113, 187, 199; PREP and, recipients, 97–99, 103–17, 121, 122; recipients, 19, 22, 97–99, 102, 105, 108, 121, 165, 187–88, 191, 199; work support benefit, 96
Terrorism, 13, 33, 179
Texas Healthy Marriage and Relationships Initiative, 18
Thomas, Adam, 9
Tierney, Tom, 73
Tipton, Steven, 16
Tolerance, 179, 180
Transition to Parenthood program, 79, 81
Transportation, 78, 94, 105
Trust, 60, 115, 165
Tying the Knot, 21

Unemployment, 194; African American male, 87
Unfaithfulness, 109
USA Today, 10

Values, 4, 5; conservative Christian, 28; dominant American, 88; taught to

students, 132–37, 140, 148; white middle class, 14, 31, 183. *See also* Family values; Institute for American Values
Victims Protective Order, 109
Violence, 24, 41, 67, 173. *See also* Domestic violence
Vision America, 30

Waite, Linda J., 2
Walker, Vaughn R., 176, 177, 224n4
Wallbuilders, 31
Wallerstein, Judith, 2
Washington Times, 189
Watt, David, 28
Waxman, Henry, A., 126
The Way We Never Were: American Families and the Nostalgia Trap (Coontz), 12
Weeks, Jeffrey, 14
Welfare, 22; benefits for poor African American women, 85–86; child, program, 3; citizenship and, 85–86; corrupting force of, 88; drop in, rolls, 18, 96, 212n7; growth, 6; history of, 86–88, 187; marriage and, 86; Oklahoma, 2–3; policies, 86, 87; for poor women, 86–87; punitive, system, 2, 95, 97, 101; race and, 88; single mothers and, 88; work requirements, 96, 97. *See also* Temporary Assistance to Needy Families
Welfare "dependency," 5, 10, 15, 77, 87, 88, 104; "welfare queen" stereotype, 88

Welfare reform, 3, 9, 18, 23, 37, 72, 87, 90, 96, 98, 126, 185; ethical reconstruction and, 98
Wetzstein, Cheryl, 189
"What is Marriage For" (Gallagher), 175
When Sex goes to School (Luker), 124
Whitehead, Barbara Dafoe, 2, 7, 48, 89, 91, 123
White middle class, 16, 32, 33, 41, 52, 90, 91; marriage initiative targeting, 69, 72, 73, 74–75, 77–79, 80–81, 85, 111, 185–86, 187; students, 142; values, 14, 31, 183
White underclass, 89–90, 124, 206n27, 224n8
Williamson, James A., 32–33, 179–80
Williamson, Sandra, 32
Wilson, James Q., 2, 93
Women, 121–22, 167, 172; emotionality of, 52, 54, 55, 181; funds for abused, 100–101; poor, 85–86, 87, 194; sexuality and, 53, 55–56, 141–42; vulnerability of, 50, 51, 55, 56; welfare benefits for poor African American, 85–86; welfare for poor, 86–87; working, 40, 86, 87, 142, 180. See also Gender; Gender hierarchy; Mothers; Single mothers/motherhood
Women's liberation movement, 6
Women's shelter, 100–101

Yakush, Jen Heitel, 10
Yarbrough, Fay, 167
Young, George, 82–85, 185

About the Author

MELANIE HEATH is Assistant Professor of Sociology at McMaster University, Ontario.